PAUSE *and* PONDER

Daily Insights from the
Doctrine and Covenants

PAUSE *and* PONDER

Daily Insights from the Doctrine and Covenants

CASEY PAUL GRIFFITHS

CFI
An imprint of Cedar Fort, Inc.
Springville, Utah

Paperback ISBN 13: 978-1-4621-4688-8
eBook ISBN 13: 978-1-4621-4832-5

Published by CFI, an imprint of Cedar Fort, Inc.
2373 W. 700 S., Suite 100, Springville, UT 84663

Distributed by Cedar Fort, Inc., www.cedarfort.com

Library of Congress Cataloging Number: 2024936346

Cover design by Shawnda Craig

Typeset by Sarina Betts

Printed in the United States of America
10 9 8 7 6 5 4 3 2 1
Printed on acid-free paper

For the grandfather I knew and the grandfather I didn't know.
I look forward to seeing both of you.

Preface

The ancient prophet Nephi challenged his readers to "feast upon the words of Christ; for behold, the words of Christ will tell you all things what ye should do" (2 Nephi 32:3). We should feast upon the scriptures daily so we can remain spiritually healthy. Despite this, we often find ourselves spiritually starving for a number of reasons. We may be too lazy or think we are too busy to read the scriptures. We may be too overwhelmed by the rich feast of knowledge presented before us. We can overcome all of these problems with a little extra effort every day. If laziness is the issue, we can increase our spiritual strength one day at a time. If busyness is our challenge, taking a little time to commune with God can bring peace to our hectic lives. If we are too overwhelmed by the scriptures, we need to remember that God doesn't expect us to know everything all at once; we just need to be nourished. A teacher I served with years ago was fond of saying, "I don't know what I ate a month ago, but I know that it nourished me." Seeking continual nourishment is one of the keys to effective scripture study.

Any scripture is nourishing, but the Doctrine and Covenants is unique among our sacred books. Readers will quickly notice that there is no storyline to the book, just a collection of revelations.

I wrote this book to provide basic historical context without overwhelming the reader with too much detail. The study strategy in the daily readings is also centered around questions, partly because the Doctrine and Covenants is a book of questions. The early Saints, led by the Prophet Joseph Smith, saw Jesus Christ as an approachable figure. They often went to him with questions and received the revelations contained in the Doctrine and Covenants as their response. From the beginning of time down to the present, the Lord has told His servants, "Ask, and ye shall receive" (Doctrine and Covenants 4:7). The Lord wants to answer our questions, He wants us to seek Him and come to know Him.

Following this pattern of asking, each short devotional begins with one question and ends with another one. You may want to write your own questions in the margins of the book. The Lord wants us to study the revelations already given, but He also wants us to seek new revelation. Reading the scriptures and asking questions of the soul can serve as a catalyst to new revelation. God is just as active in our lives today as He was in the days of the early Latter-day Saints.

He wants to give us answers. We just need to listen.

—Casey Paul Griffiths, April 2024

Day 1
Doctrine and Covenants 1:14–16

Why Do We Need a Restoration?

And the arm of the Lord shall be revealed; and the day cometh that they who will not hear the voice of the Lord, neither the voice of his servants, neither give heed to the words of the prophets and apostles, shall be cut off from among the people;

For they have strayed from mine ordinances, and have broken mine everlasting covenant;

They seek not the Lord to establish his righteousness, but every man walketh in his own way, and after the image of his own god, whose image is in the likeness of the world, and whose substance is that of an idol, which waxeth old and shall perish in Babylon, even Babylon the great, which shall fall.

The Doctrine and Covenants is the only book with a preface written by Jesus Christ. At a conference in November 1831, Church leaders tried to write their own preface, but none of them seemed right. Joseph Smith asked the Lord for a revelation to serve as a preface, and Doctrine and Covenants 1 is the result.

In Doctrine and Covenants 1, the Savior explains why we need a Restoration, what the Restoration is meant to accomplish, and how His Church will carry out its work.

But first, He starts by defining the problem. When most of us think of the Great Apostasy, we think of evil priests altering the scriptural texts, changing the ordinances of the Church, or leading vicious mobs who murdered the Apostles. These images refer to an institutional apostasy, a corrupted Christianity. It did happen to a certain degree, but that is not how the Savior defines the problem and the need for a Restoration in Doctrine and Covenants 1. The problem isn't just with the priests. It's with the people. It's with us.

In the Savior's terms, the Apostasy isn't an event in the distant historical past. It is still happening in the hearts of people. And it isn't the result of a new sin but is the result of one of the oldest sins in the book: idolatry. It is not the kind of idolatry where we bow down and worship a golden calf. The false gods of the Old Testament are in the past. Instead the Savior warns that every person "walketh in his own way, after the image of his own God" (Doctrine and Covenants 1:16).

We may have moved past the idolatrous gods of ancient times, but there are new gods that take precedence in our hearts before the real God, the Savior of the World. The Apostasy is still happening in our hearts.

What are the false gods we are worshiping in our time?

Day 2

Doctrine and Covenants 1:17–23

What Is the Restoration Meant to Accomplish?

> *Wherefore, I the Lord, knowing the calamity which should come upon the inhabitants of the earth, called upon my servant Joseph Smith, Jun., and spake unto him from heaven, and gave him commandments;*
>
> *And also gave commandments to others, that they should proclaim these things unto the world; and all this that it might be fulfilled, which was written by the prophets—*
>
> *The weak things of the world shall come forth and break down the mighty and strong ones, that man should not counsel his fellow man, neither trust in the arm of flesh—*
>
> *But that every man might speak in the name of God the Lord, even the Savior of the world;*
>
> *That faith also might increase in the earth;*
>
> *That mine everlasting covenant might be established;*
>
> *That the fulness of my gospel might be proclaimed by the weak and the simple unto the ends of the world, and before kings and rulers.*

Once the Lord defines the problem, He presents the solution. The Apostasy is leading to a series of calamities, mostly man made. Knowing the dangers ahead, the Lord called a new prophet and gave him commandments. But this new prophet, Joseph Smith Jr., was only the first of many.

The Lord promises to call others to carry out His work. Women and men will be asked to do amazing things. They will proclaim the gospel to all the world; introduce teachings and doctrines that will break down the corrupt and destructive systems that have held mankind back for millennia; bring about an increase of faith in the earth; return to the covenants made to the righteous women and men who served God anciently; and speak in the name of the Lord, even the Savior of the World.

What is the Savior's name for this amazing group, these valiant souls sent to earth in the latter days? The weak and simple.

It won't be kings and queens who will change the world. It will be the weak and the simple—the quiet disciples who faithfully carry out their duties to care for their brothers and sisters, to do what Christ would do.

After all, the Savior Himself could be seen as weak and simple. He wasn't a mighty warrior. He didn't conquer any cities, overthrow any empires, or rule with an iron first. His teachings, compared to other philosophers, were fairly simple and straightforward: Thou shalt love the Lord thy God. Thou shalt love thy neighbor as thyself. Love your enemies, and do good to those who despitefully use you.

These are all simple ideas, but they changed the world. Likewise, the complexities of the last days will be solved by weak people believing in simple truths. The Savior's greatest miracle is accomplished through the work of the most humble among us.

How have you seen the weak and simple do great things?

Day 3

Doctrine and Covenants 1:30–31

What Is a True and Living Church?

And also those to whom these commandments were given, might have power to lay the foundation of this church, and to bring it forth out of obscurity and out of darkness, the only true and living church

> *upon the face of the whole earth, with which I, the Lord, am well pleased, speaking unto the church collectively and not individually— For I the Lord cannot look upon sin with the least degree of allowance.*

One of the teachings of the Doctrine and Covenants that can be difficult for people, especially those of other faiths, is the Lord's statement that the Church is "the only true and living church upon the face of the whole earth." The statement has sometimes been misinterpreted to mean that for the Church to be true it must be the only source of truth and that the members of the Church see themselves as better than those of other faiths. Neither of these statements align with what the Lord is saying.

First, while the Church has been entrusted with sacred truths, it is not the only source of truth. God loves all of His children regardless of their religious background, and He speaks truth to all of them. The Church has been asked to safeguard sacred truths of salvation, but Church members can and should seek out truth wherever they can find it.

Second, anyone who thinks this statement means Church members think they're better than others needs to read the whole verse. After declaring that the Church is "true and living," the Savior says He is pleased with the Church collectively but not individually. Individuals, including Church leaders, struggle with their own sins and weaknesses. As the saying goes, the Church is not a monastery for perfect people; it is more like a hospital for sick people. Everyone, inside and outside of the Church, struggles and the Church exists to help people in their struggles.

Finally, any consideration of the word *true* should consider the word *living* alongside it. A living church is always growing and changing. The Lord gives out truth line upon line, precept upon precept (see Isaiah 28:13). Church members should not only learn new truths but also find delight in discovering how the Lord works among all cultures, countries, and peoples.

"Living" means the Church will always be a changing, dynamic organization. New truths are revealed all the time. The core truths of the gospel are vital in our lives and do not change. But Latter-day Saints "believe all that God has revealed, all that He does now reveal, and we believe that He will yet reveal many great and important things pertaining to the Kingdom of God" (Articles of Faith 1:9).

What are you doing to seek out new truths?

Day 4
Doctrine and Covenants 2:1–2

What Is the Purpose of Life?

Behold, I will reveal unto you the Priesthood, by the hand of Elijah the prophet, before the coming of the great and dreadful day of the Lord.

And he shall plant in the hearts of the children the promises made to the fathers, and the hearts of the children shall turn to their fathers.

If it were not so, the whole earth would be utterly wasted at his coming.

On the night of September 21, 1823 an angel appeared to a fourteen year old boy. Joseph Smith knelt down to pray, seeking to know his standing before the Lord. It had been more than three years since the his first vision, and Joseph wanted to know why he had received no further communication from the Lord.

The angel came in response to this plea. He introduced himself to Joseph, telling him that his name during his life was Moroni, and ancient Nephite prophet. He then commenced to teach the young prophet the importance of the work he was being called to. Moroni quoted dozens of scriptures to Joseph, but one in particular stood out, Malachi 4:5-6, the haunting final words of the Old Testament.

But Moroni changed the passage in subtle ways that stood out. The prophecy speaks of a new coming of the ancient prophet Elijah. But where Malachi is vague, Moroni is specific. The latter-day mission of Elijah is to reveal the Priesthood.

Malachi spoke of this appearance of Elijah turning the hearts of the fathers to the children, but Moroni inverts this, instead promises planted in the hearts of the children, and the hearts of the children turning to the fathers.

The prophecy of Malachi has fascinated millions with its mystifying predictions and prophecies. Moroni essentially stays true to the original message, but adds a few careful changes that alter the message of the prophecy. To Moroni, the coming of Elijah is call to action. The promises made to the fathers are planted in the hearts of the children, and the children must take action.

Elijah did appear in the Kirtland Temple to Joseph Smith and Oliver Cowdery on April 3, 1836. Along with Moses and Elias, Elijah restored sacred priesthood keys designed to allow family relationships endure into the eternities. When we go to the temple we use these keys to forge eternal connections with our loved ones that will last well beyond this life. This is a major part of the purpose of life, to learn to love, to connect, and to create bonds through the priesthood that will last forever.

How do we gain meaning from connection with our loved ones?

Day 5
Doctrine and Covenants 3:1–2

Why Would the Earth Be Utterly Wasted If Elijah Did Not Appear?

If it were not so, the whole earth would be utterly wasted at his coming.

When the angel Moroni quoted Malachi 4:5–6 to the young Joseph Smith, he added his own commentary to the passage. Malachi said that if Elijah's mission failed, the whole earth would be smitten with a curse (see Malachi 4:6). Moroni said it would be "utterly wasted."

Something is wasted when it isn't used for its intended purpose. What is the purpose of the earth? To connect the fathers and mothers to their children, and to connect the children to their fathers and mothers. To create connection to others—to learn every type of love but especially the connection that comes from being part of a family. If this fails to happen, the creation of the earth and the plan of God serve no purpose. They will be wasted.

Another of Malachi's most haunted prophecies speaks of those in the last days who are left without root or branch, those with no families. If we don't learn to love those around us, and those who came before us, we lose our purpose and this beautiful world loses its meaning.

Elijah did come. He revealed the priesthood and set the grand work of creating eternal families in temples in motion. The work will not fail. Only we can. When we learn to connect and love the living and the dead, this life becomes filled with meaning, and our lives gain purpose.

Elijah fulfilled his part of the mission. Whether the earth is "utterly wasted" now depends on our choices and how well we carry out our part of the plan.

How can you ensure that Elijah's mission is successful? How can you create deeper connections with the people you love?

Day 6

Doctrine and Covenants 3:1–2

Can the Works of God Be Frustrated?

> *The works, and the designs, and the purposes of God cannot be frustrated, neither can they come to naught.*
>
> *For God doth not walk in crooked paths, neither doth he turn to the right hand nor to the left, neither doth he vary from that which he hath said, therefore his paths are straight, and his course is one eternal round.*

At times we all feel that we have ruined everything. Everything fell apart, it was all our fault, there's no recovery from this. It is easy to imagine that Joseph Smith must have felt this way after the debacle with the lost manuscript of the Book of Mormon.

This revelation came in the wake of what is arguably the worst blunder of Joseph Smith's prophetic career. After several months of work on the translation of the Book of Mormon, Martin Harris, Joseph's primary scribe, asked to take the manuscript to his home in Palmyra to show to his wife. Everyone had good intentions. Martin wanted to prove to his wife that he wasn't wasting his time. Joseph wanted to help Martin have peace at home. The work of translation was going on a hiatus anyway because Emma Smith was about to give birth to their first child.

Joseph and Martin even approached the Lord in prayer to get His permission. But the answer was no. They asked again. The answer was still no. Finally the Lord gave His permission. Martin could take the manuscript if he followed a specific set of rules. Martin set off on his journey home, while Joseph and Emma prepared for the birth of their child.

When this revelation in Doctrine and Covenants 3 came several weeks later, Joseph's whole world had collapsed. His child with Emma, a baby boy, died just a few hours after birth. The manuscript was gone, lost, or stolen by ill-intentioned enemies of the work. Even the plates and the interpreters were taken by the angel. All was lost.

But the Lord assured Joseph that all was not lost. God sees the end from the beginning. He allows us to make mistakes as a way of helping us learn, but nothing ever seriously derails the work of God. This doesn't mean that we should be completely reckless in our choices, trusting that God will fix things. We cannot derail God's work, but we can recklessly leap from the train and suffer serious spiritual injuries.

When we have made a serious mistake we can also know that all is not lost. There is a way to overcome, to make things better, to be healed of the spiritual wounds we have suffered. God has already prepared it; we just have to gather the courage to ask how to get back on track.

How can you have greater faith in God's plan for you?

Day 7

Doctrine and Covenants 3:9–10

Can Prophets Make Mistakes?

> *Behold, thou art Joseph, and thou wast chosen to do the work of the Lord, but because of transgression, if thou art not aware thou wilt fall.*
>
> *But remember, God is merciful; therefore, repent of that which thou hast done which is contrary to the commandment which I gave you, and thou art still chosen, and art again called to the work.*

Doctrine and Covenants 3 is the earliest revelation in the Doctrine and Covenants. Section 1 was received as the preface in 1831, and Doctrine and Covenants 2 is an excerpt from a history written in 1838. The earliest revelation written down and then canonized is Doctrine and Covenants 3.

As the first recorded revelation, Doctrine and Covenants 3 also serves as an introduction to the Restoration. And what is the message of this earliest revelation? Prophets make mistakes—sometimes big ones.

Prophets aren't perfect. The teachings of the Church don't claim perfection or infallibility for any person who lived on earth except Jesus Christ. The earliest revelation of the Doctrine and Covenants teaches this principle forcefully. The Restoration is a story of flawed and struggling people doing their best and sometimes failing.

Any person who reads the scriptures or the history of the Church will soon find plenty of failure. But we have never been asked to put our faith in mortal men or women. That is the very mistake the Lord chastised Joseph for in this revelation. We place our faith in God and Jesus Christ. They don't make mistakes, but They do have to work through flawed men and women.

When we encounter failings in ourselves or the people the Lord has called as His servants, we need to be gentle. From time to time everyone feels like they are failing, and we don't want to contribute to their pain.

But the revelation also contains three critical words for us: God is merciful. He knows our failings and our limitations. He doesn't judge us by our mistakes but by our intentions. He chooses us to carry out His work, and He continues to choose us as long as we repent. He can turn our failures into powerful lessons that can teach us how to be better, as long as we repent.

When have you encountered failure? What did you learn from it?

Day 8

Doctrine and Covenants 4:5–6

What Qualifies a Person for the Work of God?

And faith, hope, charity and love, with an eye single to the glory of God, qualify him for the work.

Remember faith, virtue, knowledge, temperance, patience, brotherly kindness, godliness, charity, humility, diligence.

In the winter of 1829 Joseph Smith's father visited him. The young prophet was still in the doldrums over the loss of the manuscript of the Book of Mormon. Though the plates and the interpreters had been returned to his care several months earlier, Joseph seemed to have lost the heart to resume the work.

Joseph Sr. believed in his son's mission. He was one of the earliest people to believe. When the angel Moroni first visited Joseph Jr., he instructed Joseph to tell his father about his prophetic calling. Now his father was coming to him in a time of discouragement, seeking to know the Lord's will.

Sometimes when a person is disheartened, the best way to get them out of their downtrodden state isn't to help them but to ask them to help you. Father Smith asked his son for a revelation, giving the young prophet a reason to approach the Lord again.

The revelation was brief but powerful. It has become an anthem for those who want to serve God. Near the end the Lord lists the attributes He wants those who serve Him to develop.

The word *charity* appears twice in the list. The Book of Mormon teaches that "charity is the pure love of Christ" (Moroni 7:47). Paul says that charity is the greatest of the gifts God can bestow on His children. Paul also gives a lengthy list of the qualities of charity that lines up surprisingly well with the list of attributes given in Doctrine and Covenants 4. For instance, Paul teaches that "charity believeth all things" (1 Corinthians 13:7), which lines up with "faith." Charity "rejoiceth not in iniquity" (1 Corinthians 13:6), which aligns well with "virtue." Charity is "not puffed up" (1 Corinthians 13:4), which goes well with "humility." In fact, nearly every attribute Paul gives to charity has a companion in Doctrine and Covenants 4.

It seems like the Lord is trying to tell us that the most helpful attribute a person can develop in the work is Christlike love. Charity is more important than intellect. More important than scriptural knowledge. More important than our public speaking ability or our powers of persuasion. Most people can see through an insincere person, even if they are really talented. But we cannot fake the love necessary to change people. When people see that our love is genuine, they often feel inspired to do good.

Father Smith visited Joseph because he loved him. Joseph sought out a revelation for his father because he loved him. The Lord loves us and seeks to help us know that not only does He freely give His love, but we can also cultivate that love in ourselves.

How can you develop of Christlike love by giving others the chance to serve you?

Day 9

Doctrine and Covenants 5:9–10

How Does the Word of God Come to Us?

> *Behold, verily I say unto you, I have reserved those things which I have entrusted unto you, my servant Joseph, for a wise purpose in me, and it shall be made known unto future generations; But this generation shall have my word through you.*

Doctrine and Covenants 5 was given in February 1829 while Joseph Smith was still wrestling with the consequences of losing the original manuscript of the Book of Mormon. When the revelation was given, Martin Harris had returned to the Prophet's home in Harmony, Pennsylvania, seeking advice and counsel. Martin was embroiled in a lawsuit in Palmyra, New York, led by several members of the community who believed he was defrauding the community. Martin's wife, Lucy Harris, was among those accusing Martin of these crimes.

The saga of the lost manuscript, which is first addressed in Doctrine and Covenants 3, will be addressed again in Doctrine and Covenants 10. While the first revelation on the lost manuscript is a potent reminder that prophets aren't perfect, this revelation is a reminder that they are still the primary way God delivers His word to us.

In the revelation Joseph Smith is told, "This generation shall have my word through you." After telling Joseph there was a real possibility of him falling, the Lord accepted and reaffirmed Joseph's calling as a prophet of God. Joseph eventually became a dispensational prophet, the kind of prophet that not only speaks for God but also opens a new era of gospel light and knowledge.

In our day it is often common to dwell on the prophets' flaws. While it is important to remember that our faith rests in Jesus Christ, it is also important that we don't overlook the remarkable work of prophets in our attempts to humanize them.

Joseph was called to so something amazing—to bring the word of God to the entire earth in the latter days. Despite stumbles along the way, Joseph succeeded in bringing to light more scripture than any other prophet before or since. Three books of scripture, inspirational history, and dozens of discourses resulted from Joseph's labors.

The word of God comes through ordinary people like Joseph Smith. Usually someone hears the word of God from an ordinary man or woman sent with an extraordinary message. Sometimes the message isn't even shared with words but through the Christlike acts of love that often speak louder.

Prophets are humans. But they are also extraordinary messengers who carry God's authority and deliver His words. The New Testament teaches that "the testimony of Jesus is the spirit of prophecy" (Revelation 19:10). There are capital "P" Prophets and lower case "p" prophets. Both play a vital role in bringing the word of God to the children of God.

How can you bring the word of God to someone today?

Day 10

Doctrine and Covenants 5:16

How Do I Gain a Manifestation of the Spirit?

> *And behold, whosoever believeth on my words, them will I visit with the manifestation of my Spirit; and they shall be born of me, even of water and of the Spirit.*

When Martin Harris visited Joseph Smith in February 1829, he was struggling with several burdens. He doubtless felt a keen sense of guilt over losing the original manuscript of the Book of Mormon. He was struggling in his relationship with his wife, who was laboring to convince him that he was wasting his time and money supporting Joseph Smith in the work of translating the Book of Mormon. But at this time, it appears he was struggling to know if the work was real. The section heading in the original publication of this revelation reads, "Martin desired of the Lord to know whether Joseph had, in his possession, the record of the Nephites."

Martin had already received several affirmations that the record was real. Joseph was under strict command not to show the plates to anyone. But he did take the extraordinary step of transcribing characters from the plates onto a piece of paper. Martin took the paper to at least three people, Luther Bradish in Albany, Samuel Mitchell in New York City, and Charles Anthon at Columbia University. He returned home convinced the characters were authentic and eager to assist in the work.

Martin served as one of the earliest scribes of the Book of Mormon, probably for the majority of the lost manuscript. He sat for several weeks and listened to Joseph dictate the translation from the plates. We do not know the exact contents of the lost manuscript, but we know that he begged Joseph to allow him to take the manuscript home to show his wife. Apparently what was in the manuscript was powerful enough that Martin believed it could convert his skeptical spouse that the work was genuine.

Martin had all these witnesses. Yet he still doubted. Perhaps his doubts came because most of his evidence that the translation was genuine came from physical evidence—the scholars and the scribing—and not from spiritual sources.

In contrast, the Lord points to the most powerful way to know the truth—through a manifestation of the Spirit. Physical evidence can be helpful, but if it is our only source of knowledge, doubts inevitably creep in.

The manifestation of the Spirit, combined with physical evidence, can lead to a powerful witness, so the Lord counseled Martin to seek not just a manifestation but a new birth through the Spirit.

Martin eventually became one of the Three Witnesses of the Book of Mormon. He was one of only a handful of people granted the privilege of seeing the plates, the angel, and hearing the voice of God testifying of the truth of the book.

But his path to being a witness started with plea from the Lord to believe and seek a manifestation of the Spirit.

When have you received a manifestation of the Spirit? What can you do to strengthen your witness of the truth?

Day 11
Doctrine and Covenants 6:14

Does the Lord Want Us to Ask Questions?

> *Verily, verily, I say unto thee, blessed art thou for what thou hast done; for thou hast inquired of me, and behold, as often as thou hast inquired thou hast received instruction of my Spirit. If it had not been so, thou wouldst not have come to the place where thou art at this time.*

The translation of the Book of Mormon jumped back to life with the arrival of a schoolteacher named Oliver Cowdery at the home of Joseph Smith in April 1829. Oliver had boarded with the Smith family while he served as the schoolteacher in Palmyra. Though the family was hesitant at first, they eventually came to trust Oliver and opened up about the work Joseph was engaged in. Oliver became convinced he had a role to play in the work and left to travel to Joseph's home in Harmony, Pennsylvania, as soon as the school year ended. Doctrine and Covenants 6 was received on Oliver's behalf shortly after he arrived at Joseph's home. It is the beginning of a series of revelations designed to teach Oliver the process of revelation and how to get answers to his questions.

There is sometimes an unfair stereotype that being a person of faith means that you never ask questions, you just believe. A Broadway musical satirizing Latter-day Saints features a missionary singing, "I'm a Mormon, and Mormons just believe."[1] Belief is an important part of seeking spiritual knowledge, but the Lord also delights when people inquire. He loves answering our questions.

Oliver had an inquisitive mind and a natural sense of curiosity. He often inquired of the Lord through a number of different ways. When

---

1. Matt Stone, Robert Lopez, and Trey Parker, *The Book of Mormon: A Broadway Musical*, 2011.

he met Joseph Smith, he immediately asked the young prophet to inquire on his behalf, seeking to know the Lord's will for him.

Oliver is just one of dozens of people whose questions prompted revelations through Joseph Smith. The Doctrine and Covenants is filled with revelations that were initially given as answers to questions. One of the Savior's most oft-repeated sayings is, "Ask, and ye shall receive." The Savior said this to His disciples in the New Testament (see John 16:24) and to His followers in the Americas (see 3 Nephi 27:29). In the Doctrine and Covenants the phrase appears in five different revelations (see Doctrine and Covenants 4:7; 49:26; 66:9; 88:63; 103:31, 35).

Our religion does not discourage asking questions. The revelations in the Doctrine and Covenants show that we embrace questions. The inciting incident of this dispensation happened because a fourteen-year-old boy approached the Lord with a question. When done for the right reasons, asking questions becomes a doorway to greater spiritual knowledge.

When was the last time you asked the Lord a meaningful question?

Day 12
Doctrine and Covenants 6:22–23

How Do I Know When I Have Received an Answer to My Prayers?

> *Verily, verily, I say unto you, if you desire a further witness, cast your mind upon the night that you cried unto me in your heart, that you might know concerning the truth of these things.*
>
> *Did I not speak peace to your mind concerning the matter? What greater witness can you have than from God?*

Oliver Cowdery wanted to know his place in the work of the Restoration. Almost immediately after he met the Prophet, he asked for a revelation to know the Lord's will for him. He also wanted a confirmation that the work was true. He humbly went to Joseph, seeking answers and expecting to get them.

That is why he was probably surprised when the Lord told him he had already received his answer. Before Oliver ever met Joseph, he had approached the Lord in prayer. In this revelation, the Lord asked Oliver to think back to the night He had granted Oliver peace. He had given him and answer; Oliver just didn't recognize it.

We sometimes liken revelation to a light bulb suddenly turning on. While it is true that powerful spiritual insights can come in an instant, that is usually not how the Lord speaks to us. In the Doctrine and Covenants the Lord speaks of flashes of insight, but He also speaks of a continuous flow of revelation. A teacher of mine likened revelation to a radio signal. To illustrate the point, he turned on an old radio. Loud static came out of the speakers, so he adjusted the knobs and tuned the frequency. Suddenly we heard a voice. My teacher asked, "Did the voice suddenly start speaking, or was it there the whole time?"

Revelation comes when we are in tune to receive it. Oliver was in tune the night the Lord gave him his answer; he just didn't recognize it. Revelation can come in a number of different ways. Oliver was prepared to hear the voice of God when Joseph dictated the words through the Urim and Thummim. But he had never expected that the simple feeling of peace he felt after his prayer might also be the Lord speaking to him.

When we seek revelation, we need to open our minds and hearts to all of the ways the Lord can speak to us. Feelings of peace, the voice of a friend or loved one, or maybe even an angel could speak to us! There are no limits to the ways God can speak to us.

What are some of the ways God has spoken to you?

Day 13

Doctrine and Covenants 7:1

How Do Our Desires Affect the Blessings the Lord Give Us?

And the Lord said unto me: John, my beloved, what desirest thou? For if you shall ask what you will, it shall be granted unto you.

Doctrine and Covenants 7 was received sometime during the translation of the Book of Mormon. It was probably linked to questions that Joseph and Oliver asked because of things they learned in the Book of Mormon. For instance, in the book of Alma, we learn that Alma "was taken up by the Spirit, or buried by the hand of the Lord" (Alma 45:19). The record also states that Moses was taken in the same way at the end of his mortal life. Later, the Savior explains this process, which Joseph Smith called translation, in a discourse to the Nephite disciples (see 3 Nephi 28).

The revelation is a lost part or addendum to the Gospel of John. At the end of the Gospel there is a cryptic moment between Jesus Christ, Peter, and John. When Peter asked about the fate of the Apostle John, the Savior responded, "He shall not die; but, If I will that he tarry till I come, what is that to thee?" (John 21:22). This led to numerous traditions by Joseph Smith's time that John never died but continued to minster throughout the earth.

Doctrine and Covenants 7 confirms that John is still alive and continues to minister and prophesy before "nations, kindreds, tongues, and peoples" (Doctrine and Covenants 7:3).

Peter was told that he would die and come speedily into the Lord's kingdom. If you had a choice between living until the Second Coming or dying and going to heaven, which would you choose?

The Savior also told Peter, "When thou wast young, thou girdedst thyself, and walkedst whither thou wouldest: but when thou shalt be old, thou shalt stretch forth thy hands, and another shall gird thee, and carry thee whither thou wouldest not" (John 21:18). This may be a hint that Peter would literally follow Christ by dying for what he believed in. According to Christian tradition, Peter was crucified upside down. Some versions of the story say that Peter requested this because he felt he was unworthy to die the same way the Savior did.

Peter and John were both righteous souls. The Savior explained that He gave them what they wanted according to their own desires.

How do your prayers express your desires? Do you ask the Lord for specific blessings that you sincerely need?

Day 14
Doctrine and Covenants 8:2–3

How Do I Receive Personal Revelation?

Yea, behold, I will tell you in your mind and in your heart, by the Holy Ghost, which shall come upon you and which shall dwell in your heart.

Now, behold, this is the spirit of revelation; behold, this is the spirit by which Moses brought the children of Israel through the Red Sea on dry ground.

One of the most beautiful truths of the Restoration is that everyone can receive revelation from God. Scriptures and prophets play a vital role in our understanding of truth, but from the First Vision onward it was made clear that every person can approach God in prayer and seek their own revelation.

Shortly after Oliver Cowdery joined Joseph Smith as a scribe for the Book of Mormon translation, he asked if he they could trade places, with Oliver acting as the translator and Joseph as the scribe. Joseph sought the Lord to know His will, and Doctrine and Covenants 8 was the result.

What was the answer? Yes!

This was a second witness that anyone can ask the Lord for revelation. He wants us to reach out and speak to Him about our concerns. He eagerly desires us to ask for the the things that will make us happy, and provide us with the answers we seek. This was another lesson on personal revelation that the Lord delivered to Oliver Cowdery.

The Lord told Oliver, "I will tell you in your mind and in your heart, by the Holy Ghost." Sometimes revelation comes to us as sudden insights, where thoughts appear in our minds, placed there by God. Sometimes revelation comes in the form of feelings that produce hope, love, or peace in our hearts. These are not the only ways to receive revelation, but they are two of the most prominent ways the Lord speaks to us. When an idea comes to us or a strong feeling is manifested to us that aligns with the will of God prompting us to take action, we should act on it.

This is just the beginning of learning personal revelation. God can speak to us in a multitude of ways, and we must keep ourselves open to hearing His voice.

How have you heard the voice of the Lord in your mind and in your heart?

Day 15

Doctrine and Covenants 8:11

How Do I Come to Know the Mysteries of God?

> *Ask that you may know the mysteries of God, and that you may translate and receive knowledge from all those ancient records which have been hid up, that are sacred; and according to your faith shall it be done unto you.*

Near the end of His revelation to Oliver Cowdery, the Lord again emphasizes His desire to share the mysteries of God with anyone who desires to know them. The Savior wants us to know everything that He knows. All we need to do is ask. We may not always be ready for the answers or able to comprehend the truths He seeks to teach us, but He wants us to seek to know.

The word *mystery* comes from the Greek word *mystērion,* meaning a "secret rite or doctrine (known and practiced by certain initiated persons only)." This might denote a certain exclusivity to those who come to know the mysteries of God. Yet the admonition to ask and seek to learn the mysteries of God is frequently repeated throughout the scriptures. Paul spoke of knowing the mysteries of God as a spiritual gift (see 1 Corinthians 13:2). Alma the Younger taught the people in his care that "it is given unto many to know the mysteries of God" (Alma 12:9). But Alma also warned that the mysteries "are laid under a strict command that they shall not impart only according to the portion of his word which he doth grant unto the children of men, according to the heed and diligence which they give unto him" (Alma 12:9).

Greater things can be made known unto us. The key is to be diligent in our seeking and to be ready when the answers come. The mysteries of God can be as mystical as the origins and purpose of the universe or as simple and plain as the Lord's purpose for us.

He wants us to know. He wants us to ask. He wants us to seek.

What mysteries are you seeking answers to? Have you asked God?

Day 16
Doctrine and Covenants 9:7–8

What Must I Do to Receive Personal Revelation?

> *Behold, you have not understood; you have supposed that I would give it unto you, when you took no thought save it was to ask me.*
>
> *But, behold, I say unto you, that you must study it out in your mind; then you must ask me if it be right, and if it is right I will cause that your bosom shall burn within you; therefore, you shall feel that it is right.*

Oliver failed to translate. According to the history written later, Joseph and Oliver exchanged places and an attempt was made. We don't know if Oliver was able to discern a few words or phrases or if nothing at all came. The point is that Oliver failed and, stung by his failure, he asked for another revelation from the Lord to understand why he was unable to translate.

The Lord used Oliver's failure as an opportunity to teach him another lesson about person revelation: revelation takes effort.

Asking is just the first step. Once we have expressed our desire, we don't sit and wait for the Lord to give us the answer like some kind of cosmic search engine. We have to work to find the answer. In fact, the pattern presented here is less that the Lord automatically provides an answer but that He asks us to use or own gifts, our own mind, to find the answer, and then He provides confirmation that the answer is right.

This pattern is found often in scripture. When the brother of Jared asked the Lord how he could provide light in the barges his people would travel in, the Lord replied with His own question: "What will ye that I should prepare for you that ye may have light?" (Ether 2:25). The brother of Jared came up with his own solution, a crude one admittedly. What was his proposal? Rocks. But the Lord saw the sincere faith and effort behind the proposal and touched the rocks, providing them with the power to produce light.

It is often that way with our own efforts to find answers. We seek and use our God-given gifts to find them. We work with all our might. We study the problem. Then the Lord touches our crude solutions and provides light.

Revelation is always a collaboration. The Lord gently guides us, lets us find our answers, and helps us when have shown our sincere desire to know.

After asking the Lord, what efforts have you made to find the answer?

Day 17

Doctrine and Covenants 9:11–12

Why Is It Important to Move on After a Failure?

> *Behold, it was expedient when you commenced; but you feared, and the time is past, and it is not expedient now;*
>
> *For, do you not behold that I have given unto my servant Joseph sufficient strength, whereby it is made up? And neither of you have I condemned.*

Doctrine and Covenants 9 is not a rebuke of Oliver Cowdery. He was admonished and told why he failed to translate. He was then encouraged to move forward. The time for him to translate had passed, and it was time to continue with the work of translation. He failed, and the Lord was asking him to move forward.

Recognizing when it is time to move on from something we earnestly desire is not easy. We want things so badly, but our timing does not always align with the Lord's timing. We can spend days, months, even years pining after lost opportunities or reflecting on what might have been.

At times the Lord asks us to remember. Other times He asks us to look ahead. When we have encountered failure, when we have come up short, it is important that we do not lose sight of the next great challenge the Lord has given to us.

Oliver moved on. The Lord promised him opportunities to translate in the future, and he was a vital part of other great works, such as the new translation of the Bible that he and Joseph worked on, or the translation of the book of Abraham. He accepted it was time to return to the work of bringing forth the Book of Mormon. Oliver and Joseph labored diligently, and the entire text of the Book of Mormon—a 531-page book—was produced in just three months!

If Oliver had dwelled on his failure and ignored the Lord's counsel, the work might have been greatly hindered. But he had the courage to move on.

What failures are you holding on to? What is the next great challenge the Lord wants you to move on to?

Day 18

Doctrine and Covenants 10:4

Why Is It Important to Know My Limits?

Do not run faster or labor more than you have strength and means provided to enable you to translate; but be diligent unto the end.

The disciples of Jesus Christ are called upon to do mighty works, but they are also called up to know their limits. We cannot help others if we don't take care of ourselves. The Lord provides us with strength and abilities beyond what we naturally possess, but He also asks us to take the time to rest and recuperate.

When this revelation was given, Joseph Smith was engaged in one of the most important works of his prophetic ministry. After the disappointments linked to the loss of the first manuscript of the Book of Mormon, the Lord assured Joseph that he was still chosen and he still had the gift to translate. But the Lord also asked Joseph to know his limits, perhaps hinting that the young prophet was pushing himself too hard.

Righteous people filled with a desire to help others sometimes feel overwhelmed with all the tasks they face. We sometimes feel as if we are falling short of everyone's expectations. We sometimes place all of our burdens and those of our loved ones on our shoulders. The Lord's wise words to Joseph here suggest that it is okay for us to know our limits and indulge in a little self-care from time to time.

The Lord doesn't want us to burn out. When we feel that we have reached our limits, it is perfectly acceptable for us to stop, center ourselves, and take time to rest. Even the Lord needed a day of rest after six days of creation!

We can give our burdens to Him. I love the saying, "Every night when I go to bed, I turn all of my worries over to God. He's going to be up all night anyway."

We labor in partnership with a divine being. When we have reached our limits, He will carry our burdens.

What can you do to take care of yourself so that you don't exhaust your strength?

Day 19
Doctrine and Covenants 10:5

How Can I Pray Always?

> *Pray always, that you may come off conqueror; yea, that you may conquer Satan, and that you may escape the hands of the servants of Satan that do uphold his work.*

One of the central tenets of Christian thought is that there are both good and evil forces at work in the world. But these are not equal powers. The forces of good are vastly more powerful than the forces of evil. We have skipped to the end of the book and know that the good guys win. However, that doesn't make the challenge of facing evil on a daily basis any easier.

In a world in which we often feel overwhelmed by evil, it can be easy for us to become discouraged. As the Lord advises in this passage, it can help us to reconnect with the source of all good. When we approach God in prayer, He gives us power to resist evil.

Praying always doesn't mean that we have to spend all day on our knees engaged in formal prayer. The Lord asks us to be in dialogue with Him throughout the day—that when we face challenges, become discouraged, or feel alone, we can reach out and know that someone is listening. This prayer can be a formal kneeling prayer with loved ones, a quick bow of the head in a crowded room, or even a prayer in our hearts as we go about our daily tasks. If we plan to follow the Lord's admonition to pray always, we need to utilize every kind of prayer available to us.

God is always listening to us. We can share all of our fears and challenges with Him. Connected to the greatest power in the universe, we can overcome the evils we face and come off conqueror.

What does it look like for you to pray always? How can you make prayer a greater source of power?

Day 20

Doctrine and Covenants 10:37

Why Is It Important to Not Judge Others?

> *But as you cannot always judge the righteous, or as you cannot always tell the wicked from the righteous, therefore I say unto you, hold your peace until I shall see fit to make all things known unto the world concerning the matter.*

A large part of Doctrine and Covenants 10 is designed to let Joseph know that there was genuine evil facing him. Men and women wanted to destroy the work of God and stop the Book of Mormon from coming to light. At this stage in his prophetic career, Joseph was still relatively young and naive. Throughout his entire life, he often showed a tendency toward trusting too much and putting his confidence in people who didn't always deserve it. This may have caused Joseph a lot of heartache and misery, but in the end it was a good thing.

In this verse the Lord points out how difficult it can be to tell the righteous from the wicked. He also asks us to "hold our peace" or refrain from judging others until He makes all things known.

This is not to say that we don't make intermediate judgments. Every day we have to judge between good and evil. You don't have to withhold judgment when you see an unjust act. You don't have to act like nothing is wrong when you see a robber attacking a senior citizen.

What the Lord asks us to refrain from is final judgment about who is righteous or wicked. We can judge individual acts as good or evil, but we can't judge people as good or evil. We just don't have enough information to do that.

People are complex. We don't always know the story of how they became what they are or what the Lord has in store for them. The Lord knows their hearts, and often He can steer a person making terrible decisions onto a path where they find goodness and peace.

It isn't our responsibility to judge the righteous from the wicked. We seek the righteous and try to uphold the good in the world, and avoid the evils that sometimes confront us.

Realizing we don't have to make final judgments about the people around us lifts a huge burden. Our job is simply to love others.

How can you "hold your peace" and refrain from making final judgments about the people around you?

Day 21

Doctrine and Covenants 10:67–68

What Is the Church?

> *Behold, this is my doctrine—whosoever repenteth and cometh unto me, the same is my church.*
>
> *Whosoever declareth more or less than this, the same is not of me, but is against me; therefore he is not of my church.*

Most references to "the Church" refer to The Church of Jesus Christ of Latter-day Saints. Here the Lord expands the definition of "the

Church" to include anyone who repents and comes unto Him. This definition lines up well with later statements in the revelations, such as Doctrine and Covenants 97:21, which defines Zion as "the pure in heart," a term encompassing not only Latter-day Saints but all sincere people who strive to live according to the truth they possess. In this sense, the Church becomes a large typology, embracing all who do good. If we look at the concert of the Church through this lens, the Church isn't just a few million people—it might be a few billion!

Hopefully people who have joined the Lord's Church through baptism and confirmation lead the way in bringing goodness and light into the world. But there are many among all faiths and backgrounds that do good. Latter-day Saints lose nothing of their own goodness by seeing the good in all the world around them. While we work to build up the Church, we can also work to build up the Church as defined in this revelation.

If we apply this way of thinking, scriptures such as Doctrine and Covenants 10 allow us to see how the Church of the Jesus Christ can include "every thing which inviteth to do good, and to persuade to believe in Christ" (Moroni 7:16). That includes every person out there striving to live an honest life and make the world a better place. Membership in the Church of Jesus Christ can expand beyond denominational lines to include all who genuinely strive to do good according to the light they have been given.

How can you build up "the Church" as the Lord defines it here?

Day 22

Doctrine and Covenants 11:12

Am I Being Led by the Spirit?

> *And now, verily, verily, I say unto thee, put your trust in that Spirit which leadeth to do good—yea, to do justly, to walk humbly, to judge righteously; and this is my Spirit.*

Hyrum Smith, the older brother of the Prophet Joseph Smith, was a steadfast and constant support to his brother during the Restoration.

He sought diligently to sustain Joseph in his prophetic calling and even died at his side, becoming one of the dual martyrs who sealed their testimony with their blood.

But when Doctrine and Covenants 11 was given, Hyrum was just a young man, recently married and striving to know what he could do to help. While other members of Joseph's friends and family were given complex tasks, Hyrum was asked to something simple we are all called on to do—be led by the Spirit.

Every Sunday Latter-day Saints participate in a the ordinance of the sacrament and renew a straightforward covenant that comes with a simple promise. If we keep the commandments, we will have the Spirit with us.

There is a lot of complexity about the Restoration, from its sweeping history to its grand theology, but all of these lead to one simple outcome—those who call themselves Saints will follow the Spirit and do justly, walk humbly, and judge righteously.

Like Hyrum, we may not receive instructions from an angel or be called upon to translate an ancient record. But we can do the simple things that make life a bit better for the people around us.

What simple acts of goodness can you do today?

Day 23

Doctrine and Covenants 11:13

Is My Soul Filled with Joy?

Verily, verily, I say unto you, I will impart unto you of my Spirit, which shall enlighten your mind, which shall fill your soul with joy.

One of the most important gifts the gospel of Jesus Christ gives to us is an increased capacity to endure suffering. It gives meaning to our struggles, strength to cope with our daily battles, and hope for this life and the next. But the gospel is meant to be more than just a coping strategy for the sorrows of everyday life. The gospel is meant to bring us joy.

In Doctrine and Covenants 11, Hyrum Smith is told that one of the fruits of the Spirit is joy. This promise remains a vital part of the reason we put our faith and trust in Jesus Christ, because His teachings and His way of life bring us joy. Life is filled with its fair share of complexities, but the purpose of our mortal lives is to find joy. "Adam fell that men might be, and men are that they might have joy" (2 Nephi 2:25).

Joy can even co-exist with the challenges and struggles we face. President Russell M. Nelson pointed out that joy isn't just a nice thing, but it is also essential to our spiritual survival. He taught, "When the focus of our lives is on God's plan of salvation . . . and Jesus Christ and His gospel, we can feel joy regardless of what is happening—or not happening—in our lives. Joy comes from and because of Him. He is the source of all joy."[2]

How can you find greater joy today?

Day 24
Doctrine and Covenants 11:21

Am I Seeking to Obtain God's Word?

> *Seek not to declare my word, but first seek to obtain my word, and then shall your tongue be loosed; then, if you desire, you shall have my Spirit and my word, yea, the power of God unto the convincing of men.*

From the context of Doctrine and Covenants 11, it appears that Hyrum Smith was eager to share his testimony of the gospel. He eventually proved to be one of the most effective missionaries in the history of the Church, but at this time he was asked to do something that very few of us want to do.

He was asked to wait.

The Lord told Hyrum, "Seek not to declare my word, but first seek to obtain my word, then shall your tongue be loosed." Before

2. Russell M. Nelson, "Joy and Spiritual Survival," *Ensign*, October 2016.

Hyrum could be a light to others, he needed to charge his own spiritual battery.

If we want to be effective instruments in the hand of God, we have to pay the price to know His message. We have put in the time to understand and comprehend the teachings and doctrines of the scriptures and the modern prophets. We have to immerse ourselves in the word of God, and then God will give us the words to help those around us.

It can be frustrating to be told to wait. We want what we want, and we want it now. It can be even more frustrating to seek to share the word of God with others when we haven't put in the time to master it ourselves. But when we have put in the time, God will give us the words to say.

What can you do today to obtain the word of God?

Day 25
Doctrine and Covenants 12:8

Am I Humble and Full of Love?

> *And no one can assist in this work except he shall be humble and full of love, having faith, hope, and charity, being temperate in all things, whatsoever shall be entrusted to his care.*

Joseph Knight Sr., commonly referred to as Father Knight, was one of the great men of the early Restoration. He met Joseph Smith when Joseph hired him as a helping hand on his farm. Joseph Smith came to trust the Knights and eventually opened up to them about his revelatory experiences. They remained steadfast friends throughout the rest of the Prophet's ministry.

Father Knight's small acts of service had a big impact on the work of the Restoration. When Joseph Smith needed work, Knight brought him on as a hired hand. Knight encouraged Joseph when he courted his future wife, Emma Hale. During the translation of the Book of Mormon, Joseph and Oliver Cowdery often visited Father Knight, seeking help and friendship. Even the gift of some paper, a luxury at the time, helped them complete their work. Father Knight's small, simple acts of love eventually helped the Prophet accomplish a work that has touched the lives of millions around the world.

Year later, Joseph Smith wrote down several tributes to the people who assisted him in his work. He wrote of Father Knight: "Behold he is a righteous man. May God Almighty lengthen out the old man's days; and may his trembling, tortured and broken body be renewed, and the vigor of health turn upon him; if it can be thy will, consistently, O God; and it shall be said of him by the sons of Zion, while there is one of them remaining; that this man, was a faithful man in Israel; therefore his name shall never be forgotten."[3]

What humble acts of love can you carry out today to help those around you?

Day 26

Doctrine and Covenants 13:1

Who Are My Fellow Servants?

Upon you my fellow servants, in the name of Messiah I confer.

Members of The Church of Jesus Christ of Latter-day Saints should celebrate May 15, 1829, every year. On this day Joseph Smith and Oliver Cowdery knelt in prayer, once again seeking an answer to a question prompted from their translation of the Book of Mormon. They came across a passage, probably 3 Nephi 11, where Jesus Christ gave authority to His disciples to perform baptisms.

Wondering where that authority had gone, Joseph and Oliver retired to a quiet, secluded place and knelt in prayer. An angel appeared and introduced himself as John, explaining that he was the same being known as John the Baptist in the New Testament.

John the Baptist! The same person whose birth was announced by the angel Gabriel! The same person who acted as a voice in the wilderness of Judea, gathering many of the disciples who would later form the

3. "Reflections and Blessings," August 16 and 23, 1842, *The Joseph Smith Papers.*

core of the Savior's most devoted and trusted friends. The same person who baptized Jesus.

Before 1829 the last we had heard of John was his cruel death at the hands of a wicked king. After his death, Jesus declared, "Among them that are born of women there hath not risen a greater than John the Baptist: notwithstanding he that is least in the kingdom of heaven is greater than he" (Matthew 11:11).

There John stood, in resurrected glory, one of the greatest prophets who ever lived. And how did he refer to Joseph and Oliver? Not as sinners, not as subordinates, but as fellow servants.

In doing so, he preached one of the most important lessons about priesthood and service in the Lord's kingdom. In the service of the Master, we are all accounted as equal. Even the greatest prophet is seen as a fellow servant with the newest member.

How has your service in the Lord's kingdom made you a better person?

Day 27

Doctrine and Covenants 13:1

What Are the Powers of the Aaronic Priesthood?

> *The Priesthood of Aaron, which holds the keys of the ministering of angels, and of the gospel of repentance, and of baptism by immersion for the remission of sins; and this shall never be taken again from the earth, until the sons of Levi do offer again an offering unto the Lord in righteousness.*

When John the Baptist appeared to Joseph Smith and Oliver Cowdery, he gave the clearest statement we know of about the powers of the priesthood of Aaron. The keys of the Aaronic Priesthood encompass the gospel of repentance and baptism by immersion, something used on a daily basis in the Church. It also includes the keys of the ministering of angels.

To give powers like this to eleven-years-olds might seem odd in any other faith, but understanding what an angel is helps us know why this power is given to such young boys. In the Bible, the word *angel* is translated from the Hebrew word *mal'akh*, which could also be translated simply as messenger. In our culture, the word *angel* conjures to mind mighty beings of light with wings, earth-shattering voices, and transcendent powers. But in the scriptures the word just means messenger.

Angels can come in a number of different forms, including the spirits of the just or resurrected beings (see Doctrine and Covenants 129). But they are essentially messengers. They can also be mortal children of God. When a young man receives the Aaronic Priesthood, he is essentially being called as a messenger of God, or to use a more modern term, a ministering brother. Since young women also receive a call to act as ministering sisters, a part of the powers of the Aaronic Priesthood are bestowed upon them as well.

It is far more common for a mortal woman or man to act as a messenger, or angel, than a departed spirit or a resurrected being. God grants us the privilege and power to act as His messengers, a great power that comes with a great responsibility as well.

How can you minister to others today?

Day 28

Doctrine and Covenants 14:7

What Is the Greatest Gift of God?

And, if you keep my commandments and endure to the end you shall have eternal life, which gift is the greatest of all the gifts of God.

Doctrine and Covenants 14 introduces us to one of the most fascinating and complicated figures of the early Restoration, David Whitmer, who was later chosen as one of the Three Witnesses of the Book of Mormon. When this revelation was received, David was a young man, seeking to know what God wanted of him. He had only recently allowed Joseph Smith and Oliver Cowdery to relocate to his family's farm to escape persecution and complete the translation of the Book of Mormon. Bringing Joseph and Oliver into their home was a great leap of faith, not just for David but for the entire Whitmer family.

Seeing the revelatory gifts of the young prophet, David sought out his own revelation to know the Lord's will for him. The response was Doctrine and Covenants 14, where David was promised that if he kept the commandments he would have eternal life.

But what is eternal life? We speak not only of immortality, a gift that everyone receives regardless of their effort to keep the commandments. When speaking to Moses, the Lord seemed to indicate a difference between the two: "This is my work and my glory—to bring to pass the immortality and eternal life of man" (Moses 1:39). The sacrifice of Jesus Christ brought immortality to all men. Paul taught, "For as in Adam all die, even so in Christ shall all be made alive" (1 Corinthians 15:22).

If we all have the promise to live forever, what is eternal life? One more scripture might help. The Savior taught, "And this is life eternal, that they might know thee the only true God, and Jesus Christ, whom thou hast sent" (John 17:3). What was promised to David Whitmer was nothing more or less than to truly know Jesus Christ and the Father. We come to truly know Them by becoming like Them.

We gain the hope that "when he shall appear we shall be like him, for we shall see him as he is; that we may have this hope; that we may be purified even as he is pure" (Moroni 7:48).

Gaining eternal life is a process of coming to know Jesus Christ and God the Father.

What can you do today to know Jesus Christ and God the Father better?

Day 29

Doctrine and Covenants 14:8

How Can the Holy Spirit Help Me Know What to Say?

And it shall come to pass, that if you shall ask the Father in my name, in faith believing, you shall receive the Holy Ghost, which giveth utterance, that you may stand as a witness of the things of which you shall both hear and see, and also that you may declare repentance unto this generation.

Another promise given to David Whitmer was that if he approached the Father in prayer with faith, the Holy Ghost would provide him with the words he needed to stand as a witness. We all struggle with our words. We all want to know the right thing to say, and the Holy Spirit can help.

Most of us don't have the natural gift to know what to say in the moment. But most of us have also had one or two shining moments when the words just came and we said the right words to help someone. Sometimes I have walked away from a conversation wondering where my words came from, how I was given the gift of the right thing to say at that moment.

That was the simple promise given to David Whitmer. The Spirit "giveth utterance" when the moment is right. That doesn't mean that you'll always have the right words. We still stumble. But if we live worthily, the Spirit can help us through those crucial conversations where we might need to help, explain something, or lift someone who need us.

What important conversations will you face today? How can the Spirit help you find the right words?

Day 30

Doctrine and Covenants 15:3–4

What Is of the Most Worth to Me?

> *And I will tell you that which no man knoweth save me and thee alone—For many times you have desired of me to know that which would be of the most worth unto you.*

Doctrine and Covenants 15 and 16 were received on behalf of John and Peter Whitmer Jr. With the growing realization that they had a prophet among them, the brothers approached Joseph Smith for their own revelation. Addressing both John and Pete Jr., the Lord explains that He will tell that something that only they and He knows.

The idea of knowing someone fully is elusive to us. You may be friends with someone for years and then find out something completely unexpected. You may be married to someone for decades and then be surprised. You may even raise a child, nurturing them from the day of their birth, and then suddenly find out something you didn't know.

Is it ever possible to really know someone?

The truth is, we all occupy an inner world that is nearly impossible for another person to enter and come to fully understand us. But with these simple words at the beginning of sections 15 and 16, the Lord asserts that there is someone who really does know us—someone who knows and understands our deepest fears and desires. We can be honest with the Savior because He really knows us.

Empowered by this knowledge, we can reach out to the Savior. Share your deepest yearnings with Him. He will always listen, and sometimes He will even share things about yourself that you may not know yet.

How can you be more honest about your desires when you pray to the Savior?

Day 31
Doctrine and Covenants 16:6

How Can I Declare Repentance?

> *And now, behold, I say unto you, that the thing which will be of the most worth unto you will be to declare repentance unto this people, that you may bring souls unto me, that you may rest with them in the kingdom of my Father. Amen.*

Both John and Peter Whitmer Jr. approached the Lord seeking a revelation. The Lord told both of them that He knew the secret desires of their hearts. Once the Savior assured them that He really knew their desires, He told them how to make their lives meaningful: to declare repentance and bring souls unto Him.

The phrase "declare repentance" conjures up imagery of Old Testament prophets standing in high places, their arms raised in frustration, as they detail the sins of the people below. While scenes like that are found in the scriptures, declaring repentance usually takes on more of a quiet form. To repent is not to invoke punishment but to cause change in a person. Often repentance is not declared with our words but with our actions. We show people a better way.

I knew a man on my mission who was serving as a bishop. When I met him he was one of the most righteous and decent people I knew.

But years before he was an alcoholic who neglected his family and his Church responsibilities, and spent most of his time in his own selfish pursuits. He told me that one day he was lying on his couch after a long session of binging on drugs and alcohol. Hung over, he gazed out the window and saw his ministering brothers walking toward his house. He watched them walk up to his door, ring the bell, and wait.

He didn't answer. He just watched them as they waited patiently, then turned around and walked away. As he watched them walk away he realized he wanted to be like them. He wanted to have a sense of purpose, to live his life for others. Those two ministering brothers declared repentance without knowing what they had done. Their actions led this man to a life of repentance and eventually to the righteous leader I knew.

What can you do today to declare repentance?

Day 32

Doctrine and Covenants 17:1–2

How Do Faith and Observation Work Together?

> *Behold, I say unto you, that you must rely upon my word, which if you do with full purpose of heart, you shall have a view of the plates, and also of the breastplate, the sword of Laban, the Urim and Thummim, which were given to the brother of Jared upon the mount, when he talked with the Lord face to face, and the miraculous directors which were given to Lehi while in the wilderness, on the borders of the Red Sea.*
>
> *And it is by your faith that you shall obtain a view of them, even by that faith which was had by the prophets of old.*

While nearing completion of the Book of Mormon translation, Joseph learned that three witnesses would testify of the work (see Ether 5:2–4). The three chosen witnesses were Oliver Cowdery, Joseph's primary scribe in the translation; David Whitmer; and Martin Harris. Doctrine and Covenants 17 is a revelation to the Three Witnesses explaining the sacred relics that they would be privileged to see. The three men were told they would see the plates of gold, the breastplate, the sword of Laban, the Nephite interpreters, and the "miraculous directors," probably a reference to the Liahona.

When the experience actually took place, the witnesses not only saw these objects but also beheld the angel Moroni and heard the voice of the Father testifying to them that the book was true. The experience was both physical and spiritual. All three men agreed to have their testimony placed in every copy of the Book of Mormon and defended their testimony to the end of their lives, at times in the face of serious adversity.

Even though the Three Witnesses actually saw the plates and were commanded to share their observations with the world, faith was still necessary. In fact, the witnesses were told that it was only by their faith they would be able to see the sacred relics. Their faith didn't come from seeing the plates and other objects; it was the other way around.

It is the same for us today. While I don't think anyone would turn down the chance to see the gold plates or the sword of Laban, or hold the Liahona, even seeing these things would not secure your witness of the truth of the Restoration. Physical observation is always meant to work together with spiritual faith. The testimony of Three Witnesses (and later eight more witnesses) is a powerful witness of the Book of Mormon. But it is not as powerful as our own witness gained through study, faith, and the Holy Ghost testifying to us of Jesus Christ.

How can you strengthen your testimony of the Restoration?

Day 33
Doctrine and Covenants 17:8

Why Is It Important to Keep the Commandments Once I Have Received a Witness?

> *And if you do these last commandments of mine, which I have given you, the gates of hell shall not prevail against you; for my grace is sufficient for you, and you shall be lifted up at the last day.*

The Three Witnesses of the Book of Mormon gained a powerful testimony by seeing the sacred objects given to Joseph Smith. They saw the plates and other objects for themselves, beheld an angel, and heard the voice of God testify to them (see Doctrine and Covenants 128:20).

But that was not the end of their story.

All three of the witnesses, and several of the Eight Witnesses, later left the Church. It is not particularly useful, or even really possible, to fully understand why they chose to do this. Many of them, such as Oliver Cowdery and Martin Harris, later returned to the Church and died in full fellowship. But the fact remains that having a physical experience did not make them immune to temptation.

Near the end of his life, David Whitmer, the only one of the Three Witnesses who did not return to the Church, was interviewed by a young missionary named B. H. Roberts. According to Roberts, when the angel Moroni showed the plates to the witnesses, he turned and looked directly at David and said, "David, blessed is he that endureth to the end." In a talk later given in general conference, Roberts said, "It is a rather sad reflection that of these three witnesses [David] was the only one who died outside of membership in the Church. I wonder if Moroni was not trying to sound a warning to this stubborn man, that perhaps whatever his experiences and trials might be, that at the last he, too, might have been brought into the fold, and might have died within the pale of the Church."[4]

Remember, faith is a living thing that must be nourished. The Lord promised the Three Witnesses that they would only prevail if they kept the commandments. Even if you have had a profound spiritual experience, you must continue to live righteously and continue to nourish your faith.

What can you do to nourish your faith today?

Day 34

Doctrine and Covenants 18:10

What Matters the Most to God?

Remember the worth of souls is great in the sight of God.

4. Conference Report, October 5, 1926, 126.

In the average day we might see or walk past hundreds, or even thousands, of people. While we are driving to work, picking up groceries, or just going for a walk we see people going about their lives. What if while you were engaged in one of those activities you happened upon a large gold nugget on the ground? Most of us, without hesitation, would pick up the nugget, polish it, and keep it in a safe place.

Gold, silver, and other physical commodities command our attention because we see them as rare and valuable. But to God such objects are dull and not very special. What He sees as precious and valuable are the people we walk past, glance at, and sometimes outright ignore every day.

Each of those people is of inestimable value in the sight of God. Every person is precious. Because people are always all around us, we sometimes forget to see their great worth and recognize them as children of God. It might be too overwhelming to constantly look at people and see their great potential.

But the gospel teaches that each person is literally a son or daughter of God. The potential to become like God is found within every woman and man that we meet. That shouldn't overwhelm us, but it should play a vital role in how we treat others.

What can you do to recognize the value of souls today?

Day 35

Doctrine and Covenants 18:15–16

How Can I Find Joy?

And if it so be that you should labor all your days in crying repentance unto this people, and bring, save it be one soul unto me, how great shall be your joy with him in the kingdom of my Father!

And now, if your joy will be great with one soul that you have brought unto me into the kingdom of my Father, how great will be your joy if you should bring many souls unto me!

We all want joy. We all seek to be happy in the things we do each day. But we also spend a lot of time trying to find joy in the wrong places.

We pursue money, popularity, or things that don't last and don't matter in the grand scheme of things. Popularity fades, fame is fleeting, and money seems to go out the door as fast as it came in.

But there is one work that can bring true joy, not the counterfeits that the world programs us to chase after—the work of saving souls.

When we save a soul, we save something that is truly eternal. It can be challenging to soften hearts and change minds. And it can take a long time. There is no instant gratification in soul saving. But it does bring lasting happiness.

The Savior only asks for one soul. That can be your own soul. But in the work of bringing souls unto Christ you will usually find that your soul begins to naturally gravitate toward the Savior, and the promised joy comes to fill your very being.

What can you do to find joy in saving souls today?

Day 36

Doctrine and Covenants 18:34–36

How Can I Hear the Voice of God?

> *These words are not of men nor of man, but of me; wherefore, you shall testify they are of me and not of man;*
>
> *For it is my voice which speaketh them unto you; for they are given by my Spirit unto you, and by my power you can read them one to another; and save it were by my power you could not have them;*
>
> *Wherefore, you can testify that you have heard my voice, and know my words.*

Both the Book of Mormon and the Doctrine and Covenants open with a collection of witnesses who read the book, knew of its truth, and put their honor, integrity, and even their lives on the line to testify on its behalf.

In Doctrine and Covenants 18 another witness steps forward: the Savior Himself. He offers Himself as another witness of the words in the revelations. As the true author of the book, He is also willing to offer Himself as one who knows the words can change lives.

There is an old saying that when you want to speak to God you pray, and when you want God to speak to you, you open the scriptures. The words contained in the scriptures do not magically change just for us, but the Spirit has a way of guiding us to the right passages that give us the hope, courage, and fortitude to face the next challenge in our lives.

How many of us would jump at the chance to have a conversation with the Savior? Every time we open the scriptures and read, we too become witnesses that we have heard His voice and know His words.

When have you heard the voice of God through the scriptures?

Day 37

Doctrine and Covenants 19:10–12

How Does God Punish the Wicked?

> *For, behold, the mystery of godliness, how great is it! For, behold, I am endless, and the punishment which is given from my hand is endless punishment, for Endless is my name. Wherefore—*
>
> *Eternal punishment is God's punishment.*
>
> *Endless punishment is God's punishment.*

Martin Harris sought revelation from the Lord to know what his next actions should be. On the surface, Martin's concerns were financial. He was being asked to make a huge sacrifice to pay for the printing of the Book of Mormon.

But the Savior's words to Martin show there was another, deeper concern in Martin's heart. After the loss of the original manuscript of the Book of Mormon, Martin wondered about the welfare of his own soul.

Phrases such as "eternal punishment" and "endless punishment" are found in the scriptures and can strike terror into our souls, especially when we reflect on our sins and transgressions. The Savior seeks to console Martin by explaining that "endless punishment" does not last forever. It is only called that because the Savior is endless and it belongs to Him.

The Savior has no interest in punishing people for their sins for eternity. The price we have to pay for our sins is a means to an end, not the end itself. When a person has been healed of the damage inflicted by their bad decisions, the punishment ends. It can be painful and slow, but once we have repented, the punishment ends.

The only endless and eternal thing the Savior wants to give us is joy.

How does it change your perception of God to know that He does not intend to punish the wicked eternally?

Day 38

Doctrine and Covenants 19:16–19

What Did Jesus Suffer for Me?

> *For behold, I, God, have suffered these things for all, that they might not suffer if they would repent;*
>
> *But if they would not repent they must suffer even as I;*
>
> *Which suffering caused myself, even God, the greatest of all, to tremble because of pain, and to bleed at every pore, and to suffer both body and spirit—and would that I might not drink the bitter cup, and shrink—*
>
> *Nevertheless, glory be to the Father, and I partook and finished my preparations unto the children of men.*

After assuring Martin Harris that punishment for sins does not last forever, the Savior shares the most challenging moment of His life, when He suffered for our sins.

While the Savior's suffering on the cross was witnessed by hundreds of onlookers, His suffering in Gethsemane was witnessed by only the Savior Himself and an unnamed angel who came to strengthen Him (see Luke 22:43). The Savior intended for there to be witnesses in the garden with Him. He asked Peter, James, and John to accompany Him, but, exhausted, all three succumbed to sleep. Because of this, there is no firsthand account of Gethsemane in the Bible.

Instead, the only firsthand account of the Savior's suffering in the garden appears in this revelation. Jesus does not go into great detail; that is not the point here. He appears to be more concerned with us understanding why he suffered than how He suffered.

Why did He suffer? For us. He suffered to spare us pain. The grand labor of His life was to not only help us find eternal life and immortality but also to make that journey as painless as possible.

When we repent, we add meaning to the Savior's suffering. This is the greatest gift we can give Him.

What can you do today to show your gratitude for the Savior's sacrifice?

Day 39
Doctrine and Covenants 20:8–12

How Does the Book of Mormon Prove the Holy Scriptures?

And gave him power from on high, by the means which were before prepared, to translate the Book of Mormon; Which contains a record of a fallen people, and the fulness of the gospel of Jesus Christ to the Gentiles and to the Jews also;

Which was given by inspiration, and is confirmed to others by the ministering of angels, and is declared unto the world by them—

Proving to the world that the holy scriptures are true, and that God does inspire men and call them to his holy work in this age and generation, as well as in generations of old;

Thereby showing that he is the same God yesterday, today, and forever. Amen.

Early Church members referred to Doctrine and Covenants 20 as "The Articles and Covenants of the Church of Christ." Later scholars have referred to it as the Constitution of the Church. Everything needed to operate a basic unit of the Church is found in this section. It was prepared before the official organization of the Church on April 6, 1830.

To understand Latter-day Saints, it is essential to understand the history of the Church. To this end, Doctrine and Covenants 20 also presents the earliest official history of the Church, found in the first sixteen verses of the section. But these verses are more than just a history; they are a mission statement about the purpose of the Restoration.

This mission statement has one of the most direct summaries of what the Book of Mormon is all about. It was given from on high, by inspiration and through the ministering of angels. Its purpose? To prove to the world that the holy scriptures are true.

Latter-day Saints often try to use biblical passages to prove that the Book of Mormon is true. God intended it to be the other way around—we are supposed to use the Book of Mormon to prove that the Bible is true! The Book of Mormon confirms the most important stories of the Bible. God created the earth, God loves His children, and most importantly, God gave His only begotten Son to create a way for us to come home to Him. These two witnesses, the Book of Mormon and the Bible, prove that God calls and inspires men and women in our day, just as in days of old.

How has your life been blessed by your study of the Book of Mormon?

Day 40

Doctrine and Covenants 20:17–19

What Makes Me Unique Among God's Creations?

By these things we know that there is a God in heaven, who is infinite and eternal, from everlasting to everlasting the same unchangeable God, the framer of heaven and earth, and all things which are in them;

And that he created man, male and female, after his own image and in his own likeness, created he them;

And gave unto them commandments that they should love and serve him, the only living and true God, and that he should be the only being whom they should worship.

Doctrine and Covenants 20:1–16 gives a brief history of the Restoration to that point. The next section, roughly verses 17–36, provide a short overview of the most important teachings of the Church. We start with the most basic teaching of our faith—there is a God in heaven, and God created all things.

But what makes women and men unique among all of God's creations? From the beginning this teaching set apart Latter-day Saints from all other religious traditions. God loves all of His creations, but He has a unique relationship with human beings.

Human beings are created in the image of God, but Latter-day Saints believe that "all human beings—male and female—are created in the image of God. Each is a beloved spirit son or daughter of heavenly parents, and as such, each has a divine nature and destiny."[5]

God loves all of His creations, but there is a difference between loving something created by the workmanship of our hands and a child who comes into existence from our very being. Human beings are the children of God. This gives them great capacity for good but also the potential for evil. God gives us commandments not only to curb our evil impulses but also to help us achieve our greatest potential.

How does it affect you to know that you are the child of Heavenly Parents?

Day 41

Doctrine and Covenants 20:19–20

How Did the Fall of Adam and Eve Affect All of Us?

And gave unto them commandments that they should love and serve him, the only living and true God, and that he should be the only being whom they should worship.

But by the transgression of these holy laws man became sensual and devilish, and became fallen man.

The next key doctrine introduced in Doctrine and Covenants 20 is the Fall of Adam and Eve. Because of the Book of Mormon, Latter-day Saints view the Fall as positive rather than negative. Words common

5. "The Family: A Proclamation to the World," *Ensign*, November 1995, 102.

in the vocabulary of other Christians such as "original sin" are not part of Latter-day Saint beliefs. Instead Lehi taught, "Adam fell that men might be, and men are that they might have joy" (2 Nephi 2:25).

It is true that the Fall of Adam and Eve brought negative consequences. Death entered the world. Adam and Eve left their state of innocence and came to know misery and sin. But they also came to know joy and goodness (see 2 Nephi 2:22–23). Doctrine and Covenants 20—and almost all Latter-day Saint scripture on the subject—uses the word *transgression* rather than *sin* to describe the actions of Adam and Eve.

"Transgression" denotes a crossing of a boundary. First Eve, then Adam, chose to transgress the boundary set by God and partake of the fruit of the tree of knowledge of good and evil. We don't believe that women and men today are punished for what Adam and Eve did, but we do believe that each of us undergoes a similar fall as we enter this world. So, what is the difference between transgression and sin?

The difference is the saving acts of Jesus Christ. Joseph Smith's inspired translation of the Bible adds a final episode to the story of Adam and Eve. After they left the Garden of Eden, an angel appeared to them and taught them about the atoning sacrifice of Jesus. Both were left hopeful, with Eve declaring, "Were it not for our transgression we never should have had seed, and never should have known good and evil, and the joy of our redemption, and the eternal life which God giveth unto all the obedient" (Moses 5:11).

What started as a story about sin and death became a story about transgression and redemption. The difference was Christ.

How can you show your gratitude for the faith and actions of Adam and Eve?

Day 42

Doctrine and Covenants 20:21–25

What Did the Savior Do for Me?

Wherefore, the Almighty God gave his Only Begotten Son, as it is written in those scriptures which have been given of him.

> *He suffered temptations but gave no heed unto them.*
> *He was crucified, died, and rose again the third day;*
> *And ascended into heaven, to sit down on the right hand of the Father, to reign with almighty power according to the will of the Father;*
> *That as many as would believe and be baptized in his holy name, and endure in faith to the end, should be saved.*

Once when Joseph Smith was asked what Latter-day Saints believe, he quoted this passage almost precisely, stating, "The fundamental principles of our religion is the testimony of the apostles and prophets concerning Jesus Christ, 'that he died, was buried, and rose again the third day, and ascended up into heaven;' and all other things are only appendages to these, which pertain to our religion."[6]

Based on this statement, if we view our religion as a tree, the trunk of the tree is the atoning sacrifice of Jesus Christ. Everything else is a branch of that tree. Priesthood, the sacrament, baby blessings, and temple ordinances are all without meaning if there is no Atonement of Jesus Christ.

This ought to inform every part of our faith. For instance, when a person attends our church meetings, is there enough emphasis on Jesus Christ? When we share about our faith, do we center our own teachings around Jesus Christ and what He did for us? When we speak with our loved ones, do we take the time to express our gratitude for the Savior and what He did?

What can you do to make the Savior more central in your life?

---

6. "Questions and Answers," 8 May 1838, 44, *The Joseph Smith Papers*, accessed August 28, 2023, https://www.josephsmithpapers.org/paper-summary/questions-and-answers-8–may-1838/3?highlight=%E2%80%9CPertaining%20to%20our%20religion%E2%80%9D

Day 43

Doctrine and Covenants 20:30–31

What Is the Difference Between Justification and Sanctification?

And we know that justification through the grace of our Lord and Savior Jesus Christ is just and true;

And we know also, that sanctification through the grace of our Lord and Savior Jesus Christ is just and true, to all those who love and serve God with all their mights, minds, and strength.

These two short passages sound like a repeat of the same teaching but with one word changed: justification to sanctification. The use of the two different words may seem like a small matter, but contained within each of them is a world of difference.

An 1828 dictionary indicates that when this revelation was given, justification meant "[a] remission of sin and absolution from guilt and punishment; or an act of free grace by which God pardons the sinner and accepts him as righteous, on account of the atonement of Christ."[7]

You might notice words such as *pardon* or *free grace* standing out in that definition. Justification matters because it helps us to know that we are no longer facing the demands of justice, which are insurmountable for all women and men. Because of the Atonement of Jesus Christ, we no longer have to worry over the demands of justice. Jesus paid the price for our sins. We are free in that sense.

So, why worry about sanctification? The same dictionary defines sanctification as "the act of making holy . . . the act of God's grace by which the affections of men are purified or alienated from sin and the world, and exalted to a supreme love to God."[8]

Justification through Christ removes our sins. This happens the moment we accept Christ. But we still sin. Sanctification takes longer,

7. "Justification," *Webster's 1828 Dictionary,* https://webstersdictionary1828.com/Dictionary/Justification.
8. "Sanctification, *Websters 1828 Dictionary,* https://webstersdictionary1828.com/Dictionary/Sanctification.

probably most of our life, but it changes us from the kind of being who loves sin to someone who loves God with all their heart.

Think of it this way. A young man robs a store and is caught by the police. When the store owner sees how frightened and distraught the young man is, he decides not to press charges. The young man is justified. He is square with the law, but he is still the kind of person who robs innocent people. Imagine that years later the young man, now much older, goes to store owner, apologizes, and thanks him for his mercy. He is no longer the kind of person who robs stores. This is sanctification.

Christ does not want us to have to face the insurmountable demands of justice. But He also doesn't want us to stay the way we are. He wants us to work to become sanctified, to become like Him.

What can you do today to become more sanctified?

Day 44

Doctrine and Covenants 20:37

What Covenants Are Made at Baptism?

> *And again, by way of commandment to the church concerning the manner of baptism—All those who humble themselves before God, and desire to be baptized, and come forth with broken hearts and contrite spirits, and witness before the church that they have truly repented of all their sins, and are willing to take upon them the name of Jesus Christ, having a determination to serve him to the end, and truly manifest by their works that they have received of the Spirit of Christ unto the remission of their sins, shall be received by baptism into his church.*

As the first handbook of the Church, Doctrine and Covenants 20 includes instructions for the most fundamental ordinances of the Church. Verse 37 explains the requirements for a person who is being baptized. Whether a person enters the waters of baptism at age eight, thirty, or eighty-five, these simple expectations remain the same.

First, a person must come forth with a broken heart and contrite spirit. They don't have to be perfect, but they do need to show regret for their sins and a willingness to want to be better. The language of a broken heart is similar to the language we use to talk about training horses. A "broken" horse is still hearty, healthy, and happy. But it has also learned to submit to directions from its rider.

Second, a person must witness to the Church that they have repented of their sins and are willing to take upon them the name of Jesus Christ. Each of the key ordinances mentioned in Doctrine and Covenants 20 involves taking a new name. A person is given a name at birth, takes the Savior's name at baptism, and recommits to the name on a weekly basis by partaking of the sacrament.

Finally, the person shows a determination to serve Christ to the end by manifesting through their actions that they have the spirit of Christ. Our works don't save us, but we show our sincerity in the keeping of our covenants through our actions.

The covenant is the same for all members of the Lord's Church. Through temple work, we hope to extend an invitation to accept the covenant to all people, living and dead.

When was the last time you reflected on your baptismal covenants?

Day 45
Doctrine and Covenants 20:70

What Power Do I Have to Bless Others?

> *Every member of the church of Christ having children is to bring them unto the elders before the church, who are to lay their hands upon them in the name of Jesus Christ, and bless them in his name.*

Doctrine and Covenants 20—the basic operating instructions of the Church—begins with three simple ordinances: baptism, the sacrament, and the blessing of children. Two of these ordinances are essential for salvation. We have to be baptized and renew our covenants through the sacrament to enter the celestial kingdom, but we do not have to be blessed as children to receive salvation.

Why is a blessing, usually performed when a person is an infant, listed alongside these essential ordinances? Sometimes the work of the Lord's disciples isn't just about salvation in the next life. Sometimes it is about making someone's situation better in this life. There is no salvational covenant linked to a baby blessing, but the Lord commanded the early Saints to carry out this sacred act, putting alongside baptism and the sacrament as a vital way the Church can bless the lives of families and individuals.

I remember blessing each of my children. There is something very sacred and special about holding a baby in your arms and then invoking the power of heaven to give them a blessing to start them on life's journey. They may be too young to make a covenant with God, but no one is ever too young or too old to seek a blessing from God.

Is there a blessing you need to ask for today?

Day 46
Doctrine and Covenants 20:77

What Promises Are Made When I Partake of the Bread?

> *O God, the Eternal Father, we ask thee in the name of thy Son, Jesus Christ, to bless and sanctify this bread to the souls of all those who partake of it, that they may eat in remembrance of the body of thy Son, and witness unto thee, O God, the Eternal Father, that they are willing to take upon them the name of thy Son, and always remember him and keep his commandments which he has given them; that they may always have his Spirit to be with them. Amen.*

If you attend regular Sabbath services, you have heard this passage before. The sacrament prayers are said nearly every week in Latter-day Saint congregations and represent a renewal of our covenants before God and Jesus Christ.

The few minutes we spend every week closing our eyes and listening intently to these simple prayers are among the most affirming acts we can take in faith. The first prayer asks us to imagine the bread as the body of the Savior, broken, and then taken into our own bodies where it can become a part of us.

We also become a part of Christ by literally imitating His actions for the few moments of the sacrament. The priests break and bless the bread just like Christ did. The young men who pass the sacrament lovingly take it to each person just like Christ did. And each of us takes time to carefully and respectfully pass the bread to the people sitting close to us, usually beloved friends and family. If you are not sitting by your family or don't even know anyone in the congregation, the act becomes even more Christlike as you pass the bread of life to the people around you.

Outward and inwardly, the few minutes we spend each week in sacrament services act as a reminder that Christ wants to be one with us, and we become one by serving each other in love.

What can you do to make the sacrament more meaningful this week?

Day 47
Doctrine and Covenants 20:79

What Promises Are Made When I Partake of the Water?

> *O God, the Eternal Father, we ask thee in the name of thy Son, Jesus Christ, to bless and sanctify this wine to the souls of all those who drink of it, that they may do it in remembrance of the blood of thy Son, which was shed for them; that they may witness unto thee, O God, the Eternal Father, that they do always remember him, that they may have his Spirit to be with them. Amen.*

The second part of the sacramental ordinances consists of the blessing on the wine, representing the blood of Jesus Christ. Since the beginning of the twentieth century, Church members have used water instead of wine. This was in alignment with another revelation given to the Prophet Joseph Smith, where he was told, "It mattereth not what ye shall eat or what ye shall drink when ye partake of the sacrament, if it so be that ye do it with an eye single to my glory" (Doctrine and Covenants 27:2).

While wine might look more like the blood it represents, water is a better all-around symbol for the blood the Savior shed for us. Water brings life to lifelessness. Driving through the desert, the tiniest stream of water is surrounded by plant life that springs up in its presence. Just as water brings life to a desert, the blood of Christ brings life to our spiritual lives. When we take this symbolic water into our bodies, we gain new spiritual life, and God promises that we will have His spirit to be with us.

These three elements—water, blood, and spirit—were used in a lesson the Lord taught Adam long ago. The Joseph Smith Translation of Genesis reads, "Inasmuch as ye were born into the world by water, and blood, and the spirit, which I have made, and so became of dust a living soul, even so ye must be born again into the kingdom of heaven, of water, and of the Spirit, and be cleansed by blood, even the blood of mine Only Begotten; that ye might be sanctified from all sin, and enjoy the words of eternal life in this world, and eternal life in the world to come, even immortal glory" (Moses 6:59).

How can taking the sacrament every week serve as a new birth for you?

Day 48

Doctrine and Covenants 21:1

What Are the Roles of Modern Prophets?

> *Behold, there shall be a record kept among you; and in it thou shalt be called a seer, a translator, a prophet, an apostle of Jesus Christ, an elder of the church through the will of God the Father, and the grace of your Lord Jesus Christ.*

Joseph Smith received this revelation the day the Church was organized. After the small band of believers that would form the nucleus of the restored Church of Christ met together, the Prophet sought the Lord in prayer and received this revelation that outlines his five roles within the Church: a seer, translator, prophet, apostle of Jesus Christ, and elder of the Church.

Each of these roles is filled with meaning. In the Book of Mormon a seer is defined as a person that "can know of things which are past, and also of things which are to come, and by them shall all things be revealed" (Mosiah 8:17).

The Lord's designation of Joseph as a translator demonstrates that his work of translation was not complete. By this point the Book of Mormon had been published, but Joseph was only beginning his work on the Bible. Other translation projects, such as the book of Abraham, loomed on the horizon.

The last three titles—prophet, apostle, and elder—are linked together. In the book of Revelation, an angel told John that "the testimony of Jesus is the spirit of prophecy" (Revelation 19:10). In a later revelation Joseph Smith was told that apostles serve as "special witnesses of the name of Christ in all the world" (Doctrine and Covenants 107:23). Finally, the Savior teaches here that a person becomes an elder of the Church "through the will of God the Father, and the grace of your Lord Jesus Christ" (Doctrine and Covenants 21:1).

The role of the president and prophet of the Church is special in many ways. The prophet is granted greater sight as a seer and a special relationship as a translator of scripture.

However, many of the roles assigned to the president of the Church are ones we can choose for ourselves. The most important role of the prophet is to testify of Christ, bring His message to others, and serve with the power He grants through His grace.

How can you show your testimony of Christ today?

Day 49

Doctrine and Covenants 22:2–3

What Is the Purpose of Living Ordinances?

Wherefore, although a man should be baptized an hundred times it availeth him nothing, for you cannot enter in at the strait gate by the law of Moses, neither by your dead works.

For it is because of your dead works that I have caused this last covenant and this church to be built up unto me, even as in days of old.

Once the Church was organized, questions arose among the membership. What if a person had already been baptized into another church? Was a new baptism necessary, or did the previous one count toward a person's salvation? In answer to these questions, the Lord gently but directly explains that with the renewal of His church on the earth, a renewal of a person's commitment to Christ is also necessary. The Savior refers to these previous acts as "dead works" and asks His disciples to recommit by being baptized into the living church through the living priesthood. The old order of things was swept away, and a new living order was established.

While living priesthood gives life to our covenants, there is still a danger of the Savior's disciples engaging in dead works. Do our covenants give us life and joy? Does our commitment to God grow, expand, and find new purpose? If we only make a covenant once and then never think about it or act on it, it can become a dead work.

We give life the same way we nourish every living thing. We feed it, nurture it, and put it in the sunlight where it can flourish and grow.

How can you make your living covenants today?

Day 50
Doctrine and Covenants 23:3

How Can I Strengthen the Church?

Behold, I speak unto you, Hyrum, a few words; for thou also art under no condemnation, and thy heart is opened, and thy tongue loosed; and thy calling is to exhortation, and to strengthen the church continually. Wherefore thy duty is unto the church forever, and this because of thy family. Amen.

Doctrine and Covenants 23 is a collection of short revelations given to Joseph Smith shortly after the Church was organized. The first person the Lord speaks to is the Prophet's older brother Hyrum, who was one of the original six members of the Church. In a revelation given a few months earlier the Lord told Hyrum, "Seek not to declare my word, but first seek to obtain my word, and then shall your tongue be loosed" (Doctrine and Covenants 11:21).

Now the time had come. Hyrum had been patient, and the Lord tells him his heart is open and he will find the words he needs to preach the gospel. The Lord's promise to him was fulfilled.

We often find ourselves in the same situation as Hyrum, wanting to do one thing and feeling we are ready but being told to wait. Our timing and the Lord's timing don't always line up.

But there is wisdom in trusting the Lord and following His directions. Just over a year later, the Lord told Hyrum he was ready and gave him the calling to strengthen the Church continually. While we may feel like we know where we can serve best, the Lord sees the larger picture and places us where we can do the most good. If we trust in Him and His directions, we will find ourselves serving in unexpected places that use our talents and gifts in ways we never could have imagined.

What can you do to strengthen the Church today?

Day 51

Doctrine and Covenants 23:4

How Can I Be a Successful Missionary?

> *Behold, I speak a few words unto you, Samuel; for thou also art under no condemnation, and thy calling is to exhortation, and to strengthen the church; and thou art not as yet called to preach before the world. Amen.*

After addressing Hyrum, the Lord speaks to Samuel H. Smith, the younger brother of the Prophet. Samuel was a sincere seeker of truth and served as the first official missionary of the Church. Shortly after the Church was organized, Samuel took a knapsack full of copies of the Book of Mormon and set out on a journey to preach about the restored gospel.

Unfortunately, Samuel had little success. He only managed to give away a handful of copies, including one to John P. Greene, a Methodist minister, who told Samuel he would take the book on his next preaching tour to see if anyone was interested in their own copy. Samuel returned home dejected, but he continued to follow up with the Greene family.

During another visit to the Greene family, Samuel was impressed to give a copy of the Book of Mormon to Rhoda Greene, the mother. When he offered the book, Rhoda burst into tears and asked Samuel if he would pray with her. Samuel knelt in prayer and then earnestly promised Rhoda that if she read the book, the Spirit of God would give her a testimony. Within a year, Rhoda and her husband were baptized.

Sometime after her baptism, Rhoda introduced Samuel to her brother Phineas. In one of their meetings, Phineas pointed out that Samuel's name was listed in the Book of Mormon as one of the Eight Witnesses. In reply, Samuel told him, "Yes . . . I know the book to be a revelation from God."[9]

Shortly after, Phineas was baptized. He then introduced the book to his brother, Brigham Young. Samuel Smith, the first missionary, may have thought of himself as a failure, but his actions eventually led to the conversion of the second president of the Church.

What small acts can you do today to share the gospel with others?

Day 52

Doctrine and Covenants 24:1

How Have I Been Delivered From Temptation?

Behold, thou wast called and chosen to write the Book of Mormon, and to my ministry; and I have lifted thee up out of thine afflictions, and have counseled thee, that thou hast been delivered from all thine enemies, and thou hast been delivered from the powers of Satan and from darkness!

---

9. "History of Brigham Young," *Millennial Star*, vol. 25, no. 23 (June 6, 1863), 360–61; capitalization standardized; see also Ryan Carr, "The First Latter-day Missionary " *New Era*, Sept. 2004, 15.

This revelation was given when Joseph Smith and the early Saints faced an increase in persecution. At the time Joseph and his wife, Emma, were still in Harmony, Pennsylvania, near Emma's family. Emma and several other people were baptized, but before Joseph could confirm the new members of the Church, he was arrested by a local constable on the charge of being a disorderly person. Over the next few days Joseph was dragged from court to court and had several close calls with mobs hostile to his work.

In the middle of these difficulties, the Lord gave a simple assurance to Joseph that he had been delivered from troubles before and he would be again. With all that was going wrong, Joseph may have needed a reminder that he was still chosen and called.

Often the most difficult moments of our lives come when we face trials not for doing what is wrong, but for doing what is right. It can feel like there is no end to our troubles and that everyone and everything is pushing back against us.

In those moments, it is important to remember the times when the Lord has delivered us from the powers of darkness. If we reflect on our challenges, we will realize we are not alone. The Lord will deliver us from the troubles surrounding us or give us the strength to endure. If we hold on, have hope, and have faith in Him, we will find a way forward. In our moments of fear we may forget the Lord is there. But He never forsakes us.

When has the Lord delivered you from the powers of darkness?

Day 53
Doctrine and Covenants 24:8

How Can I Be More Patient in My Afflictions?

> *Be patient in afflictions, for thou shalt have many; but endure them, for, lo, I am with thee, even unto the end of thy days.*

Sometimes we assume that living the gospel will make our lives easier. It is true that making covenants with God and keeping the commandments spares us from a lot of unnecessary suffering. But it doesn't spare us from all suffering. At times it may even lead to anguish over our sins and shortcomings, or the bad choices of the people we love. That afflictions will eventually come is one of the difficult facts we have to face in life.

The Lord delivers us from many of the troubles we face but not all of them. His deliverance also doesn't always come instantaneously. It can take time. In the meantime we can be patient.

It must have been a little disheartening when Joseph Smith was told, "Be patient in afflictions," and then heard the Lord add, "for the shalt have many." But our afflictions, if faced the right way, can become blessings. They can soften our sharp edges. They can help us see when others are afflicted and help us know how we can help them. They can show us that we have strengths and skills we didn't know we had. They can help us become better people.

If we look back on the times when we experienced real spiritual growth, we'll notice that it didn't happen when things were easy. We grow when life is hard. Our afflictions, if we are patient, can help us become like Christ.

What do you need to do to cultivate more patience?

Day 54

Doctrine and Covenants 25:1

How Do I Become a Son or Daughter in God's Kingdom?

> *Hearken unto the voice of the Lord your God, while I speak unto you, Emma Smith, my daughter; for verily I say unto you, all those who receive my gospel are sons and daughters in my kingdom.*

Just as the Prophet Joseph Smith was called to be patient in his afflictions, so was his beloved wife, Emma. This revelation was received when both of them were passing through a period of trials. Emma was baptized in late June 1830, but before she was confirmed a member of the Church, Joseph was arrested and dragged to several show trials designed to discourage the work of the Lord.

During this trying time, Emma requested a revelation to know what to do. In response, the Lord tenderly addresses her as "my daughter." We take it for granted that just as men are the sons of God, women are the daughters of God. But it is nice to see it in the scriptures.

In our most difficult moments, we need to hold tightly to the knowledge that we are the children of Heavenly Parents. This is particularly true for women. We ask the young women in the Church to repeat this phrase on a weekly basis because it is so important for them to remember.

Many of us have daughters or women in our lives who we feel are like daughters to us. They need our encouragement; they need a reminder of just how special and sacred they are. They are daughters of the rulers of the universe. They have a divine parentage and the power to become like their Heavenly Parents. With a mature testimony of this sacred truth, everything changes.

How does knowing your divine parentage change the way you see yourself?

Day 55

Doctrine and Covenants 25:3

What Am I Elected to Do in My Life?

Behold, thy sins are forgiven thee, and thou art an elect lady, whom I have called.

In the summer of 1830, Emma Smith was told she was an elect lady. Twelve years passed before she found out that meant, when she was called as the first president of the Nauvoo Relief Society. When the society was organized, Joseph Smith read the revelation from more than a decade earlier and declared that the revelation had now been fulfilled.

Why wait so long to let Emma know what she was elected by the Lord to accomplish? Partially because being the first president of the Relief Society wasn't the only thing Emma was elected to do in this life. A careful reading of the revelation shows she was also elected to be a teacher, scribe, collector of hymns, comfort to her husband, and a number of other things.

Emma was elect, or chosen in a number of ways. We don't just have one mission to accomplish when we come to earth. Each of us is endowed with talents and gifts to help us make the world a better place. When the time came for Emma to serve as the leader of the Relief Society in Nauvoo, she stepped into the role and fulfilled her calling with grace and integrity. But long before that, she chose to be elected by working and serving in the Lord's kingdom.

What do you think the Lord has elected you to do?

Day 56

Doctrine and Covenants 25:4

How Can I Murmur Less?

> *Murmur not because of the things which thou hast not seen, for they are withheld from thee and from the world, which is wisdom in me in a time to come.*

Another fascinating part of Emma Smith's story is her role in the coming forth of the Book of Mormon. She was at the Hill Cumorah the night Joseph was given the plates by the angel Moroni and was among the first scribes in the translation process. She was present for all but a small part of the translation and was among the first people to read and bear testimony of the words of the book.

Even though Joseph was under a strict charge to protect the plates, he trusted Emma enough to leave the plates wrapped in a linen cloth on their table with no attempt to conceal them. Near the end of her life, Emma remarked that she moved the plates while she was cleaning! She even said that when she moved the plates they made a rustling sound like some kind of metal sheets were under the cloth.

Emma never publicly expressed any frustration over not seeing the plates, but the Lord did counsel her about not murmuring over things she hadn't seen. It is possible that she was wondering why she was unable to see the plates or see and hear the angels bringing about the Restoration.

In that way, Emma is a lot like us. Most of us will never see a resurrected heavenly messenger like Moroni during our mortal lives. Most of us aren't asked to translate sacred records or receive priesthood keys under the hands of ancient prophets.

But, like Emma, all of us can make a difference. She quietly and steadfastly supported the work in her own way. Faith is nourished and strengthened more by quiet actions than by angelic visitations. One day all things will be made known to the faithful, but for now, we serve and bless and love the people around us, and find joy in what we already know.

How can you strengthen your witness of the gospel through love and service?

Day 57
Doctrine and Covenants 25:8

Why Should I Devote Time to Writing and Learning?

> *For he shall lay his hands upon thee, and thou shalt receive the Holy Ghost, and thy time shall be given to writing, and to learning much.*

This revelation was given after Emma Smith was baptized but before she was confirmed a member of the Church and given the gift of the Holy Ghost. Once she had the gift, the Lord urged her to spend her time writing and learning.

A consistent command from the Lord in the revelations is His desire for Church members to "seek learning, even by study and also by faith" (Doctrine and Covenants 88:118). The command to Emma is particularly important, given that opportunities for women to learn and write were limited in her time. Nevertheless, the Lord saw the influence she could have through her writing. He also saw the potential for her to learn new things and grow as a person.

Each of us is capable of enlargement. One of the gifts of the spirit is the capacity to learn and seek out new things. The Lord created a marvelous world full of fascinating and wonderful new things to learn. Taking the time to acquire new knowledge increases our capacity to help others. Part of our purpose on earth is to learn as much as we can.

What can you do to learn something new today?

Day 58

Doctrine and Covenants 25:12

How Can Music Draw Me Closer to God?

> *For my soul delighteth in the song of the heart; yea, the song of the righteous is a prayer unto me, and it shall be answered with a blessing upon their heads.*

Near the end of section 25, the Lords speaks of Emma's talents and assigns her to compile a selection of sacred hymns. He then reveals something about Himself—He loves righteous music! He even says that the song of the righteous is a prayer unto Him.

When we consider how important music has become in the Latter-day Saint tradition, it is hard to imagine anyone being given a more important assignment than Emma is given here. Five years later, with help from other Church members, Emma published the Church's first collection of hymns. This tiny volume included a number of songs that still ring in the chapels of Latter-day Saints today. Among the first hymns included were classics such as "Redeemer of Israel," "The Spirit of God," and Christian hymns such as "Joy to the World."

Music plays an important role in our worship. You may be an avid singer or someone who just hums along when the music plays in church, but all of us are affected by the music we hear. There is nothing in the world that affects our emotions as quickly as the right music. It can lift us when we are sad, bring calm to us when we are feeling nervous, and help us feel the love of God through its simple harmonies.

When we hear sacred music, are we as attentive as we would be if someone was praying? The Lord compares the two things in this revelation and declares that a song by the righteous is a way of opening communication with Him. When we need to hear, feel, and know the Lord is with us, music can help us connect with Him.

What music will help you draw closer to God today?

Day 59

Doctrine and Covenants 26:2

How Can I Build Unity Among Those Around Me?

> *And all things shall be done by common consent in the church, by much prayer and faith, for all things you shall receive by faith. Amen.*

It is a common in church to see a leader walk to the stand and ask for a sustaining vote. Most of us faithfully raise our hand, even if we didn't quite hear what we are sustaining. It is rare for there to be a dissenting vote. This simple but beautiful law has been present in the Church since the beginning. One of the earliest references to it is found in Doctrine and Covenants 26, where the Lord commands that "all things shall be done by common consent in the church."

While the Church is led by revelation, the people who serve in the Church are called by the Lord. Why, then, does He ask for our consent when someone is placed into a new calling? He knows everything! He has all things laid before Him and can see the end from the beginning.

We need to remember that the Lord asking for consent is not about asking for our input on who should be called. That is occasionally sought and and can be very helpful. Giving our consent is sustaining the person whom the Lord has called. Will we stand with them? Will we help them? Will we support them if they are asked to do difficult or unpopular things?

The simple act of raising your hand shows trust and faith in the revelation given to the person. It is also a sign of our support and help anytime the person needs it. It is a simple gesture that shows our unity and goodwill to those given callings in the Church. We all need to see others sustaining us when we are called, and we all need to make sure that we live up to our covenants by providing help to the person who is called to serve.

What can you do to help those called to serve in the Church?

Day 60

Doctrine and Covenants 27:2

How Can I Make the Sacrament More Powerful?

> *For, behold, I say unto you, that it mattereth not what ye shall eat or what ye shall drink when ye partake of the sacrament, if it so be that ye do it with an eye single to my glory—remembering unto the Father my body which was laid down for you, and my blood which was shed for the remission of your sins.*

A few months after the Church was organized, Joseph Smith was visited by his friends Newell and Sally Knight. Sally and Emma Smith were newly baptized members who had not yet been confirmed as members of the Church. As part of this, Joseph Smith set out to procure wine for a sacrament service, just as he was instructed in the revelations (see Doctrine and Covenants 20:75, 78–79).

As he carried out this duty, Joseph was met by an angel who taught him an important principle. The angel remarked that what made the ceremony important wasn't the substance used but the feeling we hold in our hearts when we take the sacrament.

Today Latter-day Saints use bread and water in the sacrament services. Later revelations commanded Church members to abstain from any use of wine or strong drinks, but this revelation in not concerned with the avoidance of alcohol. Latter-day Saints actually used wine in the sacrament until the early twentieth century, when Church leaders, urging greater adherence to the Word of Wisdom, asked members to begin using water instead of wine.

But water isn't really the point of the sacrament either. We can use any number of different substances in the sacrament and it will still be meaningful to us. It isn't about the details of the ceremony as much as it is about the heart of the entire practice—which is remembering Jesus Christ, what He did for us, and how it opens the door for us to receive forgiveness. It is worth removing a few distractions to fully feel the power and spirit found in the sacrament.

What can you do to make the sacrament more meaningful the next time you take it?

Day 61

Doctrine and Covenants 27:5

How Will Angels Assist in the Restoration?

> *Behold, this is wisdom in me; wherefore, marvel not, for the hour cometh that I will drink of the fruit of the vine with you on the earth, and with Moroni, whom I have sent unto you to reveal the Book of Mormon, containing the fulness of my everlasting gospel, to whom I have committed the keys of the record of the stick of Ephraim.*

After establishing the principle that the way we take the sacrament is more important than the substance we use, this revelation points us toward the ultimate sacrament meeting. If we keep our covenants, in the future the Savior Himself will drink of the fruit of the vine with us. Every time we take the sacrament we not only look back on the Savior's Atonement but also look forward to this grand meeting.

Jesus will not be the only one with us. The revelation provides an entire list of towering figures from the scriptures who will join together at this great sacrament meeting. He begins with Moroni, the angel sent to reveal the Book of Mormon, but then quickly moves on to Elias (meaning the angel Gabriel in this context), John the Baptist, and Elijah. Continuing, he names Joseph, Jacob, Isaac, and Abraham, the ancient patriarchs from the book of Genesis.

From there he moves to Michael, the angel who cast Satan out of heaven, and reveals that this archangel came to earth as Adam, the father of all men and women. He then adds Peter, James, and John to the list, noting that they had already visited Joseph and ordained him an Apostle.

The final group invited to the meeting is perhaps the most meaningful to us. Among the noble and great ones at this sacrament meeting will be "all those whom my Father hath given me out of the world" (Doctrine and Covenants 27:14). We can assume this means a multitude of other righteous women and men, adding Sarah, Rebekah, Elizabeth, and Eve to the guest list.

And who else might be there? The Savior has invited us as well, as long as we become those who the Father gives to the Savior from the world. Anyone who receives that blessing can join the feast.

How does the sacrament help us look forward to better days to come?

Day 62
Doctrine and Covenants 27:15

How Can I Withstand Temptation?

> *Wherefore, lift up your hearts and rejoice, and gird up your loins, and take upon you my whole armor, that ye may be able to withstand the evil day, having done all, that ye may be able to stand.*

After revealing the great future sacrament meeting, the Savior reveals the dress code. All who attend must wear the armor of God. He borrows the language used by Paul to describe the kind of spiritual combat that the disciples of Christ will face in the last days (see Ephesians 6:13–17).

Paul teaches "we wrestle not against flesh and blood, but against principalities, against powers, against the rulers of the darkness of this world, against spiritual wickedness in high places" (Ephesians 6:12). What was true in Paul's day is still true in ours. The forces aligned against us exist in all levels of society, and the battles we face are more spiritual than physical, though they can be both.

Just like physical armor, every day we arise and have to take the action of putting on the armor of God. Just like physical armor, this armor has to be maintained and cared for to be effective in combat. And just like physical armor, it gives us the power to survive the attacks and ambushes that come during our time.

But unlike real armor, the weight of the armor of God is light; it is a burden that is easy to carry. It is far easier to live the commandments than it is to break them. When we put on the armor of God we surround ourselves with a layer of protection that is invisible but protects us just as surely as a suit of iron would.

How can you put on the armor of God today?

Day 63
Doctrine and Covenants 28:2

Why Is It Important to Follow the Words of the Prophet?

> *But, behold, verily, verily, I say unto thee, no one shall be appointed to receive commandments and revelations in this church excepting my servant Joseph Smith, Jun., for he receiveth them even as Moses.*

Doctrine and Covenants 28 deals with the first major doctrinal crisis in the Church. From the beginning, the Lord taught that anyone could receive revelation. So in a Church where everyone can receive revelation, can anyone get revelation for the whole Church?

Joseph sought the Lord in prayer because Hiram Page, one of the Eight Witnesses of the Book of Mormon, began to receive revelation through a seer stone. Hiram was married to Katherine Whitmer and convinced most of the Whitmer family, including Oliver Cowdery, who was close friends with the Whitmers, that his revelations were from God.

Joseph Smith was concerned because some of Hiram's revelations contradicted the scriptures and the revelations already received. Seeking to know how to move forward, all of the members of the tiny Church met together and agreed to have Joseph seek another revelation to answer their questions. The answer, given in revelation, was that only one person, in this case Joseph Smith, was appointed to receive revelation for the whole Church.

Does that mean that no one except the President of the Church can receive revelation? Of course not! Anyone can receive revelation, but revelation comes within a stewardship. A father or a mother can receive revelation for their own family. A bishop or Relief Society president can receive revelation for the people in their stewardship. The prophet can receive revelation for his entire stewardship, which is the world. The flow of revelation is steady and comes at all levels, but there has to be a system of organization or the whole Church will collapse in confusion.

God has given us prophets to provide a way for the Church to be guided by His voice. But you can be guided by His voice as well. The Lord can confirm to you the words of the prophets, or He can give you revelation within your stewardship.

What is your stewardship? Have you sought out a revelation for them?

Day 64
Doctrine and Covenants 28:11

How Can I Correct Someone Who Is in Error?

> *And again, thou shalt take thy brother, Hiram Page, between him and thee alone, and tell him that those things which he hath written from that stone are not of me and that Satan deceiveth him.*

When the questions of revelation and stewardship brought up by Hiram Page were settled, one question remained. What should happen to Hiram and his revelations? Should he be made into a public example to teach him and the Church a lesson? Should he have to admit to everyone that he was wrong and make a public penance?

Instead of a public humiliation, the Lord sought out a better way. He directed Oliver Cowdery, one of Hiram's close friends, to privately speak to Hiram. There was to be no public shaming.

This suggests that Hiram was not trying to deceive the Church but was being deceived by the adversary. There was no bad guy in the story but Satan. Forcing Hiram to recant his revelations in front of the Church may have caused more harm than good. What was necessary now was a personal visit with him to let him know that he was deceived.

Sometimes we are called upon to correct someone. Having to do this can be challenging and can often result in hurt feelings that last a long time. If someone is in error, we do need to help them but in the most tender way possible. The Lord knew Hiram's heart and knew that he was sincerely trying to do the right thing. When we are trying to bind up a person's wounds we shouldn't inflict new ones.

How can you offer correction in a way that is kind to someone else?

Day 65
Doctrine and Covenants 29:1–2

How Does the Savior Protect Me?

> *Listen to the voice of Jesus Christ, your Redeemer, the Great I Am, whose arm of mercy hath atoned for your sins;*
>
> *Who will gather his people even as a hen gathereth her chickens under her wings, even as many as will hearken to my voice and humble themselves before me, and call upon me in mighty prayer.*

Doctrine and Covenants 29 is an overview of the plan of salvation. The Lord covers the end from the beginning in one of the real doctrinal gems of the entire scriptures. But before He takes us on a journal from the war in heaven, to the Fall of Adam and Eve, to the Second Coming, He wants us to know one thing. He will take care of us. His priority as we journey through the ups and downs of this life is to keep us safe.

Prophets often use animals as metaphors for the Savior. The two most common symbols are the lion and the lamb, representing the power of Jesus Christ and His gentle and submissive nature. But when the Savior describes Himself, He uses an animal that we don't always think of as majestic—a mother hen.

A mother hen is not the most powerful or most gentle animal. But she is protective. If you have ever seen a mother hen in action, she is constantly looking for her chicks, making sure they are safe, steering them in the right direction.

In the midst of our challenges and seeing the dangers we face on all sides, it is powerful to see the imagery of the mother hen who watches over us. We need protection, we need guidance, and the Savior will do anything He can to keep us safe.

How can you show your gratitude for the Savior's protection today?

Day 66
Doctrine and Covenants 29:7

How Can I Soften My Heart?

And ye are called to bring to pass the gathering of mine elect; for mine elect hear my voice and harden not their hearts.

As the end of time approaches, the Savior seeks to gather His people to safety. Here He uses the phrase "mine elect" to describe those He will gather. Determining who the elect are has produced a lot of controversy and opinions inside the Church and in the larger Christian world.

At times the question of the elect has provoked thoughts about bloodlines, lineage, and ancestry. We have speculated that this nation or that is part of the house of Israel, or that this group of people are the true descendants of the ancient covenants. There has even been some wild speculation about the lost ten tribes of Israel being around a distant star or in the center of the earth!

But here the Lord doesn't talk about being elect in terms of bloodlines or ancestry. He only uses one qualifier to say who is elect: "mine elect hear my voice and harden not their hearts."

Saying someone is among the "elect" makes it sound like they are chosen through some mystical process, but in reality the elect choose themselves. They soften their heart, choose to repent, and listen to the directions the Lord gives His servants. They seek out the counsel of God and shape their lives to do His will.

How can you choose to be among the elect today?

Day 67
Doctrine and Covenants 29:24

How Will Old Things Become New?

For all old things shall pass away, and all things shall become new, even the heaven and the earth, and all the fulness thereof, both men and beasts, the fowls of the air, and the fishes of the sea.

Doctrine and Covenants 29 covers a lot of ground. It takes us all the way back to the Fall of Adam and Eve to the end of the world. End of the world prophecy can be very frightening. When we talk about the end of the world we tend to focus more on the death and destruction than the wonderful and amazing things that come with living in the last days. There is more to celebrate than there is to dread about living in the times before the Savior's return.

We often limit the term "Restoration" to simply mean the return of the Savior's true Church and its power and teaching in the latter days. But that is only the beginning of the Restoration. The Restoration of all things includes putting back in place everything that was lost along the way. Our loved ones will be resurrected and enjoy immortality in a physical body. Those who have made and kept their covenants with God will not only be restored to their bodies but will also enjoy a new body and become like God. According to this passage, even beloved lost pets will be restored!

And it won't just be a restoration of things lost. It will be a renewal. All things will become new, and we will find ourselves in a world where nothing was lost. The Savior came first to save the daughters and sons of God. But His full mission is much more grand: In the end He will save all things. Not one part of His creation will be lost. All things will become new.

How does it give you hope to know that all things will become new?

Day 68

Doctrine and Covenants 29:35

How Can I Use My Agency Wisely?

Behold, I gave unto him that he should be an agent unto himself; and I gave unto him commandment, but no temporal commandment gave I unto him, for my commandments are spiritual; they are not natural nor temporal, neither carnal nor sensual.

The word *agency* shows up frequently in Latter-day Saint teachings. A dictionary from Joseph Smith's time defines agency as "the quality of moving or of exerting power."[10] When God tells us in this revelation that he gave men and women the right to be agents unto themselves, He is basically saying that He gave us power. He upholds and defends this sacred right to make our own decisions, even if they aren't always the right decisions.

The fact that God honors our agency teaches us a valuable lesson about how He wields the power He possesses. God is all-powerful, and He could force us to do His will. He could simply make it so we have no choice but to love and serve Him and always do the right thing. But in His wisdom, the Lord realizes that a love that is forced isn't really love. Love is a gift that has to be given freely in order to mean something. So He allows us to choose to love Him, even though some of us choose to turn away instead.

We would do well to take this lesson into our own relationships. Honoring the agency of others can be painful. We hate to see our loved ones make the wrong choices and suffer because of it. We are sometimes hurt because others use their agency unwisely. But a world where everyone is compelled to do good is a world where there really is no such things as good. Righteousness must be a choice, or it becomes meaningless.

How can you choose the use your agency wisely today?

---

10. Noah Webster, *American Dictionary of the English Language,* 1828, https://webstersdictionary1828.com/Dictionary/Agency.

Day 69

Doctrine and Covenants 29:46–47

How Can I Help and Protect Little Children?

But behold, I say unto you, that little children are redeemed from the foundation of the world through mine Only Begotten;

Wherefore, they cannot sin, for power is not given unto Satan to tempt little children, until they begin to become accountable before me.

Near the end of this revelation the Savior repeats one of the most important and beautiful truths found in the Book of Mormon: little children are saved by Jesus Christ. Among the Christian Nephites was a controversy over whether little children needed to be baptized to be saved. The prophet Mormon emphatically declared, "Little children need no repentance, neither baptism. Behold, baptism is unto repentance to the fulfilling the commandments unto the remission of sins. But little children are alive in Christ, even from the foundation of the world" (Moroni 8:11–12).

Little children will eventually become accountable when they are old enough to understand the consequences of their choices. They need good mentors to teach and show them the way. Parents are given the primary responsibility of teaching their children, but raising good people is also a community responsibility. Great mentors can be found everywhere.

Along with this teaching comes great comfort that little children are redeemed. Among the things made new by the work of Jesus Christ are the multitudes of children who leave this life before they have the chance to experience all of its joys. These little children are redeemed by Christ and will return to their loved ones and enjoy a full life. The Savior sees the suffering and anguish of those who have known what it is like to lose a child, and He will compensate for their loss.

In the meantime, we can help Him in His word by loving and teaching the children among us.

How can you help protect a child today?

Day 70
Doctrine and Covenants 30:2

How Can I Focus on the Things of God?

But your mind has been on the things of the earth more than on the things of me, your Maker, and the ministry whereunto you have been called; and you have not given heed unto my Spirit, and to those who were set over you, but have been persuaded by those whom I have not commanded.

Our lives are busy. Despite all of the modern conveniences that make it easier for us to get to work, provide for our ourselves and our families, and get back home again, we are getting progressively busier. So many little items throughout the day that occupy our time and take us away from the things that matter most. Focusing on these smaller daily issues is often necessary and is no great sin. But over time it can progressively pull us away from the things that create a healthy spiritual life. We are often so focused on feeding our body that we neglect to feed our spirit.

While modern Latter-day Saints struggled to maintain this balance, it appears that early Church members did as well. In this case, it was David Whitmer, one of the Three Witnesses, who was chastised for focusing more on the things of the world than the things of the spirit.

I used to tell my students that they didn't have to pray every day, only on the days when they brushed their teeth. It was a quick and snappy way to tie together the idea that the simple things we do every day to maintain ourselves spiritually are just as important as the simple things we do to maintain ourselves physically. God understands that we have tasks to perform and schedules to keep, but He also asks us to take enough time out of the day to look after our spiritual health and maintain our relationship with Him.

What can you do today to focus on the things of God?

Day 71
Doctrine and Covenants 30:11

How Can I Labor With All My Soul?

And your whole labor shall be in Zion, with all your soul, from henceforth; yea, you shall ever open your mouth in my cause, not fearing what man can do, for I am with you. Amen.

In this revelation, Peter Whitmer is called to labor with his whole soul in Zion. For Peter this was literal. A few weeks after this revelation was given, he left on a mission to the borders of the United States to help locate the place for the city of Zion. Peter and his companions crossed nearly an entire continent and eventually arrived in Independence, Missouri. A few months later Joseph Smith arrived with several other missionaries and received a revelation that Independence was the chosen place for the city of Zion.

Peter never returned from this mission. He made his home in Independence, fully committing to building the city of God. He worked as a tailor, even making suits for a politician named Lilburn W. Boggs, who would eventually become one of the Saints' worst enemies. When persecutions arose in Missouri, Peter and his family were driven from place to place. In 1836, after six years in Zion, Peter passed away. His brother-in-law, Oliver Cowdery, wrote this tribute about him and his brother Christian, who also passed away near that time: "By many in this church, our brothers were personally known. They were the first to embrace the new covenant, on hearing it, and during a constant scene of persecution and perplexity, to their last moments, maintained its truth—they were both included in the list of the Eight Witnesses in the Book of Mormon, and though they have departed, it is with great satisfaction that we reflect, that they proclaimed to their last moments, the certainty of their former testimony."[11]

Peter is just one of thousands who labored in the early Church to build Zion. Most of these are little remembered, but on their sacrifices the city of God will eventually be built.

What can you do today to labor with your whole soul in Zion?

---

11. Oliver Cowdery, "The Closing Year," *Messenger and Advocate* 3, December 1836, 426.

Day 72
Doctrine and Covenants 31:2

How Can I Bless My Family?

Behold, you have had many afflictions because of your family; nevertheless, I will bless you and your family, yea, your little ones; and the day cometh that they will believe and know the truth and be one with you in my church.

Thomas B. Marsh was traveling through western New York when he started to hear strange tales of a golden bible and a frontier profit. Intrigued, he stopped in Palmyra at Grandin Press, where the Book of Mormon was being printed. The book wasn't available yet, but Thomas was able to secure a proof that had sixteen pages of text. He took the pages and returned to his family in Boston.

A few months later, convinced that the book was true, Thomas moved his family to the Palmyra area, where they soon joined the Church. A natural preacher, Thomas was called on a mission by the Lord. While we don't know much about the circumstances of this revelation, the Lord's words to Thomas seem to indicate that he was worried about his children in his absence.

Church service often pulls us away from our loved ones. We worry about children leaving home to serve missions, stressful callings, and the time our service takes away from family life. Hopefully church life and family life strengthen each other, but that doesn't always quiet our fears.

For Thomas, and us, the Lord makes a simple promise: "I will bless you and your family, yea, your little ones." While we strive to find a balance between our service and our family, we can know that the Lord blesses the families of those who serve Him. He watches over our loved ones, helps them in little ways, and compensates more than we will ever know.

How has the Lord blessed your family because of your service?

Day 73
Doctrine and Covenants 31:3

How Can I Declare Glad Tidings?

> *Lift up your heart and rejoice, for the hour of your mission is come; and your tongue shall be loosed, and you shall declare glad tidings of great joy unto this generation.*

Early Christians used the word *euaggellion* to capture the message of Jesus Christ. The prefix *eu* means "good" in Greek, while *aggelion* translates roughly to "message." A simple translation of these words into English is "good news." The Old English word used to capture this feeling is *gospel*, or glad tidings.

Sometimes we become concerned with smaller, less important details of the message of Christ and forget that at its heart is a message intended to bring joy. The gospel is supposed to be joyful. At times it may make our lives more complex, a little busier, and maybe even a little more stressful.

But in the midst of these complexities, we must not forget that the gospel of Jesus Christ is a joyful message. If we can't find joy in the teachings of Jesus, then we are doing it wrong. We find joy in having meaning. We find joy in serving others. We find joy in knowing there is someone always ready to listen to us and hear our concerns. We find joy in knowing there is a place prepared for us.

Many of the early missionaries such as Thomas B. Marsh needed this reminder. Our message is not one of gloom and doom. Our message is one of joy.

How can you find joy in the gospel today?

Day 74
Doctrine and Covenants 32:4

How Can I Give Heed to the Scriptures?

And they shall give heed to that which is written, and pretend to no other revelation; and they shall pray always that I may unfold the same to their understanding.

It is not surprising that the Lord's counsel to missionaries in the early Church—and continuing into our day—is to keep their message focused on the scriptures. There is a tendency among Church members, then and now, to head off the path into more fanciful realms of myth, rumor, and outright error when we aren't regularly and consistently studying the word of God.

The scriptures aren't the only source of truth out there. We are blessed to have modern prophets and inspired men and women who lead the Church and receive revelation. But the scriptures have been tested over a long period of time and are the most consistent and helpful guides we have to the decisions we have to make on a daily basis.

Just as the Lord counseled the missionaries in this revelation to "give headed to that which is written," it is important for use to take the time to regularly immerse ourselves in the word of God. Not only will we find answers in the scriptures, but the Lord can also use the scriptures to bring us the Spirit, which can unfold even greater connections to the deep things of God.

Parley P. Pratt, one the young missionaries that this section was received for, fell in love with the Book of Mormon, and it became the gateway to his conversion to the Church. After he was given a copy, he stayed up all night reading it. He later wrote, "I read all day; eating was a burden, I had no desire for food; sleep was a burden when the night came, for I preferred reading to sleep. As I read, the spirit of the Lord was upon me, and I knew and comprehended that the book was true, as plainly and manifestly as a man comprehends and knows that he exists. My joy was now full, as it were, and I rejoiced sufficiently to more than pay me for all the sorrows, sacrifices and toils of my life."[12]

---

12. *Autobiography of Parley P. Pratt,* 2000, 30–31.

When we give heed to the scriptures the way Parley did, they open to use the teachings of eternal life.

How can you give heed to the scriptures today?

Day 75
Doctrine and Covenants 33:2

How Can I Lift Up My Voice?

> *For verily, verily, I say unto you that ye are called to lift up your voices as with the sound of a trump, to declare my gospel unto a crooked and perverse generation.*

Living in the latter days, there is so much to be thankful for. We have modern conveniences, miracles of medicine, and modes of transportation that were undreamed of by people in previous generations. But while there is much to be grateful for, there is also much to be cautious of.

In this revelation to two young missionaries, Ezra Thayer and Northrop Sweet, the Lord warned them of the challenges they would face in teaching the gospel to "a crooked and perverse generation." While the disciples of Christ should see the good in all things around them, there is also a need to see and avoid the dishonesty and the wickedness that is so prevalent in the world around us. We live in a time of shifting society norms. Actions that may have seemed outrageous a generation ago have become commonplace and even celebrated.

At times even acts of outright dishonesty or crookedness are defended as "being smart." Life is seen as a zero-sum game, with honor and decency set aside in the name of getting ahead.

Our solution to this world of corruption and deceit? We preach the gospel of Jesus Christ. We lift up our voices and speak in the name of goodness and integrity. The Lord counsels these missionaries to lift up their voices with the sound of a trump, but we often preach the gospel just as loudly with our actions as we do with our words. We can be examples of the goodness of the gospel in word, deed, and thought. There is an old saying that "the only thing required for the triumph of evil is for good men to do nothing."

In a crooked and perverse world we can fight back by being honest and faithful.

How can you preach the gospel in word, deed, or thought today?

Day 76
Doctrine and Covenants 33:8

How Can I Be Like Nephi of Old?

Open your mouths and they shall be filled, and you shall become even as Nephi of old, who journeyed from Jerusalem in the wilderness.

As the young Church progressed and word of a new book of scripture began to spread, new scripture heroes filled the discourses of the early members of the Church. Most Christians of the time were raised on stories of Moses, Samuel, John the Baptist, or Paul the Apostle. The Book of Mormon introduced a new pantheon of heroes into the conversation.

Here the Lord uses the new scripture to point these missionaries toward a hero they had only recently learned about: Nephi, the son of Lehi. Nephi's life is worthy of emulation. He acted in faith under the most challenging of circumstances. He saw the good in his brothers and forgave them time and time again. He was courageous in his defense of what he knew was right and uncompromising in the face of evil

In the early pages of the Book of Mormon, Nephi leaves a long shadow for the prophets that followed him. We sometimes gloss over how extraordinary he was. Just the act of building a ship and then setting out without the final destination in mind required amazing faith. This was only one of the acts of faith in a life filled with amazing accomplishments.

But most importantly, Nephi was a disciple of Christ. He constantly recognized that his marvelous works only came because of his relationship with the Savior. Near the end of his life he wrote, "I glory in plainness; I glory in truth; I glory in my Jesus, for he hath redeemed my soul from hell" (2 Nephi 33:6).

While Christ is the ultimate hero in our lives, the scriptures give us hundreds of faithful men and women we can model our lives after. We can become like them, if only we have faith.

Who are your heroes from the Book of Mormon? How can you be more like them?

Day 77
Doctrine and Covenants 34:3

How Can I Become a Son or Daughter of Jesus Christ?

> *Who so loved the world that he gave his own life, that as many as would believe might become the sons of God. Wherefore you are my son.*

The revelation was given to Orson Pratt—the young, bright, and thoughtful brother of Parley P. Pratt. At the time this revelation was given, Orson was only nineteen years old. He eventually went on to become an original member of the Quorum of the Twelve called in 1835 and one of the most gifted latter-day thinkers of all time. The Lord must have sensed Orson's inquisitive mind, and so He begins the revelation with one of the most tantalizing doctrinal questions: how does a person become a son or daughter of God?

Our divine parenthood is one of the central teachings of the Church. All men and women are the children of divine parents, and because of this they have a divine nature and destiny. So why are there so many invitations in the scriptures inviting us to become the children of God? Aren't we already the children of God?

While it is true that we are children of Heavenly Parents, the invitation here is about becoming something more, specifically becoming the children of Christ. Invitations to do this are found throughout the Doctrine and Covenants, including the Lord's words to Emma Smith, where He taught that "all those who receive my gospel are sons and daughters in my kingdom" (Doctrine and Covenants 25:1).

Being a child of God is a given, but being a child of Christ is a choice. We become the children of Christ as we enter into covenants with Him. These covenants require us to offer a broken heart and a contrite spirit, but in turn Christ offers everything. He offers to make us joint-heirs with Him in receiving all that the Father hath (see Romans 8:17).

When we choose to follow Christ, we undergo a new birth, becoming the children of Christ in addition to our sacred identity as the children of Heavenly Parents.

What can you choose today to become a child of Jesus Christ?

Day 78
Doctrine and Covenants 34:10

How Can I Give My All to the Savior?

> *Wherefore, lift up your voice and spare not, for the Lord God hath spoken; therefore prophesy, and it shall be given by the power of the Holy Ghost.*

A small part of the Lord's counsel to Orson Pratt still resonates in the minds of believers today. The Lord tells him, "Lift up your voice and spare not." We sometimes enter into our responsibilities with the Lord half-heartedly. We hold back the best of ourselves for many reasons. We are afraid of being rejected, mocked, or ridiculed for our beliefs. We know that standing up for the right isn't always the most popular thing. Sometimes we are just being lazy and don't want to commit to the hard work of living the gospel. For whatever reason, we hold back.

Orson Pratt took the Lord's counsel to "spare not" to heart. He devoted his life to being a fearless advocate for the gospel. Though he still had his seasons of doubt and despair, he wholeheartedly devoted himself to the work of God. By the end of his life, Orson crossed the Atlantic Ocean sixteen times to serve missions. He published the earliest printed version of the First Vision in one of his writings. He fearlessly defended the Church, even engaging in a series of public debates with the chaplain of the United States Senate. Nearly all of his life was devoted to writing, preaching, and serving in the cause of God.

Near the end of his life when some Church members criticized Orson, Brigham Young stood up for his fellow apostle. Though they sometimes found themselves at odds with each other, Brigham declared, "If you were to chop up Elder Pratt into one inch square pieces, each piece would cry out 'Mormonism is true!'"[13] The tribute is now carved into Orson's headstone.

We hold back for a number of reasons, but when we make the choice to give our all to the service of God, we find true power in our work.

How can you "spare not" in your service to God?

Day 79
Doctrine and Covenants 35:3–4

How Can I Prepare the Way of the Lord?

> *Behold, verily, verily, I say unto my servant Sidney, I have looked upon thee and thy works. I have heard thy prayers, and prepared thee for a greater work.*
>
> *Thou art blessed, for thou shalt do great things. Behold thou wast sent forth, even as John, to prepare the way before me, and before Elijah which should come, and thou knewest it not.*

Oliver Cowdery led the first organized mission of the Church. Along with his companions, he intended to travel to the American frontier and present the Book of Mormon to the Native Americans. But an interesting thing happened along the way. One of the missionaries, Parley P. Pratt, pointed out an old friend, Sidney Rigdon, who was an influential minister in Ohio. The missionaries stopped in the area around Kirtland, Ohio, and began meeting with Sidney and members of his congregations.

---

13. Orson Pratt Headstone Inscription, https://www.findagrave.com/memorial/6279196/orson-pratt.

At first Sidney was suspicious of the missionaries and the Book of Mormon, but after talking with Oliver Cowdery and reading the book for himself, he became convinced that it was the word of God. A few days later Sidney and his wife, Phoebe, addressed their congregation in tears, explaining to them that they had to leave their church to follow their new faith. Their testimony was so powerful that a large number of Sidney's followers also began hearing the message and entered the waters of baptism.

Anxious to meet the prophet who brought forth the Book of Mormon, Sidney left Kirtland with his friend Edward Partridge and traveled nearly three hundred miles to New York, where he met with Joseph Smith. Joseph received this revelation on behalf of Sidney, who was told his work was like John the Baptist, preparing the way for the Savior and His restored Church.

Often our lives take surprising turns and we find ourselves in a new situation, just as Sidney did. At times it may feel like the Lord turns around and sends us in the opposite direction. This does not mean that our previous works and devotion are wasted. They are simply part of our preparation for the next great task the Lord has for us. If we are sincere in our service, then all of it is consecrated to God and becomes part of the story He has written for us.

How have your experiences prepared you for what the Lord is asking you to do right now?

Day 80

Doctrine and Covenants 36:2

What Are the Peaceable Things of the Kingdom?

And I will lay my hand upon you by the hand of my servant Sidney Rigdon, and you shall receive my Spirit, the Holy Ghost, even the Comforter, which shall teach you the peaceable things of the kingdom.

This revelation is addressed to Edward Partridge, the faithful friend of Sidney Rigdon, who traveled nearly three hundred miles to Church headquarters. Unlike Sidney, who was baptized before they left on their journey, Edward decided to put off joining the Church until he could meet the Prophet in person. When they met, Sidney and Edward both asked for a revelation. Doctrine and Covenants 36 is the revelation to Edward Partridge.

Not surprisingly, the Lord counseled Edward to enter the waters of baptism and promised him the Spirit once he was confirmed a member of the Church. He then gave Edward a promise that still applies to all who receive the Holy Ghost—it will "teach you the peaceable things of the kingdom."

What the peaceable things of the kingdom are may vary from person to person. But there is a peace found in serving God and our fellow brothers and sisters. Only a few months after this revelation was given, Edward was called as the first bishop in the Church. He devoted the rest of his life to caring for the poor and needy and helping to build Zion.

Though he faced numerous trials in his lifetime, Edward lived a life of peace. On one occasion he was tarred and feathered by a bloodthirsty mob. He bore his testimony to the mob and later recalled that even though his life was threatened, he felt peace.

If we live our lives to have the Spirit with us, we will still face trials, but we can also know the peace that comes only from an assurance of a pure heart and a promise of eternal life. After all, the peaceable thing taught in the kingdom is the assurance of a better world and place of rest.

What are the teachings of the gospel that bring you the greatest peace?

Day 81

Doctrine and Covenants 37:3

Why Does the Lord Gather His People?

And again, a commandment I give unto the church, that it is expedient in me that they should assemble together at the Ohio, against the time that my servant Oliver Cowdery shall return unto them.

This is the first commandment given to the Saints of our dispensation to gather. Prior to this revelation, the Saints lived in scattered communities, mostly around New York and Pennsylvania. With the success of Oliver Cowdery and the first missionaries, there were now more Church members in Ohio than in all of the eastern branches combined. The Lord would later give His reasons, but initially He simply told the Saints everywhere to gather at the Ohio River, meaning near Kirtland, Ohio.

During the following century, it was common practice for Latter-day Saints, whether they were baptized in Texas, Great Britain, or Hawaii, to seek to gather to the headquarters of the Church. Beginning in the twentieth century, the leaders of the Church asked Church members to no longer gather physically. Instead, their call was to remain in their home countries and build the Church there, planting the seeds for a new worldwide religion.

While we no longer gather physically, we continue to gather spiritually in our time. We gather on Sunday to take part in the sacrament. We gather in temples to make sacred covenants. We gather in small groups to express our love and friendship. We gather in families on a regular basis to pray, study the scriptures, and enjoy fellowship with our loved ones.

God is a gatherer. While the troubles and pressures of the world seek to split us apart, God gathers us together. As we gather there is power in unity and strength in knowing the goodness and faith of others. In this sense the gathering will always be a commandment to the Saints.

How can you gather today?

Day 82

Doctrine and Covenants 38:2

Does God Know All Things?

> *The same which knoweth all things, for all things are present before mine eyes.*

Time works differently for God. In a way that we can't comprehend right now, He sees the end from the beginning and knows all things. The Lord never makes these statements out of a sense of superiority. Instead He gives us this information to reassure us. He knows how we will escape our current troubles. He knows what we need to survive. He knows the end of our story.

Just because God knows the end of our story does not mean that we aren't free to make our own choices. God uses a light touch in how He directs our lives. Sometimes He chooses to intervene, but most of the time He allows us to make our own decisions, even if they are sometimes unwise. He knows that if He intervenes in every choice we make, our lives won't truly belong to us. Our lives are His gift to us, allowing us to gain the experiences and empathy we need to become like Him.

Instead, God guides us along our path, offering a gentle correction here and there, hoping and encouraging us to make the correct choices. One day, when we are further down the path toward becoming like God, we will look back on our life and see the order and design to our experiences. But it can be frightening to be in the middle of the journey and not see the end. That is why God shares His greater perspective with us. We might not know the end, but He does, and He is helping us to find our way back home.

It is nice to know that someone knows the end of our story and has a new chapter ready for us.

What can you do to show your trust in God's knowledge of all things?

Day 83

Doctrine and Covenants 38:8

How Can I See Past the Veil of Darkness?

> *But the day soon cometh that ye shall see me, and know that I am; for the veil of darkness shall soon be rent, and he that is not purified shall not abide the day.*

This life is only a small part of our existence. The scriptures teach that we existed long before we came to earth, and we will live forever after we leave this life. That doesn't mean that our earthly life isn't a crucial turning point in our existence. This life is a test, but all tests come to an end. When the test ends we will find ourselves with all of our knowledge restored (see Alma 11:42–43). But for now we wander in darkness.

To carry out a true test of our character, God placed a veil over our minds when we came to earth. In this revelation, the Lord refers to it as "the veil of darkness." Darkness can be terrifying because of how disorienting it can be. When I was a child, my family went to a cave in a national park. We walked what felt like a long distance into the cave with the path illuminated by electric lights. At a certain point, our guide stopped us and announced that he was going to turn off all the lights for a moment to show us how dark the cave usually was.

When the lights went out, a feeling a terror gripped me. I held my hand a few inches from my face, unable to see anything. It was so dark, my eyes couldn't adjust. There was simply no light for my eyes to take in.

In the middle of this frightening experience, I heard the voice of my father. He put his hand on my shoulder and told me that everything was going to be okay. My heart started to slow down, and I felt an overwhelming sense of calm, knowing that as long as I could hear his voice, I wouldn't be lost in the cave. We would find a way out together.

In this passage the Savior makes two important promises. First, one day we will see Him. All of our questions will be answered, and we will know for ourselves that He lives and has been there for us the whole time. Second, He promises that if we are pure, the veil of darkness will finally be taken from us. We will finally see the universe, understand its purpose, and fully appreciate its wonder.

Until then we wait in darkness. We stumble along and listen for the voice that can provide us assurance and comfort. But the day is coming when the darkness will end if we are ready.

How can you be more pure to lighten the darkness today?

Day 84
Doctrine and Covenants 38:27

Why Is Unity So Important to God?

Behold, this I have given unto you as a parable, and it is even as I am. I say unto you, be one; and if ye are not one ye are not mine.

In today's world we often celebrate diversity. This is good! The gospel brings together a wide variety of people from various backgrounds with different cultures, philosophies, and ways of life. One of the real pleasures of being part of the Church is spending time with people who are very different from you. Some of my most meaningful relationships have grown out of time spent with people not like me, learning from them and growing to appreciate their views.

But while we celebrate diversity, we must remember that the ultimate goal of the gospel is not diversity but unity in the gospel of Christ. Out of all those different backgrounds, Christ provides us with something that brings us all together and gives us a common thread of hope to cling to. He needs us to be united to survive the travails and challenges we face.

But diversity and unity are not opposites. There is a unity to be found in appreciating and celebrating the uniqueness of every individual. God wants us to be like Him, but in doing so we won't give up any of our individuality. We will come to be like God in the sense that our character and attributes will be as perfect as His are, but we will still be unique. Not everyone will look or think exactly alike in the celestial kingdom.

In becoming one, we lose the worst parts of ourselves, and the most unique and wonderful parts of our being become the best they can be.

What can you do today to increase your unity with God and the people you love?

Day 85

Doctrine and Covenants 38:32

How Can I Receive an Endowment from on High?

Wherefore, for this cause I gave unto you the commandment that ye should go to the Ohio; and there I will give unto you my law; and there you shall be endowed with power from on high.

When the Lord gave the early Saints the commandment to gather to the Ohio, He didn't gave a reason. This is often the case with some of the most important commandments we are given. We are told what to do but not given a reason. We act on faith and receive blessings for it, but it is always a little easier to do things when we know the reasons.

The Saints didn't have to wait long to find out the reasons. In a revelation given just a few days later, the Lord gave two specific reasons for the command to gather. First, once they had gathered, the Lord would give them His law. This was fulfilled just a few weeks after the Saints gathered when Joseph Smith was given the revelation, now Doctrine and Covenants 42, that contained a number of laws, including the law of consecration.

The second promise was more elusive. The Lord promised that the Saints would be "endowed with power from on high." Today the word *endowment* is almost always associated with temple worship, but when this revelation was given in 1831 there was no temple and the ordinances of the temple were yet to be revealed. The word *endowment* meant a gift of power.

The early Saints looked for that gift. After several powerful spiritual experiences, they often paused to reflect if what they had just experienced was the promised endowment from on high. In our time the endowment is one of the ceremonies performed in the temple. But the temple endowment is the beginning of the endowment promised in the revelation, not the end. It opens the door for us to receive real power.

We are endowed with power to have a greater knowledge of God. We are endowed with power to have greater love for the people in our lives. We are endowed with power to have peace in our lives. The endowment never really ends. It continues into the eternities until we are finally endowed with everything God has and we become like Him.

What can you do today to receive a greater endowment of power?

Day 86

Doctrine and Covenants 38:35

How Can I Assist the Poor And Needy?

> *And they shall look to the poor and the needy, and administer to their relief that they shall not suffer; and send them forth to the place which I have commanded them.*

While Doctrine and Covenants 37 and 38 introduce the concept of gathering, they also contain instruction about the right way and the wrong way to gather. Part of the purpose of the gathering was to allow the Saints to consecrate their resources in a way that helped everyone from the greatest to the least. The idea was never to gather as quickly as possible but to take the time to help everyone gather. Once the people were gathered, the Lord introduced the law of consecration so that they were all fed, clothed, and housed as well.

This is not easy, and it was never intended to be. Often when we see someone who is poor or needy, our tendency is to look away so that we aren't confronted with something unpleasant. But the Savior pled with the Saints to look to the poor and needy and find ways to provide comfort and alleviate their suffering.

This charge remains with us today. We must seek out the best ways to eliminate suffering and to lift all of those around us to a better place. The gathering can only happen in the right way when we look to those who struggle, are less fortunate, and need our help. There are many kinds of needs and many ways we can help. Offering this help is central to the gathering in the latter days.

How can you look to the poor and needy and administer relief to them today?

Day 87

Doctrine and Covenants 39:3

How Can I Love Those Who Have Rejected Me?

The same which came in the meridian of time unto mine own, and mine own received me not.

We all face rejection on a regular basis. It can be hard to engage in everyday life when there is so much negativity around us. Rather than face rejection and risk being hurt, many of us choose to withdraw and keep to ourselves. To those who have experienced rejection, the Savior offers this consolation—He knows rejection too.

In this passage, the Savior also effectively tells us where the center of history is found. By His own words, the Savior declares that the era of His life on earth is the "meridian of time," or the center point of all the history of the world. He came in the center of time to deliver the most important message and carry out the most important actions ever taken by one child of God on behalf of all of the other children of God.

And what did He receive for His for His efforts? Rejection.

The Savior tells us that His own people, the very people He came to save, received Him not. This isn't an indictment of all people for all time. The Book of Mormon specifies that Jesus, like any good leader, chose the most difficult group to handle Himself (see 2 Nephi 10:3). He came to them bearing a message of universal deliverance and was rejected.

He still loved them and labored to bring them around to the right way. It is telling that the Savior makes this statement to James Covel, a Methodist minister, who ultimately rejected the message (see Doctrine and Covenants 40).

The Savior knew rejection. There are still people who reject Him today, and He still loves them. We too all face rejection; that is just a given in this life. But can we do what Jesus did and continue to show love in the hope that one day we will know success?

How can you be like the Savior when you face rejection?

Day 88
Doctrine and Covenants 39:10

How Can I Choose to Be Delivered?

But, behold, the days of thy deliverance are come, if thou wilt hearken to my voice, which saith unto thee: Arise and be baptized, and wash away your sins, calling on my name, and you shall receive my Spirit, and a blessing so great as you never have known.

Doctrine and Covenants 39 was given to James Covel, a Methodist minister, who came to Joseph Smith seeking revelation. What we know about James Covel is limited, but we know that he ultimately decided to reject the message of the Restoration (see Doctrine and Covenants 40).

Given that James Covel rejected the message, the focal point of the revelation becomes the word *if.* In this early period of the Church there are many "ifs" in the revelations given to the converts who came into orbit around the Church and the Book of Mormon. Some of these early converts, such as Parley and Orson Pratt and Edward Partridge, became mighty leaders who devoted their lives to the service of God and died in the service of the Church. Others, such as James Covel, Ezra Thayre, and Northrop Sweet, stayed in the Church for a short time and then left.

These blessings, like any blessings given from God, are as much invitations as they are proclamations. The Lord always makes space for us to choose. Sometimes we make the wrong choices and find our blessings fulfilled. Sometimes we make the wrong choices and find our blessings lost. But the Lord recognizes that the only real kind of goodness and righteousness is found in what we choose, not what we are forced to do.

When we make the choice to follow Christ, the blessings flow.

What choices can you make today that will ensure you receive your blessings?

Day 89
Doctrine and Covenants 40:3

How Does the Lord Help Those Who Reject Him?

Wherefore he broke my covenant, and it remaineth with me to do with him as seemeth me good. Amen.

Doctrine and Covenants 39 is one of the most poignant revelations given to Joseph Smith. After the wonderful promises made to James Covel in the previous section, the Lord reveals that James has rejected the covenants. We know almost nothing about James Covel except what the Lord tells us here. The Lord explains that James "received the word with gladness, but straightway Satan tempted him; and the fear of persecution and the cares of the world caused him to reject the word" (Doctrine and Covenants 40:2).

From the teachings of Christ, we know that many will reject the word. The Savior shared a parable about four types of ground that seeds might be planted in: the wayside, rocky ground, among thorns, and good ground (see Matthew 13:1–8). In only one of the four places did the seeds of the gospel really take root and produce a crop.

In the same way, people sometimes reject the gospel for a number of reasons, many of which are beyond our control. When I was a young teacher, I wanted to save everyone but soon realized that it was not always possible. As long as we respect agency, we have to respect the choices of others, even when we disagree.

The most important statement in the revelation is where the Lord acknowledges James Covel's rejection but adds "it remaineth with me to do with him as seemeth me good." Our ability to help someone is limited to the extent they will allow us to help them. But the Lord was not giving up on James. We don't know how the story ends, but we know that the Lord continued to work with him even in the face of his rejection.

The Savior never gives up on people and neither should we. It can be challenging to continue to pray for and reach out to those who have turned away from the gospel, but, like the Savior, we persist.

How can you reach out to someone who has struggled or left their faith?

Day 90

Doctrine and Covenants 41:5

How Can I Be a Better Disciple?

He that receiveth my law and doeth it, the same is my disciple; and he that saith he receiveth it and doeth it not, the same is not my disciple, and shall be cast out from among you.

Disciples aren't perfect, and the Lord doesn't expect them to be. With the exception of the Savior, each of us falls short in one way or another. We all fail in one way or another in our discipleship. But the Lord doesn't expect perfection from His disciples.

Here the Lord gives a simple definition of discipleship in this revelation to Edward Partridge. "He that receiveth my law and depth it, the same is my disciple." There are two components. First, we receive the law. There are a number of ways to interpret this passage, but the most straightforward might be that we study the teachings of Christ, listen to His messengers, and then make a commitment to live by His teachings.

The second component is where things get a little trickier. We have to receive the law and do what the law tells us to do. We all fail in this sense, but the Savior is not concerned with perfect discipleship, only sincere discipleship. The Savior is more concerned with us receiving the law than following it perfectly, but if we don't make an attempt to really live the law, we are not sincere in truly receiving it.

Elder Dale G. Renlund once shared a quote from Nelson Mandela that "a saint is just a sinner who keeps on trying."[14] Discipleship doesn't have to be perfect, and the Lord can grant grace to imperfect disciples. But if we really receive the law, we will try to do what the laws to show our sincerity.

How can you strive to both receive and do the law today?

---

14. Dale G. Renlund, "Latter-day Saints Keep on Trying," *Ensign*, May 2015.

Day 91

Doctrine and Covenants 41:9

How Can I Sustain My Bishop?

And again, I have called my servant Edward Partridge; and I give a commandment, that he should be appointed by the voice of the church, and ordained a bishop unto the church, to leave his merchandise and to spend all his time in the labors of the church.

In February 1831 Edward Partridge was called as the first bishop of the Church. Before his call, Edward ran a successful business in Painesville, Ohio. But now he was asked to leave that behind and work full time to look after the needs of the members of the Church. Edward's call continued until his death nine years later in 1840.

Very few of us will be asked to make a sacrifice as significant as Edward Partridge's. The Church is filled with millions of dedicated individuals who give up time in their jobs, their families, and other ways to serve the cause of God. Being a bishop is one of the most intensive and time-consuming callings in the Church. It sometimes involves dealing with very difficult decisions, working with people who have severe challenges, and often feeling overwhelmed.

But there are many rewards for engaging in an intensive calling like that of a bishop. We learn to love people who are sometimes difficult to love. We gain the opportunity to see the hand of the Lord in the lives of our fellow Saints. We gain an understanding of how much God loves all of His sons and daughters.

Multitudes of dedicated men and women like Edward Partridge give their all to cause of Christ. We are asked to sustain them, but that involves much more than just raising our hand in support. It means that we do our best to uphold their leadership, help them in their weakness, and thank them for their service. It is never easy to hold a challenging calling in the Church, but the burden can be lighter if the people they serve are generous, kind, and understanding.

What can you do to help someone who is serving in a challenging calling?

Day 92
Doctrine and Covenants 41:11

How Can I Become a Person Without Guile?

And this because his heart is pure before me, for he is like unto Nathanael of old, in whom there is no guile.

In this section, Edward Partridge is called as the first bishop in the Church. At the time, he was a successful businessman and respected community leader, but that's not why he was called. He had a beautiful family with his wife, Lydia, but that is not why he was chosen either. He had traveled hundreds of miles to meet with the Prophet Joseph Smith and had been the recipient of a revelation given directly from Jesus Christ (Doctrine and Covenants 46), but that is also not why he was chosen.

Why was he chosen? The Lord states his reason directly. Edward was chosen because his heart was pure. The Lord even compares Edward to Nathanael in the New Testament. Nathanael was a friend of the disciple Phillip, who was invited to meet the Savior. When Nathanael was told that Jesus was from the town of Nazareth, he blurted out, "Can there any good thing come out of Nazareth?" When Nathanael was brought to meet with Jesus, the Savior looked at him and declared, "Behold an Israelite in deed, in whom there is no guile!" Nathanael immediately declared, "Rabbi, thou art the son of God; thou art the King of Israel" (John 1:46–49).

In declaring that Nathanael and Edward Partridge were both men without any guile, Jesus was making a comment on their sincerity. Possessing guile doesn't mean that a person is necessarily evil. Having guile means that a person is clever, cunning, or sophisticated. Both Nathanael and Edward were blunt and unsophisticated. But they were honest and never tried to appear as anything other than what they were in real life. They didn't feel the need to compliment or charm anyone. They were simple, pure men who did what they thought was right.

The Lord doesn't always choose the smartest, most well-educated, or most skilled person to serve. To Him the most important qualification is a pure heart and sincere desire to help.

What can you do today to have a pure heart?

Day 93
Doctrine and Covenants 42:9

How Can I Be Part of the City of God?

Until the time shall come when it shall be revealed unto you from on high, when the city of the New Jerusalem shall be prepared, that ye may be gathered in one, that ye may be my people and I will be your God.

In early February 1831, Joseph and Emma Smith made the difficult decision to leave their home and farm to obey the Lord's commandment to gather to Ohio (see Doctrine and Covenants 37). They followed this command at great personal sacrifice. Joseph's family had joined the Church and planned to travel to Ohio as well. But Emma's family chose not to believe and remained behind in Pennsylvania. Emma never saw her parents again in this life, and we do not know how much they communicated after she decided to leave home. Both Emma and Joseph left behind the childhood hometowns they grew up in, never to return.

Why leave behind everything they had known? The Lord promised that if the Saints gathered to Ohio they would receive His law and an endowment of power (see Doctrine and Covenants 38:32). The law, which is now Doctrine and Covenants 42, was given shortly after they arrived in Ohio. The Lord began the revelation by explaining that the law was only the beginning. The principles in the law would be used to build the city of Zion, a New Jerusalem in the latter days.

In leaving their home for a promised land and new life, Joseph and Emma joined the ranks of some of the most faithful women and men who have served God. Adam and Eve, Sarah and Abraham, Moses and Zipporah, and Sariah and Lehi are just a few examples of faithful people who left home filled with uncertainty but seeking a new promised land.

Today it is rare for the Lord to ask us to leave our home and find a new place. But seeking to be a part of the city of Zion can mean leaving behind old habits, incorrect beliefs, and toxic environments to seek a better way. It is never easy to leave behind what we are familiar with, but the scriptures testify that if we place our trust in God and take the leap of faith, we will find our land of promise waiting for us as well. When we arrive, the Lord will be there to greet us. We just have to take the first steps on our journey.

What do you need to leave behind to start your journey to Zion?

Day 94
Doctrine and Covenants 42:12–13

Where Can I Go to Teach the Truth?

> *And again, the elders, priests and teachers of this church shall teach the principles of my gospel, which are in the Bible and the Book of Mormon, in the which is the fulness of the gospel.*
>
> *And they shall observe the covenants and church articles to do them, and these shall be their teachings, as they shall be directed by the Spirit.*

Doctrine and Covenants 42, known as the law of the Church, is actually a series of laws that the Lord gave to the Saints to steer them toward Zion. One of the first laws given is about teaching in the Church and is what we draw our teaching from as we instruct each other. In one way or another every person in the Church is a teacher. The Lord was aware of this, so His first set of instructions was designed to steer teachers toward the best sources of truth.

It shouldn't surprise anyone that the Lord asks us to go first to the scriptures when we teach. He mentions the Bible, the Book of Mormon, and "covenants and church articles," which would later become the Doctrine and Covenants.

Today there is an abundance of lesson material that can be easily found with a few clicks and online searches. We can find stories, object lessons, and quotes from Church leaders to create our lessons from. But while the mountain of source material we have easy access to is a great blessing, it is important that we also heed the Lord's command to begin with the scriptures. However interesting or well-prepared our teaching might be, it will be a watered-down version of the truth unless the scriptures are our first source.

How often do we find ourselves talking about the word of God rather than just sharing it directly? In our classrooms, and more importantly in our homes, the scriptures are the most powerful source of truth we have access to. In a world overflowing with information, we must remember that not all of it is useful and a lot of it is superfluous. The scriptures remain the primary source of truth for us.

What can you do today to teach from the scriptures?

Day 95

Doctrine and Covenants 42:30

How Can I Remember the Poor?

> *And behold, thou wilt remember the poor, and consecrate of thy properties for their support that which thou hast to impart unto them, with a covenant and a deed which cannot be broken.*

What is the law of consecration? Doctrine and Covenants 42 contains several laws, but the centerpiece of the revelation is the law of consecration, which is found in verses 30–42. This isn't the only place the law of consecration is found. How to take care of the poor and needy and alleviate suffering is a central theme of all of the revelations given to Joseph Smith and the prophets who followed him. There are and were many adjustment to the law over time to meet the changing needs and conditions of the Church.

But the heart of the law of consecration is found right here in this verse, and perhaps in the phrase "thou wilt remember the poor."

When we have plenty of food, housing, and shelter, it is easy to forget that others might be lacking. It is also easier to avert our gaze when we see someone in a difficult place. The Lord asks us to do something harder. He asks that we not just look after our own concerns but take an interest in the suffering of others and do something about it. We remember the poor, we remember those who are suffering, and we try to help. We may not be able to solve every problem, but we acknowledge the problem and get to work.

With all of the problems in the world, where do we begin? The first step is to make a covenant with God to consecrate what we have to help Him make sure all of our brothers and sisters are taken care of. The Lord uses the word *covenant* to describe the first step in the process of helping us live the law. It is not surprising that a commitment to live the law of consecration was later revealed as one of the five sacred covenants a person makes when they enter the temple.

The Lord asks each of us to take a hard look at the ills that cause misery around us, then covenant to do something about it.

What can you do today to remember the poor?

Day 96

Doctrine and Covenants 42:42

How Can I Avoid Idleness?

> *Thou shalt not be idle; for he that is idle shall not eat the bread nor wear the garments of the laborer.*

As the Lord set down His plan to help the poor and needy in the law of consecration, He didn't shy away from a key component of making the plan a success: work! It would take a lot of work to make sure that everyone was taken care of. It required work from those who were giving assistance and from those who were receiving assistance. The law of consecration did not consist of free handouts but sincere effort on the part of all involved to end the problem of poverty. In essence, the Lord's plan was only able to help those who helped themselves.

When we are confronted with problems such as taking care of the poor, we can be tempted to look at the vastness of the challenges, feel overwhelmed, and give up. But there is a real advantage to be found in rolling up our sleeves and going to work, even if we don't quite know the whole solution yet. Answers usually don't come when we are sitting idle but when we are trying to do something to help.

Work is an offering we can give to the Lord, and when He sees our sincere effort He can open the doors for us. He can solve any problem. We just need to show that we are willing to do something, and then the Savior shows us the way or clears the path for us to accomplish what we need.

When we not only see the problem but also get to work on it, then the solutions will come.

What problem can you start to work out today?

Day 97
Doctrine and Covenants 42:48

How Can I Learn to Accept the Lord's Will?

And again, it shall come to pass that he that hath faith in me to be healed, and is not appointed unto death, shall be healed.

One of the most poignant passages in the Doctrine and Covenants is found where the Lord explains the laws of healing. One of the blessings of the priesthood is the miraculous ability to use God's power to heal the sick. Many of the stories about Jesus in the New Testament and the Book of Mormon demonstrate His compassion toward the sick and afflicted. The Savior did everything He could to ease the suffering of the people around Him. He asked His disciples to do the same, and they carried on with these efforts. When the gospel was restored to the earth, the gift of healing was made manifest again, showing that the day of miracles had not passed.

But there are limits to the power to heal. The Savior notes here that it requires faith, both on the part of the healer and the healed. The afflicted person must demonstrate faith in God or the healing may not work. Healing is a collaborative effort between the afflicted person, the healer, and the Lord. Without sufficient faith, the healing does not take effect.

The second condition is something that cannot be overcome even if the healer and the person being healed have great faith. The Lord notes a person can only be healed if they are "not appointed unto death." In other words, there are situations when we simply have to realize that our time on earth is finite—we will all eventually be called home.

In these situations, no amount of faith can overcome an illness or affliction, but faith can lessen our sorrow in losing them. Even if their time has come, our separation from those we love will only be temporary. Because of the Savior, all afflictions, even death, will eventually be overcome.

While we wait for that day, we do all in our power to help the suffering and accept the Lord's will when it overrules our desires.

What can you do today to let go and accept the will of God?

Day 98

Doctrine and Covenants 42:92

How Can I Deal with Someone Who Offends Me?

> *If any shall offend in secret, he or she shall be rebuked in secret, that he or she may have opportunity to confess in secret to him or her whom he or she has offended, and to God, that the church may not speak reproachfully of him or her.*

Even among committed disciples of Christ, offenses come. It is almost unavoidable that someone will say something or do something that upsets us. We don't have much choice in the matter. But we do have a choice in how we respond when the offense comes. Recognizing this, the Lord counsels us to seek correction and confession but not in a way that publicly embarrasses or shames someone. The smallest offense can grow into a major problem as more and more people are involved. So the Lord counsels us when we can to work out these problems amongst ourselves.

I have a son who has autism, and when he was young it was very difficult to control him during Church meetings. We did the best we could, but at times he was very disruptive. After one exhausting sacrament meeting a man in our congregation came up to me and accused me of poor parenting because my son was disruptive. He continued on a rant about my poor parenting until I interrupted him and tried to explain a little bit about my son's condition and why it was so hard to keep him reverent. The man paused but then doubled down and told me it was no excuse for his behavior.

I was offended, but I knew I could choose how I would respond. It was difficult to ignore my feelings, but I decided not to get angry. I thanked him and moved on. The next week at church the same person said he had been researching autism during the week. He apologized and gave me several articles he had printed off that he thought might be helpful. We eventually became good friends.

Offenses will come. We can choose to forgive. We can choose to resolve things privately. If we do, we can stop an offense from hardening our damaging souls.

What can you do to forgive the people who have offended you?

Day 99

Doctrine and Covenants 43:7

How Can I Enter in at the Gate?

> *For verily I say unto you, that he that is ordained of me shall come in at the gate and be ordained as I have told you before, to teach those revelations which you have received and shall receive through him whom I have appointed.*

This revelation came when a new member in Kirtland began receiving revelations that she claimed were meant to direct the entire Church. She is only identified in Joseph Smith's history as "Mrs. Hubble," and we don't know anything about her revelations, except that they alarmed Church leaders enough that they sought a revelation to clarify the matter.

The entire episode illustrates a few simple truths. First, anyone in the Church can receive revelation. But God's house is a house of order, and the revelation must come through the proper channels of stewardship. Personal revelation can lead us down dark roads if it is not constantly checked against the words of the scriptures and the prophets.

In the revelation, the Lord emphasizes this by teaching that those who receive revelations for others must "come in at the gate" or be given their authority through the proper channels. We should all seek revelation for ourselves and for those in our stewardship. That is a gift God gives us.

But there is also power in asking for revelation from those whom the Lord has placed in a stewardship role over us. Often they will have a different perspective or a better link to revelation than we have. There are those who have been asked to look after us, help us, and connect us to the Lord. When we seek guidance from those who have already entered in at the gate, we often find our own path to the Lord is clearer.

What are some good sources you can seek guidance from?

Day 100
Doctrine and Covenants 43:15–16

How Can I Best Teach Other People?

> *Again I say, hearken ye elders of my church, whom I have appointed: Ye are not sent forth to be taught, but to teach the children of men the things which I have put into your hands by the power of my Spirit;*
>
> *And ye are to be taught from on high. Sanctify yourselves and ye shall be endowed with power, that ye may give even as I have spoken.*

We all need to learn and to be taught. There is a world of knowledge out there that God has given us to use for our own benefit and to make the lives of others better. At the same time, there is a point when we need to open our mouths and share the sacred things the Lord has given us. We are often shy about sharing our faith with others, but if we are sincere and kind in the way we do it, there is nothing to fear.

In fact, we have much to gain because the truths of the gospel are designed to help lift others from their trials and troubles. This doesn't mean that we never listen to what others have to say. Real teaching is always a two-way affair, with listening and response. But we should never be ashamed to share how the gospel can help heal the wounds of others, or explain how it has helped heal us.

When I was a missionary I fell in love with a lot of other religions. I continue to study them to this day. Because of this I have found a lot of truth and beauty in the study of other faiths. But I also have gained a deeper sense of gratitude for my own faith and how profoundly true it is. When we share the gospel of Jesus Christ and how it has helped us to overcome the challenges we face, we open the door for others to share the same power and gain the same sense of belonging.

We go forth to teach because that is how we can help save the world.

How can you teach the gospel today in words or in deeds?

Day 101

Doctrine and Covenants 44:6

How Can I Administer Relief to Others?

> *Behold, I say unto you, that ye must visit the poor and the needy and administer to their relief, that they may be kept until all things may be done according to my law which ye have received. Amen.*

Shortly after Joseph Smith arrived in Ohio and received the law of the Church, the Lord provided the instructions in Doctrine and Covenants 44. This revelation instructed Church leaders to gather together all of the elders serving in one place so that the Lord could "pour out my Spirit upon them in the day that they assemble themselves together" (Doctrine and Covenants 44:2).

The Lord was taking the first steps to implement the law of consecration, one of the first steps on the road to building the city of Zion. He further instructed the elders to "visit the poor and needy and administer to their relief." This remains a vital part of the reason elders, now joined with the sisters of the Church, act as ministering servants to their fellow saints.

The law of consecration is still administered by leaders of the Church on all levels. But ministering brothers and sisters effectively act as the eyes and ears of Church leadership to know what they can do to help those who are struggling. Sometimes their actions can help get food and the necessities of life on the table of those who are in physical need. Sometimes their actions can help get emotional support to those families who are in need of love and fellowship.

The most important thing is that a visit or a check-in on the families you serve is not just a nice thing to do. It is a commandment of the Lord, a way of following His law for caring for the poor and needy. They need you, and the Lord needs you to go into their homes so that His servants can know how to help.

What can you do to visit and administer to someone today?

Day 102
Doctrine and Covenants 45:9

How Can I Be a Light to the World?

> *And even so I have sent mine everlasting covenant into the world, to be a light to the world, and to be a standard for my people, and for the Gentiles to seek to it, and to be a messenger before my face to prepare the way before me.*

In March 1831 Joseph Smith received a revelation that is one of the most comprehensive lists of the signs of the last days ever given. Doctrine and Covenants 45 brings together the prophecies of thousands of years into one revelation that contains a step-by-step account of events leading up to the Second Coming of Jesus Christ.

Events linked to the last days are often portrayed as frightening and dark. But in contrast to this, the Savior begins the revelation by talking about light, specifically the light of the gospel. We sometimes forget that the prophecies of the last days contain as much about great events as they do about terrible events. While it is true that the Saints who live in the last days will face many challenges, they will also see wondrous miracles.

What is the light that will emerge in these darkest of times? The Savior explains that the everlasting covenant will be a light and messenger to all the world. We are seeing this play out literally with the building of hundreds of temples in different locations around the world. These physical structures of light offer a chance for those who qualify to enter and receive the blessings of the everlasting covenant. When they emerge they join in sharing the light as they demonstrate how the covenants of the temple bring joy to a darkened world.

Yes, there is a growing darkness in the world. But there is also a growing light.

What can you do to bring the light of the gospel to the people around you?

Day 103

Doctrine and Covenants 45:17

How Can I Show Appreciation for the Gift of a Physical Body?

For as ye have looked upon the long absence of your spirits from your bodies to be a bondage, I will show unto you how the day of redemption shall come, and also the restoration of the scattered Israel.

Many religious traditions view our bodies as a trial to overcome. At best, our physical body is seen as a hold for a luminescent spirit, and at worst as a prison for our spirit. Latter-day Saints are somewhat unique for seeing our bodies as a blessing from God. We believe that having a physical body is an important step toward becoming like God. In Doctrine and Covenants 45 the Lord even declares that not having a body is a kind of bondage that keeps us from reaching our full potential. For Latter-day Saints, not having a body is the prison.

But we are also blessed to know that those who have lost their physical body will get it back. They will not only have the chance to dwell in a physical body again but also to know the joy that comes from living in a gloried, resurrected body. Because of Jesus Christ and His resurrection, every daughter or son of God who comes to earth will be resurrected as well. We will know each other, hold each other, and feel the joy of having a physical body forever.

In the meantime, instead of complaining about the aches and pains that sometimes are part of having a physical body, we can celebrate it. We have the ability to taste, smell, touch, and hold. We can cradle an infant in our arms. We can behold with wonder the physical world around us and labor to make it a better place. Rather than dwelling on the pain of life, we can focus on the promise of a glorious physical body while still enjoying the imperfect but wonderful body we now live in.

What can you do to show your appreciation for your body?

Day 104
Doctrine and Covenants 45:35

How Can I Escape Being Troubled?

> *And I said unto them: Be not troubled, for, when all these things shall come to pass, ye may know that the promises which have been made unto you shall be fulfilled.*

There are a lot of troubling things about living in the last days. Scrolling through the news, it is easy to feel like the world is spinning out of control and there is nothing we can do about it. Even those who believe in a better world to come can find themselves in distress about the state of the world we live in right now. There is a lot to worry about.

However, in all ages of the world, the Savior has offered this simple advice to His disciples: be not troubled.

That is, of course, easier said than done. But if we really understand the message of the gospel, it will help us to manage our anxiety over the state of the world. Things might be bad, but they are going to get better. The seemingly random nature of our lives has a purpose and a goal. We are going somewhere, and it is better than where we are right now.

Even the events that seem like they are spinning out of control are one of the signs that God is preparing to fulfill His covenant with us. He always keeps His promises. And if we have the faith to hold on, have courage, and do what we can to make things better, we will find those promises fulfilled. It takes mental effort, but we can be not troubled. We can know that things are going to be okay.

How can you choose to be not troubled today?

Day 105
Doctrine and Covenants 45:57

How Can I Take the Holy Spirit as My Guide?

> *For they that are wise and have received the truth, and have taken the Holy Spirit for their guide, and have not been deceived—verily I say unto you, they shall not be hewn down and cast into the fire, but shall abide the day.*

One of the most haunting teachings of the Savior is the parable of the ten virgins, found in Matthew 25:1–13. In the story, the Savior told of a group of young women invited to a marriage feast. Five of the virgins prepared by storing oil for their lamps, and five delayed getting oil for their lamps. When the marriage feast came in the middle of the night, the five wise virgins were able to join the caravan, while the five foolish ones were left behind. The Savior references this parable in Doctrine and Covenants 45 and gives a few more specifics about what makes a person prepared for the Second Coming. He states, "They that are wise and have received the truth, and have taken the Holy Spirit for their guide, and have not been deceived."

In the parable the five wise virgins relied on their lamps to guide the way to the marriage feast. The Savior likens the lamps in the parable to the Holy Spirit, which acts as our guide in the latter days. While we are blessed to have scripture, prophets, and a mountain of Church material to help guide us in our decisions, nothing can take the place of the Holy Spirit as a guide in our daily lives.

The Holy Spirit is the most immediate and essential of the guides God has given to us to help us avoid the dangers and pitfalls of the last days. If we live worthy of the Holy Spirit, its gentle whispering and promptings can help us know the best way to navigate the challenges of the latter days. The Spirit can give us guidance in every situation. We may not always have time to pull out the correct scripture or the right talk, but the Spirit can put inspired words into our mouths to help us know the right thing to say or do. If we have this guide with us, we will be like the five wise virgins, finding a light to show the way through dark times.

What can you do to have the Holy Spirit as your guide today?

Day 106
Doctrine and Covenants 45:66

How Can I Create Places of Refuge?

And it shall be called the New Jerusalem, a land of peace, a city of refuge, a place of safety for the saints of the Most High God.

As one of the most comprehensive lists of the signs leading up to the Savior's Second Coming, Doctrine and Covenants 45 warns us that the world will experience turmoil and upheaval in the latter days. It is perhaps our natural tendency to focus on the bad things about the Second Coming and ignore the prophecies that speak of the good things that will take place during that time. If we only focus on the bad, however, we miss an essential part of the mission of the Saints of the last days, specifically our call to build places of refuge.

The early Saints focused their hopes on building a New Jerusalem, a city where they could live in peace, take care of the poor among them, and dwell with the Savior. Their struggles to build this city is major part of the Doctrine and Covenants. But what was the city for? After the Lord lists the signs leading up to the Second Coming, He describes the New Jerusalem as "a city of refuge, a place of safety for the saints of the Most High God."

The commandment to build a city of refuge remains with the Church today. But now instead of a single city in one location, our charge is to build places of refuge around the world. The Lord urges us to create places where people can find safety, acceptance, and the love of Christ. There is so much in the world that seeks to abuse, hurt, or tear down. Are our homes and our churches places where people can come and feel safe and uplifted? Do we find ways to invite people to find safety among us?

The greatest safety is found in making covenants with God that allow us to have His grace to assist. But even small acts of refuge such as a kind smile, an encouraging word, or other expressions of love can create refuge in a troubled and tiring world.

What can you do to create a place of refuge for others today?

Day 107
Doctrine and Covenants 46:8

How Can I Seek the Best Gifts?

> *Wherefore, beware lest ye are deceived; and that ye may not be deceived seek ye earnestly the best gifts, always remembering for what they are given.*

Doctrine and Covenants 46 is one of three lists in the scriptures about the gifts of the Spirit. The other two lists were written by Paul (see 1 Corinthians 12–13) and Moroni (see Moroni 10). These gifts are a kind of spiritual superpower given by God to His children. They are meant to bless the people around us and assist us as we navigate the challenges of our daily lives. Everyone has a spiritual gift.

One of the wonderful things about these gifts is that we don't just have to be content with the gifts we already have and leave it at that. The Lord counsels us to seek out the best gifts and obtain them through our faith and effort. As with most things with the Lord, all we need to do is sincerely ask, and He will generously give.

It is tempting to seek out some of the most obvious spiritual gifts such as the gift of healing or the gift of prophecy. But there are other, quieter spiritual gifts that can be just as powerful, even if they are less well known. Being able to listen and empathize, being able to comfort, or knowing the right thing to say are all spiritual gifts as well. Spiritual gifts are God's way of compensating for our weaknesses by giving us power to do extraordinary things. But it is up to us to know what gifts to seek.

What spiritual gift can you seek to be a better disciple?

Day 108

Doctrine and Covenants 46:10

What Are My Spiritual Gifts?

> *And again, verily I say unto you, I would that ye should always remember, and always retain in your minds what those gifts are, that are given unto the church.*

The list of spiritual gifts in Doctrine and Covenants 46 is only the beginning of the gifts that God offers His children. Some of the gifts, such as the power to heal or be healed, can be seen easily. Others, such as the differences of administration, are more difficult to define clearly. The Lord also makes some interesting distinctions among the gifts. As just one example, He speaks of a person having the gift of the word of wisdom and another gift as the word of knowledge.

The "word of wisdom" mentioned here is not a reference to the health code followed by the Church, which was given some time later. Instead, here the Lord is making a distinction between wisdom and knowledge. Knowledge is information, while wisdom is information applied in everyday life. I know some of the most knowledgeable and educated people on earth. These scholars have worked hard to educate themselves at some of the finest schools in the world. But some of the wisest people I know have little education. They seem to be able to naturally know how to handle themselves and how to help others.

There is great value in seeking to know what your gifts are, and there are many ways to find out. Patriarchal blessings often provide a person with a few hints toward knowing their gifts. Studying the word of God and serving others are also effective ways of discovering your gifts and knowing how they can be used to benefit the people around you. You can also just ask in prayer to know what your gifts are; they are often manifested to you by the power of the Spirit.

Everyone has a gift and can seek new gifts. Once we know our gifts, we have an obligation to use them to help others.

How can you seek to know your gifts?

Day 109

Doctrine and Covenants 46:11–12

How Can I Help Others Find Their Gifts?

> *For all have not every gift given unto them; for there are many gifts, and to every man is given a gift by the Spirit of God.*
>
> *To some is given one, and to some is given another, that all may be profited thereby.*

One of the Lord's final teachings about spiritual gifts is that while everyone has them, only a small number of people can use all of them. This is by design. The Lord distributes the gifts among His children in a way that leads us to reach out to the people around us to use their gifts. We all need connection, and the Lord uses our spiritual gifts to bring us together.

It can take humility to ask another person for help, but it is essential to our spiritual survival to reach out to others who can use their gifts to help us. It can also strengthen our testimony to see the power of God manifest through the spiritual gifts of others. At times asking someone else to use their gifts to help you might be just the kind of lift they need to know that God has given them power.

The Lord's Church is a vast storehouse of talent and spiritual gifts. When we seek to bring out others' gifts, all of us are raised to a higher level. The manner in which the Lord grants spiritual gifts is intended to forge friendships, create connection, and truly allow the members of the Church to not just be a light to the world but a light to each other.

How can you help others to use their spiritual gifts?

Day 110
Doctrine and Covenants 47:1

How Can I Fulfill My Callings?

Behold, it is expedient in me that my servant John should write and keep a regular history, and assist you, my servant Joseph, in transcribing all things which shall be given you, until he is called to further duties.

John Whitmer was called in a revelation to serve as Church historian and immediately felt overwhelmed. He was asked to replace Oliver Cowdery, one of the most gifted thinkers and writers in the Church. Oliver was called to lead a mission to the Native Americans, and the Lord asked John to take over the role of Church historian.

John may have thought he didn't have the literary talent necessary to fill the job. But the Lord didn't ask for literary flair in fulfilling this calling. Instead the word the Lord used to describe the way He wanted the history written was "regular." John didn't have to be brilliant; he just had to be consistent.

In our own callings, the Lord values consistency and sincerity over brilliance. You don't have to be the best missionary or speaker or writer. You just have to humbly do the job you were given, and the Lord will help you accomplish it. There is an old saying in the Church that "whom the Lord calls, He qualifies."

We see that with John Whitmer. He wasn't the most skilled writer in the Church, but he worked hard to carry out his job. He started collecting documents, taking minutes, and making records of Church events. The amount of material we have to write Church history started to multiply after John was placed in the position, and today we have a bounty of historical information from his time to help us know our story.

John wasn't the most brilliant historian, but he was a faithful one and that was enough.

How can you be most consistent in your service to God?

Day 111
Doctrine and Covenants 48:4

How Can I Prepare for the Future?

It must needs be necessary that ye save all the money that ye can, and that ye obtain all that ye can in righteousness, that in time ye may be enabled to purchase land for an inheritance, even the city.

Following the Lord's commandment to gather to the Ohio, the Saints in the New York and Pennsylvania branches of the Church began making preparations to relocate. This came at great sacrifice, with most of the Saints from the east selling their homes, businesses, and farms. The Saints in Ohio also prepared to sacrifice to find ways to provide food, shelter, and housing for the arriving Saints.

The newly revealed law of consecration pointed to how the Ohio Saints could provide for the new arrivals, but it was only in its early stages of implementation. In addition, the Lord was continuing to reveal the principles of consecration line upon line. In Doctrine and Covenants 48, the Lord emphasized two more principles: saving for a future time and obtaining our livelihood in righteousness. These are still important principles of provident living for Latter-day Saints.

Saving was a challenge for the Saints in the 1830s, and it is still a challenge for Saints today. We are constantly bombarded by messages and advertising pushing us to buy the newest and latest things. There is also a tendency to try to keep up with the purchases of the people around us. But a little patience and thrift in our purchases can go a long way toward building financial security. A little saving right now can go a long way toward preparing us for the difficult times ahead.

Righteous work is another principle the Lord emphasized, telling the Saints to "obtain all that ye can in righteousness." When it comes to making money, sometimes Christlike attributes fly out the window. Doing anything just to get ahead can eventually corrupt and destroy a person's soul. Honesty, kindness, and charity are all vital in our professional lives. We don't want to gain the whole world but lose our soul along the way.

What can you do right now to save and prepare for the future?

Day 112
Doctrine and Covenants 49:5

How Can I Receive the Savior?

Thus saith the Lord; for I am God, and have sent mine Only Begotten Son into the world for the redemption of the world, and have decreed that he that receiveth him shall be saved, and he that receiveth him not shall be damned.

Just up the road from where the Saints had gathered in Kirtland lived another peculiar people called the Shakers. The Shakers, officially called the United Society of Believers in Christ's Second Appearing, were a religious group centered around the teachings of Ann Lee. They existed in several communities throughout the United States, including Shaker Heights, near the gathering place in Ohio. As word of the Book of Mormon spread throughout the area, Leman Copley, a former Shaker, was baptized. Leman approached Joseph Smith and asked for a revelation about the Shakers.

The Shakers had some beliefs in common with Latter-day Saints and some that conflicted. Shakers believed in continuing revelation, the equality of men and women, and sharing goods to help the poor. But Shakers also believed that baptism was unnecessary, that celibacy was a higher form of living, that the vicarious Atonement of Jesus Christ was not real, and several other untrue teachings.

Doctrine and Covenants 49 was intended to correct the Shakers' false beliefs. But with so many points of disagreement, where was the best place to begin?

In the revelation, the Lord began with the most important doctrine the Saints could share—that Jesus came to earth for the redemption of the world. Only in His teachings and His sacrifice can salvation be found.

In our dealings with people of different beliefs we can look for common beliefs to build on. We can also disagree in a friendly way that helps them feel our love. But we must also be clear about what our core beliefs are and that our lives and faith are centered on Jesus Christ and His atoning sacrifice. The Lord set the example by leading with a declaration of what He did and how He saves.

How can you show your faith in Jesus Christ to others today?

Day 113

Doctrine and Covenants 49:15–16

Why Are Marriage and Family So Important?

And again, verily I say unto you, that whoso forbiddeth to marry is not ordained of God, for marriage is ordained of God unto man.

Wherefore, it is lawful that he should have one wife, and they twain shall be one flesh, and all this that the earth might answer the end of its creation.

The Shakers, who this revelation was addressed to, didn't forbid marriage altogether, but they did believe that celibacy was a higher form of life. When a person joined the Shakers, whether they were married or unmarried, they were expected to be celibate. In addressing these beliefs, the Lord provided one of the key statements that still is taught frequently by Latter-day Saints—marriage is ordained of God.

The Lord even goes one step further. He places the union of man and woman as one of the purposes for the earth's creation. Not everyone in this life will marry, but family life is a major reason we came to earth. Connection with other children of God, whether as husband and wife, parent and child, or through the fellowship of the gospel is a vital part of our eternal progression.

Though family life can bring a lot of ups and downs, no experience on earth helps us understand God more than being part of a family. God asks us to address Him as Father, and knowing the kind of love that comes from being a part of a family is a vital part of becoming like God. As the Lord explains, the purpose of this earth and the end of its creation is to allow the sons and daughters of God to know what it means to be part of a family.

How can you show love toward a member of your family today?

Day 114
Doctrine and Covenants 49:24–25

How Can I Help Others Flourish?

But before the great day of the Lord shall come, Jacob shall flourish in the wilderness, and the Lamanites shall blossom as the rose.

Zion shall flourish upon the hills and rejoice upon the mountains, and shall be assembled together unto the place which I have appointed.

As the Lord concluded His address to the Shakers, He also made another remarkable prophecy—Jacob, or Israel, would flourish in the wilderness and the Lamanites would blossom as the rose. There are many ways this prophecy could be fulfilled. On a surface level, the Church, the modern-day house of Israel, was driven into the Rocky Mountains of western North America, where they flourished and became a mighty people.

If the wilderness is a metaphor for all of the persecution faced by the Latter-day Saints, the prophecy is still true. All around the world, the house of Israel has gathered and flourished wherever they are planted. That story still continues to be written in hundreds of countries around the world.

The second part of the prophecy may be even more valuable. We are still discovering where the children of Lehi live and how they are gathered, but we know that the early members of the Church believed that the Native Americans were the Lamanites. At the time this prophecy was given, the Native Americans were a despised and driven people. The Lord saw them not as they were but as they could be. He urged the Saints to look past the racial prejudices they grew up with and do all they could to assist their brothers and sisters to reach their full potential.

These prophecies are still coming true. The Lord sees the despised and outcast, and He raises them to a height level. He can do the same with us, if we only allow Him to do so.

How can you see and nourish the potential in others today?

Day 115

Doctrine and Covenants 50:11–12

How Does the Lord Use Reason to Teach Us?

Let us reason even as a man reasoneth one with another face to face. Now, when a man reasoneth he is understood of man, because he reasoneth as a man; even so will I, the Lord, reason with you that you may understand.

A few months after Joseph Smith arrived in Kirtland, the Saints there began experiencing unusual spiritual manifestations. The Prophet later recorded in his history, "Many false spirits were introduced, many strange visions were seen, and wild, enthusiastic notions were entertained; men ran out of doors under the influence of this spirit, and some of them got upon the stumps of trees and shouted, and all kinds of extravagances were entered into by them."[15] One Church member was almost injured chasing a ball of light that led him to jump off a cliff, but he was caught in a tree below. Faced with these unusual challenges, Joseph Smith sought out a revelation to know what to do.

In the revelation the Lord confirmed that the spiritual manifestations were not inspired by Him, and He warned the Saints against following false spirits. But rather than just asking the Saints to have faith in His word on the matter, He also offered to use reason to prove that the manifestations were false.

In doing so, the Lord illustrates that reason and faith are not opposed to each other. In fact, they are intended to work together. Paul taught that "faith is the substance of things not seen" (Hebrews 11:1). Faith is useful in helping us find the truth when we don't have all the information.

Reason is useful when we do have information. The Saints could clearly see that the manifestations were harmful—one person was almost killed by running off a cliff! The Lord expected them to use their reason

15. *Times and Seasons*, April 1, 1842, 747; *The Joseph Smith Papers*, accessed October 10, 2023, https://www.josephsmithpapers.org/paper-summary/times-and-seasons-1–april-1842/13?

to know what came from Him and what did not. Likewise, we use reason and faith to tackle the problems of our daily lives. The Lord gave us a mind capable of taking in information and making good decisions, and faith to help us when we don't have all of the information. We use both together and in that way we grow to become more like God.

How can you use reason and faith together more effectively?

Day 116

Doctrine and Covenants 50:21–22

How Do I Know if I Have Taught by the Spirit?

> *Therefore, why is it that ye cannot understand and know, that he that receiveth the word by the Spirit of truth receiveth it as it is preached by the Spirit of truth?*
>
> *Wherefore, he that preacheth and he that receiveth, understand one another, and both are edified and rejoice together.*

When the gospel is taught correctly, the Spirit is present. The fruits of the Spirit bring us love, joy, peace, goodness, and understanding (see Galatians 5:22–23). But gospel teaching is also a two-person process. The teacher must teach by the Spirit, and the learner must learn by the Spirit. If the teacher is unprepared, unfaithful, or tries to use worldly persuasion, the Spirit will not be present. If the learner is unprepared, uninterested, or too embroiled in sin, the message can often miss the mark. When both are prepared and ready to learn, the Spirit can flow properly and both learn.

It has been said that true education is not the filling of a vessel but the lighting of a fire. In this revelation, the Lord adds that when the Spirit is truly present, the teacher will learn as much as the student. Marion G. Romney, a former member of the First Presidency, once said, "I always know when I am speaking under the inspiration of the Holy Ghost because I always learn something from what I've said."[16]

16 Quoted in Boyd K. Packer, *Teach Ye Diligently,* (Salt Lake City: Deseret Book, 1975, 304).

True teaching is inspiring to both the teacher and the learner. The Lord says it as edifying, which means it builds the person who receives it. Sometimes we will be edified as the teacher, and sometimes we must focus so that as a learner we can be edified as well. When both the teacher and the learner are in sync with each other and the Spirit, the classroom can become one of the most enlightening places in the Church.

What can you do to better teach and learn by the Spirit?

Day 117

Doctrine and Covenants 50:23–24

How Can I Know if Something Comes from God?

And that which doth not edify is not of God, and is darkness.

That which is of God is light; and he that receiveth light, and continueth in God, receiveth more light; and that light groweth brighter and brighter until the perfect day.

Every day we are confronted by hundreds of choices about what we watch, read, or take into our minds. This can be a little overwhelming, and it can be difficult to know what is best to nourish our minds and spirits. Much of what we consume as part of our media diet is good, uplifting, and wholesome. But much of what is out there is degrading, destruction, and toxic. How do we know what choices to make?

In Doctrine and Covenants 50, the Lord provides a simple formula for the choices we make. He teaches "that which doth not edify is not of God, and is darkness." An important action to take before we make a choice is to ask, Is this edifying?

A dictionary from the time of this revelation defined *edify* as "to instruct and improve the mind in knowledge generally, and particularly in moral and religious knowledge, in faith and holiness," or more simply, "to build in a literal sense."[17] Before we watch, listen to, or read

17. Noah Webster, *American Dictionary of the English Language*, 1828, https://webstersdictionary1828.com/Dictionary/Edify.

something, we can ask ourselves, Is this going to build me into a better person? If not, then it doesn't come from God and it may be best to avoid it.

This doesn't mean that we have to confine ourselves strictly to materials produced by the Church. There is a lot of edifying music, drama, comedy, and other material out there that comes from talented and wonderful people outside of the Church. God inspires people of all faiths and backgrounds to produce edifying content. But there is also a lot of material out there that tears us down, makes us small, and puts us in a bad place. That is not of God and should be avoided.

How can you seek out materials that are edifying to you?

Day 118
Doctrine and Covenants 50:26

How Can I Be a Good Leader?

He that is ordained of God and sent forth, the same is appointed to be the greatest, notwithstanding he is the least and the servant of all.

The Lord's leadership model is completely different than what most of us are taught to think of leaders. We normally think of a good leader as dynamic and challenging, at the center of every crisis, and decisive at issuing orders. But when the Lord defines leadership, He doesn't speak of someone who dominates the people around them. Quite to the contrary, in the Lord's model of leadership, a good leader looks for ways to serve those around them.

The Lord teaches that the greatest shall be the least and the servant of all. Rather than seeing themselves as above everyone around them, a good leader places themself below everyone around them by finding ways to help. The largest rivers are at the lowest elevations. All of the water from the streams around flow into them, and this gives them their power to move and change the landscape.

Likewise, leaders who position themselves as servants below the people they lead have the trust and confidence of the people flow into them. This empowers them to be the kind of leader people love and respect.

In the end, true Christlike leadership has never been about acquiring the most power. It has been about using your power to bring about the most good.

What can you do to serve those that you lead today?

Day 119

Doctrine and Covenants 51:3

How Can I Help Others Equally?

> *Wherefore, let my servant Edward Partridge, and those whom he has chosen, in whom I am well pleased, appoint unto this people their portions, every man equal according to his family, according to his circumstances and his wants and needs.*

The revelations in the Doctrine and Covenants show how the Lord was deeply involved in the lives of His Saints and how He helped them find solutions to their problems. In Doctrine and Covenants 51, Edward Partridge, the first bishop of the Church, was struggling with how to distribute the limited resources of the Church in a fair and equitable way. The law of consecration had only been revealed a few months earlier, and working out the practical aspects of the law was a major challenge.

The Lord counseled Bishop Partridge to distribute resources equally among the families in his charge but to also consider their circumstances, wants, and needs. Then, as well as now, consecration was never a one-size-fits-all proposition. It was the duty of the bishop to get to know each family and their needs and then find out how to help.

It is the same in our day. Loving Church leaders and ministering sisters and brothers should get to know their families and seek out the best way to help them. Consecration is only partly about physical wants and needs. The servants of God must seek to know the spiritual, emotional, and spiritual needs of the families in their care, and then seek the best ways to provide for them. These dedicated ministers act as the Lord's hands in lifting the down-hearted, feeding the poor, and providing for the children of God.

What can you do to help a family in your care today?

Day 120

Doctrine and Covenants 52:5

How Can I Come to Know My Inheritance?

And it shall also, inasmuch as they are faithful, be made known unto them the land of your inheritance.

Following the Lord's commandment to gather, Joseph Smith and other Church leaders gathered together nearly all of the priesthood holders in the early Church to Kirtland, Ohio, for a conference. This group of Saints, not more than a few dozen souls, met together and experienced a great spiritual outpouring. During this time Doctrine and Covenants 52 was received. In the revelation the Lord commanded Joseph and most of the men present to travel to the edge of the frontier in Missouri for their next conference. Once they had gathered there, the Lord promised to make known the land of their inheritance.

While the Lord still promises physical inheritances to His children, the most importance inheritance we can receive and pass on to our loved ones is spiritual. Our inheritance is coming to know that there is a place prepared for us in the eternities where we can grow and progress. The lands of inheritance promised in the scriptures are symbolic reminders of the real inheritance promised to every son or daughter of God—a place in the celestial kingdom.

The land of Canaan was the promised inheritance to the Israelites. The new world was a land of promise for the children of Lehi. Eventually the land of Missouri was promised to the early Saints of the Church. But all of these lands, beautiful as they are, are but pale shadows of the real inheritance waiting for us in the very land where God and Jesus Christ dwell.

How can you come to better know what your inheritance is?

Day 121

Doctrine and Covenants 52:16–17

How Can Being Meek Help Me to Be Strong?

He that speaketh, whose spirit is contrite, whose language is meek and edifieth, the same is of God if he obey mine ordinances.

And again, he that trembleth under my power shall be made strong, and shall bring forth fruits of praise and wisdom, according to the revelations and truths which I have given you.

In Doctrine and Covenants 52, the Lord called several sets of missionaries to travel to Missouri, where their inheritance would be made known to them. Along the way they were instructed to preach the gospel to the people they met. The Lord told them if they used meek and edifying language they would find success.

Meekness is often thought of as weakness, but the opposite is actually true. It can take a lot of courage to show humility in the face of opposition. The most meek among us are usually the strongest. Moses, for instance, was said to be "very meek, above all the men which were upon the face of the earth" (Number 12:3). Reading the story of Moses, no one would assume that this mighty prophet, who challenged the leaders of one of the most powerful empires and freed his people from slavery, was meek.

But Moses was meek because he showed humility in accepting the Lord's counsel and the counsel of those around him. This wasn't a sign of weakness but a sign of strength. It showed that he had enough faith in God, faith in the people around him, and faith in himself to find the best solutions to the challenges he faced.

If we can show similar meekness, we can become strong as well and maybe even become a great leader like Moses.

How can you show meekness today?

Day 122
Doctrine and Covenants 52:33

How Can I Find My Own Path in My Journey?

Yea, verily I say, let all these take their journey unto one place, in their several courses, and one man shall not build upon another's foundation, neither journey in another's track.

In His commandment to the missionaries to travel to the frontier, the Lord also included instructions that each pair of companions should take a different route, preaching along the way. This meant that they didn't all arrive in Missouri at the same time, but they would reach more people along the way. The goal was to make it to Independence and find Zion, but there were multiple paths to that goal.

In our day, we are still trying to reach Zion, but we need to recognize that there are many paths that end in the heavenly city. While the Lord has one grand plan for all of the children of the covenant, there are multiple paths we can choose along the way.

While not all paths lead to Zion, we should recognize that there are many different paths that do lead there. We must resist the temptation to judge or belittle someone because they walk a different path than we do. We don't know where the Lord is leading them and what plans He has in store for them along the way. Our task is simply to follow the path the Lord has laid out for us and find our own way to Zion. He is leading all of those who keep true to their covenants, but the paths and the tasks He gives us can very widely.

In the end, all that matters is that we find our way to Zion.

How can you love and help someone who might be on a different path to Zion than you?

Day 123
Doctrine and Covenants 53:2

How Can I Forsake the World?

Behold, I, the Lord, who was crucified for the sins of the world, give unto you a commandment that you shall forsake the world.

Algernon Sidney Gilbert was a successful businessman when he was called to travel to Zion. He and his business partner, Newell K. Whitney, ran a successful store in Kirtland, Ohio. Business was booming and both men were pillars of the community, enjoying respect and prosperity because of their hard work.

Because of this it is understandable that Sidney Gilbert felt some hesitation when he was asked to travel to Zion with the missionaries called by the Lord a few days earlier. At times all of us feel the struggle between the calls the Lord extends to us and the desire to pursue worldly things. Nevertheless, the commandment came directly from the Lord to forsake the world and travel to Zion.

Despite his fears, Sidney packed up his goods and made the trek to Zion. Once he arrived in the place of the future city of God he opened another successful store and found prosperity for a short time.

But it was only a few months later that persecutions arose against the Saints and Sidney's store was ransacked and destroyed. In the aftermath, he generously gave away nearly everything that he had to help the Saints who were thrown out of their homes. The cruelty of the Missouri mobs stripped away nearly every worldly possession Sidney had, but his faith never wavered.

When a cholera epidemic broke out among the Saints, Sidney welcomed many of the victims into his home, caring for them until he too fell victim to the deadly disease.

Sidney Gilbert lost just about everything he had in this world to obey the command to gather to Zion. But in forsaking this world, he gained eternal life in the world to come.

What can you do today to forsake the world?

Day 124
Doctrine and Covenants 53:7

How Can I Endure to the End?

And again, I would that ye should learn that he only is saved who endureth unto the end. Even so. Amen.

Another item of counsel that the Lord gave to Sidney Gilbert was this short admonition that salvation comes in enduring to the end. This simple principle is found in the scriptures alongside faith, repentance, baptism, and the gift of the Holy Ghost, as one of the essentials of salvation.

Being a disciple of Jesus Christ comes with ups and downs. There are days when the gifts of God flow freely and it is easy to see the benefits of following the covenant path. But there are also days when it is difficult to see the hand of God in our lives, and the blessings of heaven feel distant.

In my life I have definitely seen more good days than bad because of my discipleship. But good days are perhaps a lesser measure of discipleship. It is when we have to endure trials and challenges that our real discipleship becomes refined and purified. There are also days when we fall short, when we sin, and when our commitment to the gospel wavers.

But God does not expect perfection from us. Worthiness is not flawlessness.[18] What God expects from us is just a sincere, earnest effort to keep the commandments and help the people around us. Enduring to the end might be the most challenging of the first principles of the gospel, but it also allows us to build a life of meaning. When we look back on the paths we have traveled, we will finally see the purpose of the journey. We will realize that we weren't enduring to the end; we were persevering until we reached a wonderful new beginning, a life of joy in the presence of God.

Why is perseverance more important than perfection when it comes to living the gospel of Jesus Christ?

---

18. See Bradley R. Wilcox, "Worthiness Is Not Flawlessness," *Ensign*, November 2021.

Day 125
Doctrine and Covenants 54:6

How Do My Covenants Bring Blessings?

But blessed are they who have kept the covenant and observed the commandment, for they shall obtain mercy.

Living the law of consecration is not easy. While a commitment to live the law of consecration is one of the essential covenants a person makes at baptism and in the temple, these sacrifices do not come all at once. The challenges of living the law of consecration can also be increased when others refuse to consecrate.

Doctrine and Covenants 54 came in response to challenges linked to the law of consecration. A group of Saints gathering to Kirtland from Colesville, New York, were assigned to settle on consecrated land provided by a new convert from Ohio, Leman Copley. The Colesville Saints set about the arduous task of building new homes and farming the land, when Copley's faith wavered and he withdrew from his covenant of consecration. The Colesville Saints suddenly found themselves without a place to live, and they sought guidance from the Lord.

The Lord urged them to keep their covenants, despite the fact that Leman failed to keep his promises to the Lord. We cannot control the actions of others; we can only determine our own choices. In our time we often face the same dilemma in our service to God, but if someone else fails to live up to their promises, we must stay true to our covenants.

The Lord promises that if we keep our covenant we will receive blessings. That must have been difficult for the Colesville Saints to hear now that they had no place to live. But the Lord asked them to forgive and move on, and promised them a new home in Zion. Arrival in their promised land was delayed but only temporarily. There was something even better waiting down the road.

People can disappoint us. We should still forgive. Plans might fall through. We can still move on. The blessing we want may not be what we receive. There is always a promised land waiting for those who keep their covenants.

How can you stay true to your covenants today?

Day 126
Doctrine and Covenants 54:10

How Can I Seek the Lord Early?

And again, be patient in tribulation until I come; and, behold, I come quickly, and my reward is with me, and they who have sought me early shall find rest to their souls. Even so. Amen.

Because of the actions of one unfaithful Church member, the Colesville Saints found themselves without a home and place to settle. Seeking to comfort them, the Lord asked them to be patient and promised a coming reward. He noted that the Colesville Saints, who were some of the earliest converts to the Church, would eventually find a home.

He also counseled that "they who have sought me early shall find rest to their souls." What does it mean to seek the Lord early? In part it might mean that we seek out the Lord before trouble comes our way and not after. Of course, the Savior is pleased whenever we find Him. But the promise here is that when we seek the Lord early—before our time of trouble—we will find greater rest. When we only find God in our difficulties, we might miss out on all the good things He has in store for us at all times.

Finding rest to your soul—being at peace with your life—is something we can all seek. It is common for us to talk about faith in crisis. This is a real thing and should never be dismissed. But our faith doesn't have to be in constant crisis. We can find rest in simply finding the Savior early, trusting in His plan, and seeking to reassure others that everything is going to be okay. When we invite God to join us early on in our journey, the rest of the passage becomes more peaceful and enjoyable.

How can you seek the Lord early?

Day 127
Doctrine and Covenants 55:1

How Can I Have an Eye Single to the Glory of God?

Behold, thus saith the Lord unto you, my servant William, yea, even the Lord of the whole earth, thou art called and chosen; and after thou hast been baptized by water, which if you do with an eye single to my glory, you shall have a remission of your sins and a reception of the Holy Spirit by the laying on of hands.

William W. Phelps was a gifted writer. As a young man, he used his talents and gifts for political causes he strongly believed in. He edited several newspapers and became known as a fierce advocate for what he thought was right. He purchased a copy of the Book of Mormon from Parley P. Pratt in April 1830, then stayed up all night comparing it with the Bible. He later said, "From the first time I read this volume of volumes, even till now. I have been struck with a kind of sacred joy at its title page. . . . What a wonderful volume!"[19]

But William's path to conversion was not easy. Some of his colleagues charged him with indebtedness and forced him to go to prison for thirty days. Debt was common among those in William's profession, and once he was in prison the people who charged him admitted their real motive for putting him behind bars. These men told William they had jailed him to keep him from "joining the Mormons."[20]

William spent thirty days in prison because of his refusal to give up his study of the Church. When he was finally let out, Phelps gave up his life as a newspaper editor in New York to gather with the Saints in Kirtland, Ohio. But he put off being baptized until he could meet with the Prophet himself. Once he met with Joseph he announced that he was willing to do anything to follow the will of the Lord. In response,

---

19. Letter from W.W. Phelps to Oliver Cowdery, *Messenger and Advocate* 1 (February 1835), 177.
20. Bruce A. Van Orden, We'll Sing and We'll Shout: The Life and Times of W.W. Phelps (Salt Lake City: Deseret Book, 2018), 34.

Joseph received a revelation for William calling him to be baptized and lead a life "with an eye single to my glory."

Like William, each of us is called to make sacrifices for the gospel. With his literary gifts, William could have had a bright future as a writer, but he chose to devote all of his time to God, eventually becoming the author of many beloved works of Latter-day Saint literature, including the hymns "The Spirit of God," "Redeemer of Israel," "Praise to the Man," and many others. If we have an eye single to the glory of God we can find our reward as well.

What can you do today to show you have an eye single to the glory of God?

Day 128
Doctrine and Covenants 55:4

How Can I Teach the Little Children in My Care?

> *And again, you shall be ordained to assist my servant Oliver Cowdery to do the work of printing, and of selecting and writing books for schools in this church, that little children also may receive instruction before me as is pleasing unto me.*

William W. Phelps is one of the most gifted writers in the history of the Church. His eloquent poetry is found in some of the most beloved hymns of the Restoration. He had a way of turning a phrase that could be humorous, insightful, and moving. And how did the Lord direct him to use his talents? What was the most important audience for William to write for? In the revelation given to William the Lord directed this master of the English language to write first and foremost to little children.

The Lord delights in the instruction and learning of little children. If He directed one of the most gifted writers in the Church to focus his efforts on teaching children, it underlines for us how important it is to take time to make sure that our little ones are taught the gospel and all of the things that will help them be happy and successful in this life. Teaching children is among the most noble callings given to women and men in this life. Whether this means in a classroom, at home, or in church, those who teach our children deserve our thanks and support because it is pleasing to the Lord "that little children also may receive."

What can you do today to help instruct a little child?

Day 129
Doctrine and Covenants 56:16

How Can I Use My Resources to Help the Poor?

> *Wo unto you rich men, that will not give your substance to the poor, for your riches will canker your souls; and this shall be your lamentation in the day of visitation, and of judgment, and of indignation: The harvest is past, the summer is ended, and my soul is not saved!*

In the Doctrine and Covenants the Lord reserves some of His most strict chastisement for those who refuse to share their substance to help their brothers and sisters. In Doctrine and Covenants 56, Ezra Thayer, one of the missionaries called by the Lord to travel to Zion, was reproved by the Lord and released from his mission call. We do not know the exact reason for this action, but the context from the section indicates that Ezra was probably murmuring because of the financial sacrifices relating to giving up his time and possibly his property to travel to Zion.

The Lord warns Ezra that "your riches will canker your souls." It isn't riches or money that has that effect on people; it is greed that ultimately hurts a person's soul. People often misquote the Bible by saying that "money is the root of all evil," but Paul actually wrote that "*the love of* money is the root of all evil" (1 Timothy 6:10; emphasis added). Money isn't intrinsically good or evil. It is how we choose to use it that corrupts us or blesses others.

As part of our covenants of consecration, the Lord asks us to generously and selflessly give what we can to help others. When we hang on too closely to our riches, they can become an anchor that weighs us down and keeps us from ascending toward the presence of God.

What can you do today to be unselfish with what the Lord has blessed you with?

Day 130
Doctrine and Covenants 56:17

How Can I Be Satisfied With What I Have?

> *Wo unto you poor men, whose hearts are not broken, whose spirits are not contrite, and whose bellies are not satisfied, and whose hands are not stayed from laying hold upon other men's goods, whose eyes are full of greediness, and who will not labor with your own hands!*

Doctrine and Covenants 56 presents an interesting contrast. In verse 16 the Lord rebukes rich men for selfishly hoarding their riches instead of helping the poor. In the next verse, the Lord reproves poor people who are greedy and refuse to work to improve their situation. It becomes clear from this sharp contrast that righteousness or wickedness has less to do with our personal possessions and a lot more to do with how we choose to use them. This all goes back to the most universal of sins, pride.

We often think of being prideful as something people do when looking at others, such as a rich person who scoffs at their less well-off neighbors. But prophets have also warned against pride from the bottom looking up, when we feel anger toward people who have more than us. We often become jealous of the things other people have. The adversary doesn't care if we are guilty of looking down on others or looking up with envy; he just wants us to get angry and blame our problems on others. In both cases, the Lord seeks to have us see our possessions as only tools to help us improve our situation or bless the lives of others. If we focus too much on what we have and not the good we can do with it, it can also canker our souls. It can be just as hard for a poor and greedy person to enter the kingdom of heaven as it can be for a rich and selfish person.

What can you do to avoid comparing yourself in a negative way to others?

Day 131
Doctrine and Covenants 56:18

How Can I Be Pure in Heart?

But blessed are the poor who are pure in heart, whose hearts are broken, and whose spirits are contrite, for they shall see the kingdom of God coming in power and great glory unto their deliverance; for the fatness of the earth shall be theirs.

After chastising both the rich and the poor who are greedy, the Lord softens His tone and addresses one last audience, the poor who are pure in heart. Being poor in heart has nothing to do with the amount of money in your bank account. In the verse just before this one, the Lord rebukes the poor who "will not labor with your own hands" (v. 17). But some people who experience poverty aren't in that situation because they refuse to work. They can suffer because of health, lost opportunities, or just plain bad luck. This is the kind of poverty the Saints of God are charged to help with in any way they can.

In the scriptures the Lord frequently refers to the need to help the widows, the fatherless, and others struggling with adversity. Many of these brothers and sisters are among the best people among us and the most generous with what they have. When I was a young missionary serving in Florida, I was deeply moved when an immigrant family who joined the Church offered to feed us dinner. I saw their humble home and realized that they didn't have much to share. When I tried to decline their offer, the father of the family looked me straight in the eye and said, "You bless my family when you let us feed you." This family had next to nothing, but because they were pure in heart they had everything. It can be the same with us. Our happiness is less about what's in our bank account and more about what is in our heart.

What changes can you make to be more pure in heart today?

Day 132
Doctrine and Covenants 57:2–3

How Can I Find Zion?

Wherefore, this is the land of promise, and the place for the city of Zion.

And thus saith the Lord your God, if you will receive wisdom here is wisdom. Behold, the place which is now called Independence is the center place; and a spot for the temple is lying westward, upon a lot which is not far from the courthouse.

After weeks of travel, Joseph Smith and his companions arrived in Independence, Missouri, in late July 1831. The Lord had promised that when they arrived in Missouri He would reveal to them the place of the city of Zion—the New Jerusalem promised in the Book of Mormon (see Ether 13:6). When the missionaries arrived at their destination on the edge of the American frontier, the Lord kept His promise and in revelation told them this was the place where Zion would rise in the latter days.

The land before them was rich and green, but at the time it was only a tiny village filled with rough-hewn frontier characters. It is difficult to imagine a more challenging place for them to build the city. The Lord asked them to build a city where all people could be of one heart and one mind and with no poor among them (see Moses 7:18). But at the time Missouri was wracked with poverty, greed, and racism. The European settlers brought slaves with them, and they despised the Native Americans who only lived a few miles from them on the other side of the Missouri River. Building Zion in this place was going to be a challenge, as the Saints soon found out.

We still wrestle with the challenge of Zion in our time. We may not solve this problem until the Savior returns. But there is much to be gained on the road to Zion as there is in traveling there. The problems of racism, equality, and selfishness are still with us. But the challenge of Zion is to do what we can to not ignore those problems and lay the foundations of the city of God where we can all live in peace.

What can you do to help build Zion today?

Day 133
Doctrine and Covenants 57:14–15

How Can I Be Planted in My Inheritance?

And thus let those of whom I have spoken be planted in the land of Zion, as speedily as can be, with their families, to do those things even as I have spoken.

And now concerning the gathering—Let the bishop and the agent make preparations for those families which have been commanded to come to this land, as soon as possible, and plant them in their inheritance.

Now that the place for the city of Zion was known, the Lord commanded the early Saints to immediately start the process of building the city. This was where the real challenge began. Up to this point Zion was an ideal and a point in the distance. Now they had arrived at their destination, and it was time for them to begin the painstaking work of building the actual city. The task of helping families relocate to Zion fell into the hands of the bishop of the Church, Edward Partridge. Bishop Partridge immediately began to make the New Jerusalem a real place on the American frontier.

We often face the challenge of taking our good intentions and translating them into real actions. It can be a real challenge to follow through and live up to the ideals we hold in our hearts. I can't count how many times I have thought about visiting a friend, contacting a neighbor, or doing some other deed, only to become distracted. The Lord does judge us by our intentions and not just our actions, but He also wants us to do something. In this revelation the Lord instructs Bishop Partridge to "plant" the Saints in their inheritances. The seeds planted under Bishop Partridge's care did not immediately bear fruit. Persecution and other challenges kept the Saints of the early Restoration from establishing the physical city of Zion, but the seeds they planted led to later city in Nauvoo, the mountains of the West, and communities of Saints all over the world today.

What is an action you can take today to help build up Zion?

Day 134
Doctrine and Covenants 58:3–4

How Can I See the Designs of God?

Ye cannot behold with your natural eyes, for the present time, the design of your God concerning those things which shall come hereafter, and the glory which shall follow after much tribulation.

For after much tribulation come the blessings. Wherefore the day cometh that ye shall be crowned with much glory; the hour is not yet, but is nigh at hand.

Joseph Smith and the missionaries called to travel with him arrived in Zion with dreams of a glorious city on their minds. The Lord encouraged this group by showing them the place where the temple would stand in the latter days, and revealing at last the place for the New Jerusalem. Only a few days after the missionaries arrived, the first settlers, led by the family of Joseph and Polly Knight, arrived in Zion. These faithful members had given up their homes in Colesville, New York, to follow the Lord's commandment to relocate to Ohio. Once they arrived in Ohio, they were given an inheritance that was snatched away from them by the selfish actions of Leman Copley (see Doctrine and Covenants 54). With no place to settle in Ohio, the Lord commanded these stalwart Saints to travel another eight hundred miles to settle among the first Saints in the place for Zion.

The happy arrival of the Colesville Saints was tempered by the Lord's warning that the road to Zion was still difficult. The Lord counseled that it would be difficult from their perspective to see the designs of God and that much tribulation ahead. It is the same with us today. We often lack the perception to see the grand tapestry of our lives that the Lord is weaving. We may not appreciate how all of the good times and bad times of our lives come together to create a masterpiece. No great work is accomplished easily, but beyond the tribulations we face right now there is a great future.

How have your tribulations helped you grow into the person the Lord wants you to become?

Day 135
Doctrine and Covenants 58:26–27

How Can I Be Anxiously Engaged?

For behold, it is not meet that I should command in all things; for he that is compelled in all things, the same is a slothful and not a wise servant; wherefore he receiveth no reward.

Verily I say, men should be anxiously engaged in a good cause, and do many things of their own free will, and bring to pass much righteousness.

Speaking to the Saints who were beginning the work of building the city of Zion, the Lord revealed one of the most important truths of the gospel, specifically that we shouldn't always have to be told what to do. We value revelation and guidance from the Holy Spirit as one of the great blessings of this life. But alongside the gifts of the spirit, God also gave us the gift of a mind capable of independent thought. Most of the time we know what we can do to make things better around us. It just take courage and determination to do the things that we already know are right.

God wants us to cultivate our sense of right and wrong alongside our capacity to receive guidance from Him. There are dozens of things we can do right now to build the kingdom of God. We don't always need a revelation to explain what our duty is. We can just go and do good things. We are servants of God, capable of making our own decisions. In this sense, we aren't just God's helpers on earth but also His partners in making the world a better place.

What can you do to be more "anxiously engaged" today?

Day 136
Doctrine and Covenants 58:55–56

How Can I Be Patient in Accomplishing My Work?

> *Let all these things be done in order; and let the privileges of the lands be made known from time to time, by the bishop or the agent of the church.*
>
> *And let the work of the gathering be not in haste, nor by flight; but let it be done as it shall be counseled by the elders of the church at the conferences, according to the knowledge which they receive from time to time.*

After the Lord revealed the location for the city of Zion, He urged the Saints to be planted in Zion "as speedily as can be" (Doctrine and Covenants 57:14) but also urged them that "the work of gathering be not in haste, nor by flight" (Doctrine and Covenants 58:55). How do we reconcile these two seemingly contradictory statements? It lies in counseling with the Lord and other trusted voices to find the right balance between doing things quickly but also doing them the right way. Sometimes it can seem like the demands in our life come at an overwhelming pace, and other times it can seem like it takes forever to get anything done.

Finding the right mixture of action and reflection can be a real challenge. But notice here that the Lord asks the Saints to gather as "counseled by the elders of the church." There are times for action and times for patience. Hopefully we are always moving forward in our faith, but taking a few brief moments to counsel with the Lord or the other trusted voices in our lives can help us develop the courage to do what is right when it is needed, and the patience to know when to slow down.

What can you do to find the right balance between action and patience in the challenges you face?

Day 137

Doctrine and Covenants 59:3

How Can I Receive the Good Things of the Earth?

Yea, blessed are they whose feet stand upon the land of Zion, who have obeyed my gospel; for they shall receive for their reward the good things of the earth, and it shall bring forth in its strength.

The first group of Saints to arrive in Zion consisted of the Colesville branch, led by the family of Joseph and Polly Knight. They had traveled all the way from New York to Missouri in the span of only a few months. The journey was particularly challenging for Polly Knight, who was in advance age and was sick during the entire trip. Her son, Newell Knight, was so concerned about his mother that he purchased lumber during the trip just in case he needed to make a coffin for her. But Polly endured and eventually saw the promised land of Zion before she passed. In his journal Newell Knight wrote, "The Lord gave her the desire of her heart, for she lived to stand upon that land [Missouri]." Polly died just a few days after her arrival in Zion.[21]

Joseph Smith was close friends with the Knight family. This revelation was received near the time of Polly's funeral. The Lord was likely referring to Polly when He declared that "those who die shall rest from all their labors" (Doctrine and Covenants 59:2). Polly only stood in Zion for a few days before she was called home, but she showed her commitment to the gospel by enduring to the end. Though her time in Zion was short, she will inherit all the good things of the earth because of her faith.

It is the same with us. The Lord loves effort, and our journey here on earth is less about our destination and more about what we can learn on the way there.

What have you learned and gained because of your struggles?

---

21. Newell Knight, *The Rise of the Latter-day Saints*, (Provo, UT: Religious Studies Center, 2019), 36–39

Day 138

Doctrine and Covenants 59:9–10

How Can I Keep the Sabbath Day Holy?

And that thou mayest more fully keep thyself unspotted from the world, thou shalt go to the house of prayer and offer up thy sacraments upon my holy day;

For verily this is a day appointed unto you to rest from your labors, and to pay thy devotions unto the Most High.

The previous revelations given when Joseph Smith arrived in Missouri (sections 57 and 58) were about finding the land of Zion. Doctrine and Covenants 59 is about life in Zion. The Lord recognized the sacrifices of those who traveled to Zion and now made known His expectations for the people who would build Zion.

Not surprisingly, among the first commandments given was to honor the Sabbath Day. The Lord asks the Saints to go to the house of prayer, offer up their sacraments, and rest from their labors. We sometimes complicate the Sabbath day by coming up with complicated lists of "do's" and "don'ts" that get tangled up in complicated arguments. Even President Russell M. Nelson noted that when he was a young man he tried to create his own set of strict guidelines for what was and wasn't appropriate for the Sabbath. In the end he realized that the Sabbath wasn't about rules but about paying devotion to God. He settled on a simple question: "What sign do I want to give to God?" After that, Sabbath day worship became simple, and the Sabbath became a delight.[22]

The Lord intended for the Sabbath day to be a key part of life in Zion. For those who still long to build Zion, it remains a key part of how we demonstrate our devotion to God.

What sign can you give to God about your worship on the Sabbath day?

---

22. Russell M. Nelson, "The Sabbath Is a Delight," *Ensign*, May 2015.

Day 139
Doctrine and Covenants 60:2

How Can I Overcome My Fear of Using My Talents?

> *But with some I am not well pleased, for they will not open their mouths, but they hide the talent which I have given unto them, because of the fear of man. Wo unto such, for mine anger is kindled against them.*

As the missionaries who traveled to Zion prepared for the journey home, the Lord offered a few words of counsel before they started on their way. In general, He was pleased with their efforts to locate the land of Zion, but He did reserve a few choice words for those who hesitated to share the gospel, admonishing them for hiding "the talent which I have given unto them, because of the fear of man."

In this context the Lord was speaking about preaching the gospel, but it can readily apply to any talent that we have been given. We all have talents and gifts that the Lord gave us to build His kingdom and help the people around us. Whether your talent is preaching, singing, dancing, athletics, or just providing a friendly smile or an uplifting comment, don't hide it! The Lord is correct in saying that we hide our talents because of the fear of men. In fact, we sometimes keep back the better parts of ourselves because we are so worried what others will think of us.

Everyone is talented in their own way, and all of us can use our talents for good. Don't keep your talents from the world.

What can you do to share your talents today?

Day 140
Doctrine and Covenants 60:13

How Can I Keep from Idling Away My Time?

Behold, they have been sent to preach my gospel among the congregations of the wicked; wherefore, I give unto them a commandment, thus: Thou shalt not idle away thy time, neither shalt thou bury thy talent that it may not be known.

Sometimes we don't share our talents because we are scared of others (see Doctrine and Covenants 60:2), and sometimes we don't share our talents because we are lazy. As the missionaries prepared for their journey home from Zion, the Lord counseled them not to "idle away thy time, neither shalt thou bury thy talent that it may not be known." We might just be too lazy to do what we can to bless and uplift the lives of others!

Idling away our time isn't always the result of laziness. Sometimes our talents are buried by doing nonessential things that waste our time. How many of us have idled away our time watching screens, mindlessly scrolling, or playing games alone? There is nothing inherently evil about any of these things, but they aren't always the best way to use our talents. Most of the time using our talents entails focus, effort, and hard work. Just a few small adjustments here and there can make a big difference in the lives of others and in our own lives. The amount of good we can do increases when we focus on the important things and set aside the less essential things.

What can you do to keep from being idle today?

Day 141

Doctrine and Covenants 61:2

How Can I Obtain the Lord's Mercy?

Behold, verily thus saith the Lord unto you, O ye elders of my church, who are assembled upon this spot, whose sins are now forgiven you, for I, the Lord, forgive sins, and am merciful unto those who confess their sins with humble hearts.

Doctrine and Covenants 61 has one of the strangest contexts of any section in the book. Joseph Smith and his companions were traveling home from the land of Zion by canoe. They were on the Missouri River when fights and contentions broke out among the men. The ill-tempered group was suddenly stopped in their journey when an underwater tree nearly capsized one of the canoes, giving all of the man a fright. They stopped to rest and regroup along the banks of the river, and William W. Phelps saw an open vision of the destroyer riding upon the face of the waters. It seems that from this one curious incident came the popular Latter-day Saint folklore that Satan controls the waters.

In reality, the men never identified who "the destroyer" was. The term "destroyer" is found in the scriptures in several places and more often refers to an angel from God than to Satan. The purpose of the destroyer that day is unknown as well. What we do know is that the men were barely spared from disaster because of their own contention and murmuring. Once the men made it to shore, the Lord counseled them to humble themselves and confess their sins.

The destroyers we face rarely have power unless we give it to them. When we are humble and seek the Lord's mercy, He can protect us from evil or strengthen us so that we can resist it. We don't know if Satan controls the water, but we know that he does gain a fair degree of control when we aren't humble, when we seek fault in others, and when we look for the worst around us.

What can you do to be more humble today?

Day 142
Doctrine and Covenants 61:14

How Can I Greater Respect the Power of God?

Behold, I, the Lord, in the beginning blessed the waters; but in the last days, by the mouth of my servant John, I cursed the waters.

Doctrine and Covenants 61 gave rise to the Latter-day Saint folk belief that Satan controls the waters. In truth, the revelation never teaches this. There is no mention of Satan controlling the waters anywhere in the text. But the Lord did tell those assembled on the banks of the Missouri River that the waters were cursed. We are not given the full meaning of the cursing, only that it happened by the hand the Lord's servant John. This passage's meaning is open for interpretation. Are the great waterborne calamities of the last days linked to this cursing? Do the tornadoes, hurricanes, and tsunamis we have witnessed fulfill this promise? How does the Lord use the elements around us to further His will?

We may not know the answers to these questions, but we do know who is in control. The scriptures emphasize that the struggle between Satan and God is not a war between equal powers. We know who will win in the end. Satan is a side character. The main story is between you and God, and how you can find a way to connect to Him to enjoy peace, safety, and joy on your journey through this life. We may not always be able to comprehend the purposes of God, but a healthy respect for His vast power leads us to make wiser choices.

How can you show respect for God's power today?

Day 143
Doctrine and Covenants 62:3

Why Is It Important to Share My Testimony?

Nevertheless, ye are blessed, for the testimony which ye have borne is recorded in heaven for the angels to look upon; and they rejoice over you, and your sins are forgiven you.

On his way home from Missouri, Joseph Smith and his companions ran into a group of missionaries led by the Prophet's brother Hyrum Smith. Hyrum's company was expected to join the other missionaries in Zion, but they were held up when a member of their group, John Murdock, became too ill to travel. Hyrum and the other missionaries decided to care for John until he was well enough to travel. Instead of reproving Hyrum's group for missing their rendezvous in Zion, the Lord blessed them for their compassion and the sincere testimonies they shared along the way. He even told them that because of the testimonies they had shared along their journey, their sins were forgiven.

Does sharing your testimony cause your sins to be forgiven? We need to be careful not to see our relationship with God as a kind of cosmic vending machine where we put in a testimony and get back forgiveness. God can see our sincerity when we share our testimony and does forgive those who believe in Jesus Christ and seek to follow His teachings. If we are sharing our testimony sincerely, then we are growing in faith, and that does result in forgiveness for our sins.

Testimony can be shared through words or actions. It doesn't always need to take place at a pulpit or in front of a congregation. You can bear your testimony in a number of quiet ways throughout the day. It can be a simple affirmation of your faith to a loved one, an act of kindness, or a silent prayer offering thanks.

How can you bear your testimony today?

Day 144
Doctrine and Covenants 62:9

How Can I Have the Savior as My Constant Companion?

Behold, the kingdom is yours. And behold, and lo, I am with the faithful always. Even so. Amen.

The final blessing given to Hyrum Smith and his faithful band of missionaries was that the kingdom was theirs and the Lord would be with them always. They went on their way rejoicing and knowing that through they may have been a little late in arriving to Zion, they found Zion along the way. Hyrum and his companions were only late because they stopped to care for one of their company, and caring for the people around us is a vital part of Zion. Because of how they acted, the Lord was their constant companion.

We believe the Savior is a living, resurrected person. He is somewhere right now teaching or ministering. So how can He be with us always? There are several ways to answer this paradox. First, the Savior is with us through the Holy Spirit. When we take the sacrament, we are promised to always have His spirit with us. Second, time and distance work differently for the Savior. In a later revelation, the Saints were taught that the Light of Christ is present in all things (see Doctrine and Covenants 88:13). Finally, the Savior taught His disciples that "inasmuch as ye have done it unto one of the least of these my brethren, ye have done it unto me" (Matthew 25:40). When we follow the Savior's example, we see all people as if they were Him and treat them as we would the Savior Himself.

What can you do have the Savior with you today?

Day 145
Doctrine and Covenants 63:9–10

How Do Signs Connect to Faith?

But, behold, faith cometh not by signs, but signs follow those that believe.

Yea, signs come by faith, not by the will of men, nor as they please, but by the will of God.

After several months of traveling to and from Missouri to identify the place for the city of Zion, Joseph Smith at last returned home to Kirtland, Ohio, with the happy news that he had found the place for the city of Zion. But to his dismay, the Church in Kirtland had fallen into some disarray while Joseph and many of the leaders of the Church were away. Everyone was anxious to know how to start the work of gathering to Zion, so Joseph approached the Lord for a revelation. The Lord responded by first working to correct some of the errors Church members in Kirtland had fallen into. One of the biggest problems in Kirtland appears to have been a desire to seek for grand, dramatic signs.

The Lord had already addressed the topic of sign-seeking through several revelations (see Doctrine and Covenants 43, 46, and 50). But the Kirtland Saints were addicted to seeking signs. Signs can be a great blessing for the faithful, but the Savior correctly points out that signs come after we have demonstrated faith, not the other way around. Miracles are real, but a person who bases their faith on signs is building on a shaky foundation. Faith is mostly built through small, simple acts of devotion, carried out on a regular basis. Occasionally the Lord opens the heavens and shows us a sign but usually only after a thousand tiny acts of faith that have led us to that point.

What can you do to demonstrate your faith today?

Day 146
Doctrine and Covenants 63:21

What Did the Apostles See on the Mount of Transfiguration?

When the earth shall be transfigured, even according to the pattern which was shown unto mine apostles upon the mount; of which account the fulness ye have not yet received.

One of the most mysterious events in the New Testament came when Jesus invited three of His disciples to join Him on a hike to the top of a nearby mountain. Peter, James, and John left the rest of the Apostles and joined Jesus. When they arrived at the top of the mountain, Jesus was transfigured so that His skin shone like the sun. The Apostles saw Moses and Elias (probably the Old Testament prophet Elijah) and then heard the voice of God the Father testify of Jesus Christ. The three Apostles were given the keys of the kingdom, and they later passed them on to rest of their brethren.

Doctrine and Covenants 63 illuminates what happened on the top of the Mount of Transfiguration. According to this revelation, Peter, James, and John not only saw Jesus transfigured, but they also saw the entire earth transfigured. They saw a pattern of how the entire world would be lifted into a higher and holier state. Why show this to them? Sometimes we need to see the big picture. It can be easy for us to get caught up in the daily tasks of our lives and forget that all of this is building up to something great and wonderful. The Apostles were about to endure the trials of the Savior's arrest, crucifixion, and resurrection. They needed to see the better world they were fighting for. That vision sustained them through the rest of their trials.

Every once in a while we need to pull back from our daily struggles and see how the Lord is helping us work toward something wonderful. We change the world one small act at a time, but it is nice to know that all of those small acts will eventually add up to an entire world transformed.

What helps you to see the big picture so that you aren't discouraged?

Day 147

Doctrine and Covenants 63:49

How Can I Have Hope for Those Who Have Passed Away?

Yea, and blessed are the dead that die in the Lord, from henceforth, when the Lord shall come, and old things shall pass away, and all things become new, they shall rise from the dead and shall not die after, and shall receive an inheritance before the Lord, in the holy city.

As much as we try to put it out of our mind, it is sometimes difficult to escape the sense of a looming catastrophe. Every one of us has lost someone we love, and the end of our life is a reality that we must all face someday. One of the reasons the gospel of Jesus Christ is so important is that it gives us hope for ourselves and those we have lost. We will miss those we lose, but our separation is only temporary.

The promise of Zion is not a vague promise that we will live again but an assurance that we will be resurrected and live in meaningful ways. The city will not only be built by mortal hands, but after the Resurrection, eternal hands will join in the process as well. We will not just spend eternity floating on clouds and singing praises building the ever-expanding city of Zion. The Savior's promise gives us peace in this life, and that is the most important thing. But it is also nice to know that we will have a fulfilling, interesting life in the eternities as well.

How does the knowledge of an afterlife help you in your daily life?

Day 148

Doctrine and Covenants 63:64

Why Is Important to Be Careful with Sacred Things?

Remember that that which cometh from above is sacred, and must be spoken with care, and by constraint of the Spirit; and in this there is no condemnation, and ye receive the Spirit through prayer; wherefore, without this there remaineth condemnation.

President Boyd K. Packer once counseled, "I have come to believe also that it is not wise to continually talk of unusual spiritual experiences. They are to be guarded with care and shared only when the Spirit itself prompts you to use them to the blessing of others."[23] In our time there is an acute loss of the sacred. Almost everything is shared constantly, and very little is kept and held close to our own hearts.

In Doctrine and Covenants 63, the Lord urges the Saints to remember that there are sacred things in the world. Experiences, knowledge, and the gift of a testimony are all sacred and must be treated as such. At times the Lord blesses us with an assurance, a prompting, or a just a simple feeling, and these are sacred experiences. A genuine testimony stems from these small, personal experiences. There is a time and place to share our testimony with others, and there are also times when it is best to allow ourselves to ponder and take time to reflect on our blessings. I have always been touched by the simple phrase in the New Testament that after the momentous events surrounding the birth of the Savior, Mary "kept all these things, and pondered them in her heart" (Luke 2:19).

What sacred experiences have you had that you can reflect on?

Day 149
Doctrine and Covenants 64:10

Why Are We Commanded to Forgive All People?

> *I, the Lord, will forgive whom I will forgive, but of you it is required to forgive all men.*

After Joseph Smith arrived home from his trip to the land of Zion, there was a lot of housekeeping to do in Kirtland. First, he received a revelation addressing the excessive sign-seeking that was happening among the Saints. Then a more mundane concern was raised, specifically that resentments had arisen among the Saints and they were beginning to get out of hand. In this revelation the Lord reminds the

23. Boyd K. Packer, "The Candle of the Lord," *Ensign,* January 1983, 51–56.

Saints that this problem also existed in New Testament church and probably exists anytime a group of people are asked to work together. Small arguments happen, resentment festers, and sometimes these turn into real concerns.

The solution to these problems isn't complicated. We just have to forgive each other. I know that is easier said than done. Sometimes we are genuinely wrong. Sometimes people act out of malice and deliberately do things to harm us. We still must make the effort to forgive. A friend of mine said that not forgiving someone is like taking poison and then expecting it to hurt the other person.

The reason we forgive isn't because the other person was right but because if we don't forgive we harm ourselves. The Savior settled the matter for us permanently by saying that it is a commandment to forgive. If we do not forgive, not only does the greater sin lie with us, but also the greater harm.

Is there someone you can forgive today?

Day 150

Doctrine and Covenants 64:23

What Kind of Sacrifices Does the Savior Ask For?

> *Behold, now it is called today until the coming of the Son of Man, and verily it is a day of sacrifice, and a day for the tithing of my people; for he that is tithed shall not be burned at his coming.*

Though tithing as we understand it would not be fully defined until a revelation given a few years later, the Lord speaks here of tithing as a command to sacrifice. Here the Lord was referring to the command to live the law of consecration as a way of providing for the poor and needy and helping build Zion. One of the basic principles of the law of consecration is that we start with the knowledge that everything we have really belongs to God. So how do we sacrifice when we never truly own anything in the first place? And why has God commanded sacrifice in all ages of the world when we never really had anything to sacrifice?

There is something that we own, something that is uniquely ours to give up. Elder Neal A. Maxwell taught, "The submission of one's will is really the only uniquely personal thing we have to place on God's altar. The many other things we 'give,' brothers and sisters, are actually the things He has already given or loaned to us. However, when you and I finally submit ourselves, by letting our individual wills be swallowed up in God's will, then we are really giving something to Him! It is the only possession which is truly ours to give!"[24]

We can sacrifice the most personal thing we have to give. We can give up our will to God.

What can you sacrifice to more fully align your will with God?

Day 151

Doctrine and Covenants 64:33

What Are Some Small Things I Can Do to Make Things Better?

> *Wherefore, be not weary in well-doing, for ye are laying the foundation of a great work. And out of small things proceedeth that which is great.*

Of all the principles and ordinances of the gospel, perhaps the most challenging is enduring to the end. The Savior helps us with all of our burdens, but living the gospel is still hard work that requires continual effort. Sometimes it can feel like all of our good deeds go unnoticed, but God always sees the good that we do. Small acts of devotion can add up to something great over a lifetime of discipleship.

At times it can be difficult to see the long-range impact of all the good that we do on a regular basis. But remember that the Restoration of the gospel is a generational project. The simple acts of goodness that we carry out on a regular basis can eventually add up to something powerful

24. Neal A. Maxwell, "Swallowed Up in the Will of the Father," *Ensign*, November 1995.

and grand in the great plan of God. Each of us is laying a stone that will eventually become the kingdom of God. Just like the early Saints who built the first temples, we can only see the individual stones with their flaws and imperfections, or we can have the perspective to know that enough stones can eventually become a beautiful temple.

What small things can you do today to build the kingdom?

Day 152
Doctrine and Covenants 64:34

What Does the Lord Require of His Disciples?

Behold, the Lord requireth the heart and a willing mind; and the willing and obedient shall eat the good of the land of Zion in these last days.

Each of us spends a fair amount of time wrestling with expectations. What does my job, spouse, or children really require of me? Perhaps most important, what does God require of me? How do I know if I am a good person? Am I putting in enough effort? Is there something more I could be doing?

While it is important to ask ourselves these questions on a regular basis, we shouldn't become so fixated on them that they stop us from doing good. The Lord simply states in this section that what He requires is "the heart and a willing mind." That can mean very different things for different people based on their age, experience, health, and too many other factors to list. In the end it is really between ourselves and God as to whether we gave our full heart or had a willing mind.

If you can honestly say that you have given you heart and your mind to God, it is okay for you to mentally rest for a moment and partake of the joy that comes from being a disciple. Self-improvement is something that God expects of us, but even He paused every now and then to reflect and enjoy His work.

What are some things in your life that show you have given your heart and willing mind to God?

Day 153
Doctrine and Covenants 65:2

How Can I Help the Kingdom of God Fill the Earth?

The keys of the kingdom of God are committed unto man on the earth, and from thence shall the gospel roll forth unto the ends of the earth, as the stone which is cut out of the mountain without hands shall roll forth, until it has filled the whole earth.

One of the most curious episodes in all of scripture happened when Nebuchadnezzar, the King of Babylon, had a dream that he could not explain. In the dream, the king saw a large statue with a head made of gold, chest and arms of silver, a belly of brass, legs of iron, and feet of iron mingled with clay. Then in the dream he saw a stone cut out of a mountain without hands that rolled forth, growing larger and larger. It smashed the statue to bits and then filled the entire earth. Eventually Nebuchadnezzar sought out the prophet Daniel to interpret the dream. Daniel informed the king that the statue represented the kingdoms of the earth, including the golden head, which symbolized the king's own empire. The stone was a kingdom set up in the last days that would end the kingdoms of men and fill the whole earth.

Doctrine and Covenants 65 reveals that the keys of that kingdom are now on earth, and the work is beginning to accelerate. The rapid changes witnessed since the time of the Restoration attest to how the Lord is bringing about His final work and throwing down the centuries of corruption and greed that oppressed and hurt billions of people. While the stone rolling forth might represent a supernatural work carried out by God, men and women are given the keys to assist Him in restoring the world to a place of peace and justice. God can fix all that is wrong, but He gives us the keys and asks us to help Him create a new world.

Why do you think God gives His children glimpses of His future victory like this?

Day 154

Doctrine and Covenants 66:3

How Can I Repent of My Sins?

Verily I say unto you, my servant William, that you are clean, but not all; repent, therefore, of those things which are not pleasing in my sight, saith the Lord, for the Lord will show them unto you.

Doctrine and Covenants 66 was given to William McLellin, a new convert to the Church who was seeking spiritual guidance. William was skeptical by nature, and he decided to test whether Joseph Smith's revelations were authentic by writing down five questions privately before seeking the revelation. He didn't show the questions to Joseph, and to this day the questions are lost, though after the revelation was received William declared that every one of his questions was answered to his "full and entire satisfaction."[25]

Working backward from the text of the revelation, it is clear that many of William's questions centered around his worthiness before God. William's wife had died a short time before he joined the Church. The Lord warned him to repent and not be tempted to commit adultery. Though we may not know the precise questions William asked the Lord, it is clear that many of us struggle with the same issues he did. We ask, Am I worthy? How can I change? Will the Lord accept me?

It's clear from this revelation that the answer to each of us would probably also be similar to what the Lord said to William. Yes, you are clean, but you still have some work to do. Yes, I accept you, but I ask you to continue to better yourself. Yes, you have begun to repent, but repentance is a lifelong process, not a single event. Like William, most of us are heading in the right direction, but the road of repentance is long and winding.

What can you do to move further down the road of repentance today?

---

25. See Matthew C. Godfrey, "William McLellin's Five Questions," *Revelations in Context,* https://www.churchofjesuschrist.org/study/manual/revelations-in-context/william-mclellins-five-questions?lang=eng.

Day 155
Doctrine and Covenants 66:9

How Can I Learn to Be Patient in My Afflictions?

Lay your hands upon the sick, and they shall recover. Return not till I, the Lord, shall send you. Be patient in affliction. Ask, and ye shall receive; knock, and it shall be opened unto you.

Though the Lord told William that he was still in need of repentance, the Lord also assured the young convert that he didn't need to be perfect to use the powers of the priesthood. William had already seen Joseph and Hyrum Smith use the power of the priesthood to heal him when he was sick and injured. Now he longed to know if he could use the same power. In response the Lord assured him that he would be able to lay his hands on the sick and they would be healed. Just because William wasn't flawless didn't mean that he wasn't worthy.

The Lord also counseled William to be patient when he faced trials. He was at the beginning of his ministry and had already faced many afflictions, including the death of his wife a short time before he was baptized. Making covenants with God never comes with the assurance that our lives will be free from trial. In fact, we sometimes experience an increase in our trials as we work to better ourselves. But covenants bring us greater power to overcome trials and strength to endure. Sometimes all the strength we need is a little more patience to trust in God, have faith in His goodness, and be willing to endure the tough times.

What can you do to be a little more patient today?

Day 156
Doctrine and Covenants 67:5

How Can I Learn to Accept Imperfection in the Lord's Servants?

Your eyes have been upon my servant Joseph Smith, Jun., and his language you have known, and his imperfections you have known; and you have sought in your hearts knowledge that you might express beyond his language; this you also know.

Doctrine and Covenants 67 was received during a conference held by Church leaders to determine if they should create a new book of scripture. The new book, first called the Book of Commandments, would later expand and become the Doctrine and Covenants. However, at the conference, several of the elders expressed concern over the language used in the revelations and its imperfections. The Lord even challenged those present to choose someone to see if they could create their own revelation. Joseph Smith later noted that William McLellin, a new convert and "the wisest man in his own estimation, having more learning than sense, endeavored to write a commandment like unto one of the least of the Lord's, but failed." Joseph then commented "It was an awful responsibility to write in the name of the Lord." After McLellin's favor, "the elders, and all present, that witnessed this vain attempt of a man to imitate the language of Jesus Christ, renewed their faith in the fulness of the gospel and in the truth of the commandments and revelations which the Lord had given to the church."[26]

Like some of the elders at this meeting, we can be tempted to see the imperfections in the men and women called to lead. But the people called to lead the Church are still people, flawed and struggling, just like us. Revelation comes from a God who is perfect but who chooses to work through imperfect beings to carry out His will. The Lord spoke in the revelation of the challenge Joseph Smith faced in expressing heavenly concepts "beyond his language." Rather than our

26. History, 1838–1856, volume A-1 [23 December 1805–30 August 1834], *The Joseph Smith Papers*, 162.

judgment and condemnation, Church leaders need our love and support. When we see our leaders as the imperfect beings they really are, our hearts soften and we see our own struggles and how the Lord can and will help us overcome them.

What can you do to show your love and support for a Church leader today?

Day 157
Doctrine and Covenants 67:10

How Can I Overcome My Jealousies and Fears?

> *And again, verily I say unto you that it is your privilege, and a promise I give unto you that have been ordained unto this ministry, that inasmuch as you strip yourselves from jealousies and fears, and humble yourselves before me, for ye are not sufficiently humble, the veil shall be rent and you shall see me and know that I am—not with the carnal neither natural mind, but with the spiritual.*

At the Church conference to decide whether to publish the Doctrine and Covenants, several members questioned the authenticity of the revelations given to Joseph Smith. In response the Lord challenged the elders present to recreate one of the revelations on their own. William McLellin attempted to do so and failed, prompting the Lord to gently rebuke all of those at the conference. The Lord noted that imperfections in the revelations came because He works through imperfect beings like Joseph Smith. But the Lord also warned those at the conference that some of their questions came because of jealousy and fear.

The Lord links jealousy and fear together here and notes the cure for these afflictions: choosing to humble ourselves. When we compare ourselves to others, we open the door to making ourselves miserable. We aren't really jealous of what the other person has; we are jealous of what we don't have. Most jealously grows out of fears that we are really inadequate in some way. It is natural for us to feel this way, but the gospel asks us to take a higher path. Instead of getting jealous over the success of others, we can rejoice in their success. Instead of seeing what others have and we don't, we can rejoice over what the Lord has already given us. We can seek to lift others, not to tear them down.

What can you do today to choose to be more humble?

Day 158
Doctrine and Covenants 68:4

What Is Scripture?

> *And whatsoever they shall speak when moved upon by the Holy Ghost shall be scripture, shall be the will of the Lord, shall be the mind of the Lord, shall be the word of the Lord, shall be the voice of the Lord, and the power of God unto salvation.*

This revelation was given to several elders, specifically Orson Hyde, William McLellin, and the brothers Luke and Lyman Johnson. Each of these men were eventually ordained Apostles, but here they were rank and file priesthood holders being sent out to preach. The Lord told them they would have the ability to speak scripture and even gave His definition of scripture to them. Scripture comes when the servants God speak by the Holy Ghost and represent the mind, word, and voice of the Lord.

Does this mean that anytime a person speaks by the Holy Ghost they are creating scripture? Yes! If you give a great lesson in Sunday School, share your testimony, or share wise counsel with a loved one through the Holy Spirit, that is scripture. The Lord doesn't intend for us to think of scripture merely as a collection of writings given thousands of years ago. He wants us to know that new scripture is given every day, every time someone speaks by the power of the Spirit.

Along with this comes a caution. There is an authoritative collection of writings known as the standard works that is authenticated scripture. The reason we call them the standard works is not because they are the only scripture but because we use them as the standard to measure new scripture. If something contradicts what is found in the Bible, the Book of Mormon, the Doctrine and Covenants, or the Pearl of Great Price, we should approach it with extreme caution because it might not be scripture. The Lord intends the scriptural canon and the words given by the Holy Ghost to work together, not against each other.

Accepting this, it is amazing to contemplate that the Lord didn't just intend for ancient prophets to give us scripture. Anyone speaking by the Holy Ghost can provide scripture that guides in the ways of happiness and eternal life.

When was the last time you felt you spoke by the power of the Spirit?

Day 159
Doctrine and Covenants 68:6

How Can I Overcome My Fears?

> *Wherefore, be of good cheer, and do not fear, for I the Lord am with you, and will stand by you; and ye shall bear record of me, even Jesus Christ, that I am the Son of the living God, that I was, that I am, and that I am to come.*

The Lord told the missionaries addressed in Doctrine and Covenants 68 that their words would be His words because He would be their companion in their trials and journeys. The Lord promised that He would accompany them and stand with them as they went forward to testify of the gospel. The Savior also directs the missionaries to testify of three specific things about Him: that He was, that He is, and that He is to come. Let's consider each of these separately.

That I was. Jesus Christ was a real person who lived, loved, died, and then was resurrected and overcame death. His life has changed the world in a way that we cannot fully comprehend. His teachings have spread throughout the world and caused a revolution in the way humanity sees right and wrong. His Resurrection provides all of us with the hope that we will gain eternal life and live in happiness with our loved ones.

That I am. "I am" is title the Savior asked Moses to address Him by in the Old Testament (see Exodus 3:14). There are a number of ways to interpret this name, but one of its richest applications comes from knowing that the Savior is not a figure of the past but of the present. He is with us. He can provide courage, hope, and inspiration to all people in the moment they need it. He is not a historical figure from the distant past but the main figure behind all the moments of goodness and joy we experience right now.

That I am to come. Finally, there is the Christ of the future. There is an assurance that the sufferings of our daily lives are leading to something glorious. The followers of Christ are fundamentally optimistic about the fate of the world. There is a time ahead when the Savior will return to earth, the story we are currently living will end, and the real story will begin. We can all look forward to that time.

The Savior asks us to see Him as our Savior in the past, present, and future. Each of us can see Him as our friend and guide in all phases of our existence.

What has the Savior done for you in the past? What is He doing for you right now? What do you think He will do for you in the future?

Day 160
Doctrine and Covenants 68:25–26

How Can I Be a Good Parent?

And again, inasmuch as parents have children in Zion, or in any of her stakes which are organized, that teach them not to understand the doctrine of repentance, faith in Christ the Son of the living God, and of baptism and the gift of the Holy Ghost by the laying on of the hands, when eight years old, the sin be upon the heads of the parents.

For this shall be a law unto the inhabitants of Zion, or in any of her stakes which are organized.

In Doctrine and Covenants 68 the Lord addresses the role of parents. He summarizes parents' responsibilities by stating that they should teach their children to understand repentance, faith in Jesus Christ, the covenants made at baptism, and the gift of the Holy Ghost. There is a lot to unpack there, but the central message appears to be that the most important gospel teachers for almost all children are their parents. The home is the most effective place to create disciples of Jesus Christ.

One of the most frustrating but also wonderful things about being a parent is learning that your children have free will. The Lord doesn't expect us to control every aspect of our children's lives, and this is impossible anyway. All He expects is that we will love them, teach them, and lead them. If we neglect these duties we share in the sins our children commit. But if we do teach them, even if they stumble or make poor decisions, we can find joy in knowing that we have seen a little of what God experiences. Parenting, with all of its challenges and joys, is the school of godhood.

What lessons have you learned from being a parent, or did you learn from those who parented you?

Day 161
Doctrine and Covenants 69:7–8

How Can My Story Help Future Generations?

> *Nevertheless, let my servant John Whitmer travel many times from place to place, and from church to church, that he may the more easily obtain knowledge—*
>
> *Preaching and expounding, writing, copying, selecting, and obtaining all things which shall be for the good of the church, and for the rising generations that shall grow up on the land of Zion, to possess it from generation to generation, forever and ever. Amen.*

This revelation was further counsel to John Whitmer, the Church historian. The Lord expressed to John the importance of filling his calling by seeking knowledge. John struggled with feelings of inadequacy in his calling, something a lot of us can relate to. He didn't think that he had literary gifts or the education to be a good historian. But the Lord points out to John that sometimes our talents aren't as important as our effort. Some of the things He asked John to do, such as copying, selecting, and just obtaining knowledge, didn't require him to be a great thinker or writer. They just required him to get to work.

It can be the same in any calling. You may not be the most gifted speaker, singer, or writer. But you can put in the effort and work to become better. The Lord counseled John that whatever he did would be for "the good of the church, and for the rising generations that shall grow up in the land of Zion." In the end, John never became a great writer of history, but the thousands of documents he collected form the core of the rich history of the Church. His work really did bless the rising generations.

It can be the same with us as it was with John Whitmer. Each day that we do our best to live a good life is a page in a story that will inspire others and give them the courage to do the same.

What part of your story could help inspire the rising generation?

Day 162

Doctrine and Covenants 70:7–8

How Can I Help Fill the Lord's Storehouse?

> *Nevertheless, inasmuch as they receive more than is needful for their necessities and their wants, it shall be given into my storehouse;*
>
> *And the benefits shall be consecrated unto the inhabitants of Zion, and unto their generations, inasmuch as they become heirs according to the laws of the kingdom.*

In Doctrine and Covenants 70 the Lord set up a new extension of the law of consecration. Called the Literary Firm, the purpose of the organization was to publish the scriptures fully to the world. Several Church leaders, including Joseph Smith, committed everything they had to publishing the scriptures and in return were promised that their families would be provided for out of any profits that came from the project. To avoid any appearance of Church leaders getting rich off the sale of the scriptures, the Lord commanded the participants in the Literary Firm to only take what was "needful for their necessities and their wants" and give the rest to the storehouse so that everyone in the Church could benefit.

This is one of the fundamental principles of consecration. The Lord wants us to be provided for but not to excess. What we obtain that goes beyond our means should be generously shared with those in need. In the Book of Mormon, the prophet Jacob counseled, "But before ye seek for riches, seek ye for the kingdom of God. And after ye have obtained a hope in Christ ye shall obtain riches, if ye seek them; and ye will seek them for the intent to do good—to clothe the naked, and to feed the hungry, and to liberate the captive, and administer relief to the sick and the afflicted" (Jacob 2:18–19).

The list Jacob provides here is a good starting point for what we can do if we have more than we need. How many people can benefit from our extra time or resources? How many of us have something we can give?

If your needs are being met, what is something you could do today to make sure that someone else's needs are met?

Day 163
Doctrine and Covenants 70:14

How Can I Give in an Ungrudging Way?

> *Nevertheless, in your temporal things you shall be equal, and this not grudgingly, otherwise the abundance of the manifestations of the Spirit shall be withheld.*

In the book of Acts, the Apostle Paul taught, "It is more blessed to give than to receive" (Acts 20:35). But we can sometimes be robbed of the joys that comes from giving by doing so grudgingly, or only out of a sense of obligation. Mormon counseled, "If a man being evil giveth a gift, he doeth it grudgingly; wherefore it is counted unto him the same as if he had retained the gift; wherefore he is counted evil before God" (Moroni 7:8). All of this seems to lead back to the basic principle that our motives matter more than our actions.

Some people have little to give but have a great desire to share with others. Others have more than they need but no desire to give to others. The Lord doesn't count the size of our donations as much as He does the size of our hearts. It should be a joy to give of our time and our substance to others. Giving grudgingly or resentfully takes away the beauty of our sacrifice and can lead us away from God. On the other hand, finding joy in our sacrifice and seeing the blessings in helping others meet their needs make us more willing to give in the future.

What is your attitude towards giving, and how can you improve it?

Day 164
Doctrine and Covenants 71:7

How Can I Confound My Enemies?

> *Wherefore, confound your enemies; call upon them to meet you both in public and in private; and inasmuch as ye are faithful their shame shall be made manifest.*

This revelation was given to Joseph Smith and Sidney Rigdon when Ezra Booth, a disgruntled former member, began publishing attacks on the Church in the *Ohio Star*, a local newspaper. The attacks became severe enough that Joseph and Sidney were instructed to set aside their work of translating the Bible and confront the allegations that Booth and others were making against the Church. Following the Lord's commands, Joseph and Sidney temporarily laid aside their work and began to defend the faith publicly. Joseph later wrote that their preaching "did much towards allaying the excited feelings which were growing out of the scandalous letters then being published in the Ohio Star."[27]

In my experience, most Latter-day Saints are fairly non-confrontational. We don't like to argue, and we see contention as a way of driving

---

27. Joseph Smith—History, vol. A-1, *Joseph Smith Papers*, 179.

the Spirit away more than answering concerns. But revelations like this one show that there is a time and a place to defend the gospel. We can and should answer falsehoods about our faith. It is possible to do this in a kind and friendly way. The Savior demonstrated how to do this in His own confrontations with others. We don't need to apologize for the truth, and we can help others by clearing up falsehoods about our faith, our history, and ourselves. Being kind doesn't mean being silent.

What can you do to defend your faith today?

Day 165

Doctrine and Covenants 72:3

How Can I Be a Good Steward?

> *And verily in this thing ye have done wisely, for it is required of the Lord, at the hand of every steward, to render an account of his stewardship, both in time and in eternity.*

This revelation called the second bishop in the Church, Newell K. Whitney, to serve and look after the needs of Church members in Ohio. In the revelation the Lord returns to the teaching of stewardships given under the law of consecration but gives this concept a stronger link to our eternal welfare. Consider what He teaches here as a kind of preview of final judgment. The Lord says that He will require of every person an account of their stewardship, both in time and in eternity. That is a powerful request, and it benefits every one of us to occasionally do a self-examination to see if we are good stewards.

The Lord also emphasizes that our stewardships will be examined in time and eternity. For our purposes here, let's say that time refers to the things we have stewardship over during our time on earth, and eternity refers to the things we have stewardship over here and into the next life. Our earthly stewardships are an important part of our survival and happiness here on earth and should not be neglected. But the Lord may be emphasizing that the eternal parts of our stewardship take top priority. What is our eternal stewardship? The first thing that comes to mind is our relationships. Do we spend as much time on our relationships with our loved ones as we do on our work or other projects? Do we spend as much time listening to and caring for those around us as we do seeking our pleasure?

The Lord wants us to be happy, but true happiness comes from seeing the things that really matter and spending our time there.

Have you been giving enough time to the eternal parts of your stewardship?

Day 166

Doctrine and Covenants 72:19

How Can I Be Recommended of the Lord?

> *And now, verily I say unto you, let every elder who shall give an account unto the bishop of the church in this part of the vineyard be recommended by the church or churches, in which he labors, that he may render himself and his accounts approved in all things.*

In calling Newell K. Whitney as a new bishop in the Church, the Lord introduced a new practice as well. The bishop would provide recommends for the members in his stewardships. These recommends allowed members in different places to know that someone was in good standing in the Church and worthy to serve wherever they went. This practice continues today. Bishops and other Church leaders provide recommends for Church members who want to attend the temple, go to Church-sponsored schools, or enter into missionary service.

It can be a little nerve-wracking to go before a Church leader and answer the questions honestly and openly. But remember that the leaders are only acting as a stand-in for the Lord. The Lord is the one who judges us, and He loves us with a perfect love. The leader sitting in front of you is there to act as representative of the Lord. If you have a recommend from him, then you are worthy to enter the presence of the Lord. They don't ask us for perfection, only honest, genuine striving to be better and keep the commandments. If you are struggling, the Lord wants to help. If you want to know your standing before Him, seeking a recommend is a good place to begin.

How have your experiences seeking recommends strengthened your relationship with the Lord?

Day 167

Doctrine and Covenants 73:3

How Can I Translate the Scriptures?

> *Now, verily I say unto you my servants, Joseph Smith, Jun., and Sidney Rigdon, saith the Lord, it is expedient to translate again.*

Doctrine and Covenants 73 is a sequel to section 71, where Joseph and Sidney Rigdon were commanded to set aside the work of translating the Bible in order to combat falsehoods being spread by Ezra Booth, a disgruntled former member of the Church. After several weeks of successfully confronting Booth and his accusations, the Lord asked Joseph and Sidney to take up the work of translating the scriptures again.

Though it is a relatively unknown part of Joseph Smith's work, he considered the translation of the Bible to be a major part of his prophetic calling. Even the word *translation* can be confusing because it wasn't a process of translating from one language to another. One scholar who studied Joseph's translation efforts of the Bible carefully defined it as "recasting the text into a new form by means of inspiration from the Holy Spirit."[28] In one sense, this is something that only authorized prophets can do under the direction of the Savior. No other prophet in our time has been asked to take on a similar work.

But in another sense, this kind of translation is something that any of us can do by the aid of the Holy Spirit. Joseph and Sidney were wrestling with the scriptures, diving in deep, and searching for ways to make them more relevant to our lives. One of the meanings of "trans-

28. Kent P. Jackson, "Joseph Smith's New Translation of the Bible," in *Joseph Smith, the Prophet and Seer* (Salt Lake City: Deseret Book), 2010, 51–76.

lation" from Joseph Smith's time was interpretation, and we all need to make the effort to interpret the meaning of God's word for us. In this sense, we can all take part in translation on a regular basis.

Have you done any work to "translate" the scriptures today?

Day 168
Doctrine and Covenants 74:1

How Can I Make My Family Holier?

> *For the unbelieving husband is sanctified by the wife, and the unbelieving wife is sanctified by the husband; else were your children unclean, but now are they holy.*

This revelation appears to have come from Joseph Smith tackling the meaning of 1 Corinthians 7:14, where Paul wrote, "For the unbelieving husband is sanctified by the wife, and the unbelieving wife is sanctified by the husband: else were your children unclean; but now are they holy." The revelation clarifies that this was counsel given by the Apostle Paul, though it specifies that it was not a direct commandment of the Lord (see Doctrine and Covenants 74:5). Paul taught that if a wife who was a believer was married to a non-believer, she should not end the marriage just for that reason. Paul believed that her good influence might change her husband's heart and make him more likely to gain salvation.

Similar situations still cause heartache among believers in our time. Whether challenges stem from a mixed-faith marriage or other reasons, Paul counsels believers to try to find a way to use the light of the gospel to help their loved ones. But Paul's counsel to stay with an unbelieving spouse is his own counsel and not a command of the Lord. At times a believing spouse can lift their partner onto higher ground. At other times the Spirit may direct a spouse in a different direction. Paul's point is that holiness can be contagious, and at times the love, light, and understanding of the gospel can lift everyone around you.

How can your actions help sanctity and lift the lives of your family members?

Day 169
Doctrine and Covenants 74:7

How Does Jesus Christ Sanctify Little Children?

But little children are holy, being sanctified through the atonement of Jesus Christ; and this is what the scriptures mean.

In writing about mixed-faith marriages, Paul also addressed the subject that might be the most painful to bring up. He specifically addressed the status of children produced in those marriages, assuring that the Atonement of Jesus Christ will sanctify and make children holy. This does not mean that children are always well behaved or easy to manage. Children are not holy because they always make the right decisions. Children don't start out this life being inherently good or bad. Instead, the Lord says in a later revelation that children "become again, in their infant state, innocent before God" (Doctrine and Covenants 93:38).

Doctrine and Covenants 74 emphasizes that children are innocent before God because of Jesus Christ and His atoning sacrifice. This has provided immense hope to those who have lost children, and even to those who have simply wondered if little children are in need of baptism. The Lord paid the price for every child who passes away before they are accountable for their actions and for all those who are baptized and honor their covenants. The Savior's work provides a way for everyone to return to Him. The little children we have lost are waiting for us. It is up to us to live so that we are worthy to return to them.

How does the teaching that Jesus Christ saves little children affect your view of the gospel?

Day 170
Doctrine and Covenants 75:24

How Can I Support the Families of Missionaries?

Behold, I say unto you, that it is the duty of the church to assist in supporting the families of those, and also to support the families of those who are called and must needs be sent unto the world to proclaim the gospel unto the world.

Missionaries have always been a stirring symbol of the latter-day restoration of the gospel of Jesus Christ. They leave their homes at great sacrifice to spread the word and to help others make sacred covenants with God. While most missionaries today are young women, young men, or retired couples, when this revelation was received most missionaries were married men with wives and children. For a father who acted as the primary provider, leaving on a mission was a great sacrifice for his family. Every tale of a valiant missionary who traveled to preach the gospel has an equally harrowing tale about how his wife and children endured hardship in his absence. To name just one, while Brigham Young led the Quorum of the Twelve Apostles on their mission to the British Isles in 1840, Mary Ann Angel Young lived in an abandoned army barrack on the bank of the Mississippi River.

In this revelation, the Lord directs the Church to look after the needs of the family of the missionaries. This counsel remains sound in the Church today. Although families of today's missionaries may not make as great of a temporal sacrifice, sending a missionary out into the world can be a huge spiritual and emotional sacrifice. These families need our love and support. In reality, when a missionary leaves home, their entire family goes on a mission, and their extended Church family can help by looking after their needs.

How can you lend support to a family of missionary?

Day 171
Doctrine and Covenants 75:28

How Can I Provide for My Family?

And again, verily I say unto you, that every man who is obliged to provide for his own family, let him provide, and he shall in nowise lose his crown; and let him labor in the church.

This revelation addresses a number of practical concerns, including how to help the families of missionaries and how men should provide for their families. The Church still supports these ideals today. The Family Proclamation states, "By divine design, fathers are to preside over their families in love and righteousness and are responsible to provide the necessities of life and protection for their families. Mothers are primarily responsible for the nurture of their children. In these sacred responsibilities, fathers and mothers are obligated to help one another as equal partners."[29]

Many of us read through the first two sentences of this statement where the duties of fathers and mothers are explained but neglect to read the next sentence, which states that fathers and mothers are obligated to help one another as equal partners. No two families are exactly the same, and there may be a number of different ways that parents ensure that everyone is taken care of, fed, and clothed. The Lord asks that we make the care of our family first priority. Parents have an obligation to provide temporally and spiritually for their families.

How are you providing for the spiritual and temporal needs of your loved ones?

29. "The Family: A Proclamation to the World," *Ensign*, November 1995, 102.

Day 172
Doctrine and Covenants 75:29

How Can I Refrain from Idleness?

Let every man be diligent in all things. And the idler shall not have place in the church, except he repent and mend his ways.

Another neglected part of the law of consecration is the Lord's teachings concerning idleness. Consecration was never designed to just allow the Saints to sit back and partake of the fat of the land. Consecration is hard work! Every member of the community worked and sacrificed to make sure that everyone was taken care of and had their basic needs met. Not every member of the community was capable of putting in eight hours of hard labor, but everyone could contribute in their own way.

Consecration was a positive way of looking at the people around you and expecting the best of them. It asked the Saints to see the possibilities in the world and then work in unity to make them real. Throughout our history when the Saints have pulled together and committed fully to consecrate themselves to God, amazing things have happened. Impoverished Saints built the first temples in Kirtland and Nauvoo. Saints who committed to live consecration in the Nauvoo Temple crossed the plains of North America and founded many of the cities of the Intermountain West. Today devoted Saints all around the world labor to make their communities better, provide for their families, and be good neighbors to those around them. There is so much good for us to do. There isn't time to be idle.

What can you do to avoid idleness today?

Day 173
Doctrine and Covenants 76:22–23

How Can I Come to Know that Jesus Christ Lives?

And now, after the many testimonies which have been given of him, this is the testimony, last of all, which we give of him: That he lives!

For we saw him, even on the right hand of God; and we heard the voice bearing record that he is the Only Begotten of the Father.

Often referred to simply as "The Vision," Doctrine and Covenants 76 is actually a series of six different visions given to Joseph Smith and Sidney Rigdon during their efforts to translate the Bible. These visions took the men on a sweeping journey from seeing the best of the best (the Father and the Son) to the worst of the worst (the fall of Lucifer and the sons of perdition). The vision begins by correctly focusing our attention on the true center of the plan of salvation, the living Christ.

Joseph and Sidney begin their account of the vision by describing their witness of Jesus Christ as a living, resurrected being who stands on the right hand of God. Before this vast vision of the afterlife and all its possibilities really starts, the Lord wanted us to know one thing: Jesus Christ lives. If we have a testimony of that simple fact, then the rest of the questions surrounding life after death become relatively simple. Jesus Christ lives, so we will live too. Jesus Christ loves us, so our fate will be decided by someone who is deeply invested in only doing what will help us the most. Jesus Christ is just and merciful, so we can expect our final fate to be as merciful as it is fair.

Every discussion of the plan of salvation begins with Christ. Once we get our facts straight concerning Him, then the rest of the discussion can happen in its proper light.

Do you have a testimony that Jesus Christ lives?

Day 174
Doctrine and Covenants 76:24

How Can I Appreciate the Infinite Nature of the Savior's Work?

> *That by him, and through him, and of him, the worlds are and were created, and the inhabitants thereof are begotten sons and daughters unto God.*

The vision in Doctrine and Covenants 76 not only tells us the fate of women and men on earth but also briefly pulls back the curtain on the role of Jesus Christ in the entire cosmos. Joseph and Sidney both state that through Christ, the worlds, not just the world, are and were created. The inhabitants of those worlds become sons or daughters of God through Christ as well.

A few years after Doctrine and Covenants 76 was received, Joseph Smith, with a little help from his friend William W. Phelps, rewrote the entire section as an epic poem. This poem, which can be found fairly easily online, is one of the most useful commentaries on the vision. For instance, Joseph and William rewrote this section as follows:

> *And I heard a great voice, bearing record from heav'n,*
> *He's the Saviour, and only begotten of God—*
> *By him, of him, and through him, the worlds were all made,*
> *Even all that career in the heavens so broad,*
> *Whose inhabitants, too, from the first to the last,*
> *Are sav'd by the very same Saviour of ours;*
> *And, of course, are begotten God's daughters and sons,*
> *By the very same truths, and the very same pow'rs.*[30]

In the poem, Joseph teaches that not only were all the worlds created by the Savior, but He redeems them as well. All of the sons and daughters of God on those worlds are saved by the same

30. Poem from William W. Phelps, between 1 and 20 January 1843, *Joseph Smith Papers*.

truths. It isn't essential to our salvation to know this, but it is exciting to know that the gospel is the same throughout the entire universe. The Savior's work is intimate in its healing and infinite in its scope.

How does a knowledge of the Savior's infinite Atonement change the way you see the universe?

Day 175

Doctrine and Covenants 76:25–26

How Can I Mourn over Those Who Choose the Wrong Path?

> *And this we saw also, and bear record, that an angel of God who was in authority in the presence of God, who rebelled against the Only Begotten Son whom the Father loved and who was in the bosom of the Father, was thrust down from the presence of God and the Son,*
>
> *And was called Perdition, for the heavens wept over him—he was Lucifer, a son of the morning.*

The first vision in Doctrine and Covenants 76 is of the Father and the Son. The second vision goes from the highest heights to the lowest depths, showing us the fall of Lucifer. If Jesus Christ shows the potential of how high a son of God can ascend, then Lucifer shows how far a son of God can descend. But in providing the backstory for the adversary of all righteousness, the vision also teaches an important principle: God created Lucifer, but He didn't create evil. God gave His son Lucifer the agency to make his own decision. In order for agency to exist, there must be good and bad choices. It appears that Lucifer started out on the right path but then fell from grace.

Lucifer's fall is reflected in the names he is given in these passages. The name Lucifer is Latin for "the bearer of light," while the name he received after his fall, perdition, means "ruined." The passage also notes that the heavens mourned the loss of such a gifted person. But make no mistake, Lucifer was not created to be evil. He misused his agency and fell. By placing the visions of the Father and Son next to the vision of this fallen being, God wanted us to contrast our potential for goodness with our potential for evil.

Why is it important to know the story of Lucifer's fall?

Day 176

Doctrine and Covenants 76:38

Why Include the Sons of Perdition?

> *Yea, verily, the only ones who shall not be redeemed in the due time of the Lord, after the sufferings of his wrath.*

The third vision given to Joseph and Sidney is the vision of the sons of perdition. Among the children of God who accepted the Father's plan, the sons of perdition are a relatively small number. Joseph Smith even described the sons of perdition by saying, "He has got to say that the sun does not shine while he sees it; he has got to deny Jesus Christ when the heavens have been opened unto him, and to deny the plan of salvation with his eyes open to the truth of it."[31] Most of us will never possess this kind of knowledge in this life, so why does the vision spend so much time on the fate of the sons of perdition? In the entirety of the vision, only the vision of the celestial glory takes up more space.

One possibility is that the Lord wanted to emphasize that He always weighs our accountability against our knowledge. In another revelation, the Savior taught, "Where much is given much is required, and he that sins against the greater light shall receive the greater condemnation" (Doctrine and Covenants 82:3). The Lord doesn't punish people for things they don't know, but He has high expectations for those of us who qualify for greater knowledge. In other words, He doesn't see us as one great mass of saints or sinners. He see individuals who He is trying as hard as He can to help. But He also honors the agency of those who refuse to get help. I am sure the Savior mourns over the sons

31. *Teachings of the Prophet Joseph Smith*, 358.

of perdition, but He holds their agency too sacred to keep them from the fate they have chosen for themselves.

Why do you think the Savior sees agency as so important?

Day 177
Doctrine and Covenants 76:69

What Is the Glory of the Celestial?

> *These are they who are just men made perfect through Jesus the mediator of the new covenant, who wrought out this perfect atonement through the shedding of his own blood.*

The next vision shows the glory of the celestial kingdom, the highest of the degrees of glory shown in the vision. The people of the celestial glory become perfect through the blood of Christ. They are not perfect on their own but become perfected through their covenants with the Savior. You don't have to be perfect to go to the celestial kingdom; you just have to accept Christ fully, rely on His grace, and strive to keep His commandments.

The celestial glory is a place of infinite possibilities. But while we often picture the celestial kingdom as a place where we can test out God's cosmic powers of creation, we sometimes forget that the most important powers of God are already in our grasp. In the celestial kingdom we will know perfect compassion, perfect empathy, perfect understanding. We will love as God and the Savior love, and we will experience the kind of joy They experience. We will reach our full potential and then find an infinity of fulfillment in helping others along the same path. In the celestial kingdom, because of Christ, our real life will finally begin with the ones who love us the most.

How does a knowledge of the celestial kingdom give you hope?

Day 178

Doctrine and Covenants 76:71

What Is the Glory of the Terrestrial?

And again, we saw the terrestrial world, and behold and lo, these are they who are of the terrestrial, whose glory differs from that of the church of the Firstborn who have received the fulness of the Father, even as that of the moon differs from the sun in the firmament.

Originally Joseph Smith and Sidney Rigdon included a short introduction to Doctrine and Covenants 76 describing the scope of the vision. They described the experience as a vision "which they saw concerning the church of the first born and concerning the economy of God and his vast creation throughout all eternity."[32] From the text of the vision, the "church of the Firstborn" clearly refers to the celestial glory, those who are saved by God's Firstborn Son, Jesus Christ. But they also stated that the vision concerned "the economy of God and his vast creation." Today, the word *economy* brings to mind stocks, bonds, and trading, but one of the uses of the word from Joseph and Sidney's time was "the management, regulation, and government of a family or the concerns of a household."[33] One of the main reasons the vision was so powerful was that it didn't just show how God deals with the best and the worst but how He manages the entire family.

In this spirit, the next vision showed the terrestrial glory. People who go to the terrestrial world are not bad people. The Lord even describes them as honorable. They also will not suffer but will find themselves in a lesser glory. The vision of the terrestrial demonstrates that the old binary model of heaven and hell doesn't take into account the complexities of human nature. A simple line between the good and the bad does account for those who are honorable but perhaps not valiant in their covenants. Rather than thinking that the Lord sets out

---

32. Vision, February 16, 1832 [D&C 76], *The Joseph Smith Papers*,1.
33. "Economy," *American Dictionary of the English Language,* https://webstersdictionary1828.com/Dictionary/Economy.

to punish the wicked, the vision asks us to change our mindset and accept that His intent is to reward people as much as they are willing to be rewarded. People are complicated, and so a little complexity in the afterlife is necessary.

Why is it helpful to know there are degrees of glory in the afterlife?

Day 179
Doctrine and Covenants 76:81

What Is the Glory of the Terrestrial?

> *And again, we saw the glory of the telestial, which glory is that of the lesser, even as the glory of the stars differs from that of the glory of the moon in the firmament.*

The final vision given to Joseph and Sidney shows the overwhelming mercy of the plan of God. Here they see the telestial glory, or the glory of the stars. The people of the telestial glory are shown as an unsavory bunch, but it is not in God's character to punish them eternally either. They do accept what Jesus Christ is, even if they do not choose to follow Him. They do receive a reward and find happiness in the glory they are assigned to. Part of the aim of the vision is to show that God is intent on giving His children as much of a reward as they are prepared to receive. He wants to reward even those who are guilty of serious sins and longs for them to have a home in His many mansions.

Lorenzo Snow summarized this principle: "God loves His offspring, the human family. His design is not simply to furnish happiness to the few here, called Latter-day Saints. The plan and scheme that He is now carrying out is for universal salvation; not only for the salvation of the Latter-day Saints, but for the salvation of every man and woman on the face of the earth, for those also in the spirit world, and for those who may hereafter come upon the face of the earth. It is for the salvation of every son and daughter of Adam. They are the offspring of the Almighty, He loves them all and His plans are for the salvation of the whole, and He will bring all up into that position in which they will be as happy and as comfortable as they are willing to be."[34]

How does the vision help you to understand the merciful nature of God?

Day 180
Doctrine and Covenants 77:6

How Can I Better Understand the Revelation of John?

> *Q. What are we to understand by the book which John saw, which was sealed on the back with seven seals?*
>
> *A. We are to understand that it contains the revealed will, mysteries, and the works of God; the hidden things of his economy concerning this earth during the seven thousand years of its continuance, or its temporal existence.*

Doctrine and Covenants 77 is unique among the revelations because it functions as a Q&A about the book of Revelation. The content only asks questions of the content up to about Revelation 11, but the answers provide important clues in unlocking the larger meaning of the book. The book of Revelation uses rich symbolism to teach about the return of Jesus Christ and the cosmic struggle between good and evil. One of the most valuable contributions is to help us understand that the book John saw with seven seals represents seven thousand years of the history of the earth. The first seal represents the first thousand years, the second seal represents the second seal, and so on down to the present.

We do not know exactly where in the story we fit in, but a direct reading of the scriptures places us somewhere near the sixth and seventh thousand years. This time period, where the world is undergoing the radical transformation from a world of sin to its paradisiacal state, is where the book of Revelation spends the majority of its time. The first five thousand years are covered in just eleven verses. The sixth seal,

34. *Teachings of Lorenzo Snow*, 91.

a description of terrible calamities, is covered in twenty-two verses. But the seventh seal, which describes the Second Coming of Jesus Christ and His return to the earth, is described in 218 verses! The majority of the book of Revelation is devoted to helping us understand the events before the Second Coming of Christ. This key from Doctrine and Covenants 77 helps us understand how important the last days are in God's plan. When an ancient prophet like John needed hope, he was shown the last days, our time, when the Saints are at last victorious.

Why is it a blessing to live in the latter days?

Day 181
Doctrine and Covenants 77:12

How Will God Complete the Salvation of Man?

> *Q. What are we to understand by the sounding of the trumpets, mentioned in the 8th chapter of Revelation?*
>
> *A. We are to understand that as God made the world in six days, and on the seventh day he finished his work, and sanctified it, and also formed man out of the dust of the earth, even so, in the beginning of the seventh thousand years will the Lord God sanctify the earth, and complete the salvation of man, and judge all things, and shall redeem all things, except that which he hath not put into his power, when he shall have sealed all things, unto the end of all things; and the sounding of the trumpets of the seven angels are the preparing and finishing of his work, in the beginning of the seventh thousand years—the preparing of the way before the time of his coming.*

According to the keys given in Doctrine and Covenants 77, the seven seals represent seven thousand years of the history of the earth. The revelation also compares the seven thousand years to the seven creative periods spoken of in the book of Genesis and other places. As it was in the beginning, the last time period was devoted to the work of God, rest, and finding joy in the beauty of creation. The seventh thousand years, sometimes referred to as the Millennium, was the Sabbath day in the history of earth. While the Sabbath is intended to be a day of rest, it is also a day set aside to carry out the work of God.

Doctrine and Covenants 77 says that during this time God will "complete the salvation of man." One way this might be fulfilled is through the work that will happen in temples during the Millennium. The vast majority of our brothers and sisters left this life without knowing the gospel, and it might take a thousand years to ensure that all of them have the opportunity to make covenants with God. Like the Sabbath, the Millennium will be a time when the earth can rest from the wickedness it has seen, but the work of God will go forward, unhindered, and open the door of salvation for all women and men who choose it.

What do you look forward to most about the Millennium?

Day 182

Doctrine and Covenants 77:14

What Role Will Ancient Prophets Play in the Last Days?

> *Q. What are we to understand by the little book which was eaten by John, as mentioned in the 10th chapter of Revelation?*
>
> *A. We are to understand that it was a mission, and an ordinance, for him to gather the tribes of Israel; behold, this is Elias, who, as it is written, must come and restore all things.*

One of the most curious episodes in the book of Revelation occurs when John is shown a small book, which he is then commanded to eat. John described this event as follows: "And I took the little book out of the angel's hand, and ate it up; and it was in my mouth sweet as honey: and as soon as I had eaten it, my belly was bitter" (Revelation 10:9–10). Doctrine and Covenants 77 clarifies that the little book was a mission for him to gather the tribes of Israel before the end times. Like much of the work God asks us to perform, this commission was sweet for John but also a little bitter.

Because we are only given glimpses of their lives, the prophets like John found in scripture sometimes seem like larger-than-life figures. It is a little encouraging to know that John got a little bit of a stomachache when he realized how vast and all-encompassing his mission would be. Other revelations in the Doctrine and Covenants speak of John becoming as "flaming fire and a ministering angel" (Doctrine and Covenants 6:6). But behind the fire and the glory is a person striving to carry out a mighty work. The callings we receive can also be a little bittersweet. Our tasks probably won't take a few millennia to accomplish like John's, but they are also part of the great work he is taking part in. One of the powerful truths of the Restoration comes in knowing the ancient Saints are our partners in carrying out the Lord's great work.

How has your service for God been both bitter and sweet?

Day 183
Doctrine and Covenants 77:15

What Role Will Modern Prophets Play in the Last Days?

> *Q. What is to be understood by the two witnesses, in the eleventh chapter of Revelation?*
>
> *A. They are two prophets that are to be raised up to the Jewish nation in the last days, at the time of the restoration, and to prophesy to the Jews after they are gathered and have built the city of Jerusalem in the land of their fathers.*

Another mysterious passage in the book of Revelation is found in chapter 11, which describes the ministry of two witnesses in Jerusalem during the last days. The two witnesses prophesy in the city and call down the power of heaven, sending fire and plagues on the armies that assail the city. Eventually the two witnesses are killed and their bodies lie in the street for three and a half days. Then life will be restored to their bodies and they will ascend into heaven. Like most of the book of Revelation, the wording, numerology, and descriptions of the two witnesses is deeply symbolic. But at the same time, Doctrine and Covenants 77 steers away from a completely symbolic interpretation of this passage and points toward a literal ministry of the two witnesses.

Section 77 identifies the two witnesses as "prophets that are to be raised up to the Jewish nation in the last days." While we do not know exactly how and when this will be fulfilled, it is reasonable to assume that these prophets will hold the priesthood and be sustained as prophets by the Church. The important thing to remember is that modern prophets have a substantial role to play in the last days. The Lord has sent His prophets to guide us through the trials and tribulations leading up to the Second Coming. If we follow their counsel and teachings, we can endure the challenges of the last days and emerge triumphant as well.

How has the counsel of modern prophets helped you navigate the challenges of the last days?

Day 184

Doctrine and Covenants 78:5-6

How Can I Be Equal in Heavenly Things?

> *That you may be equal in the bonds of heavenly things, yea, and earthly things also, for the obtaining of heavenly things.*
>
> *For if ye are not equal in earthly things ye cannot be equal in obtaining heavenly things.*

In the spring of 1832, Joseph Smith and Sidney Rigdon were commanded to travel to Missouri to reorganize some of the businesses of the Church to better help the members there live the law of consecration and stewardship. This might seem like a purely earthly matter, but the Lord reminded them there is only a thin line that separates our spiritual and temporal welfare. Because the Saints in Missouri were given the task of building the city of Zion, they needed to be sync in temporal matters to be have the blessings of the Lord to excel spiritually.

We tend to separate the spiritual and the physical, but the Lord worked in the revelations to help the Saints understand how closely related the two really are. While prayer, meditation, and reflection have their place in our lives, the Lord also expects us to do daily acts of physical service to bless the lives of those around us. Whether a person is rich or poor, in good health or bad health, there is always something we can do to lift others. The Lord didn't intend for us to just look after ourselves and not worry about other people. Sometimes an act of kindness is a profound act of spirituality.

What can you do to help lift others today?

Day 185

Doctrine and Covenants 78:14

Why Must the Church Stand Independent?

> *That through my providence, notwithstanding the tribulation which shall descend upon you, that the church may stand independent above all other creatures beneath the celestial world.*

While the Lord emphasizes the interconnection among the Saints by teaching them the law of consecration and stewardship, the Lord also emphasizes the independence of the Saints from the world. It might seem paradoxical to seek to be both interconnected and independent, but the Lord sometimes deals in paradoxes. We are interconnected in the sense that we see ourselves and all the people around us as part of the family of God. God has given us all that we have. That is the starting point of consecration.

But God also asks us to work to be independent so that we can grow and prosper. You cannot always help others until you yourself are secure. God asked the Church to be independent so that it could have more power to assist others and help them become independent. Becoming a Zion people was always a gentle push and pull between interdependence and independence. We want to see the connections we have to other people while we strive to make our connection with God and our power to help others even stronger. This is part of the reason we sometimes speak of these commandments as the law of consecration and stewardship. Consecration allows us to see each other as part of God's bounty, interconnected and tied together. Stewardship is demonstrated when we show that we can manage the blessings God has given us on our own. All of this is part of the process of becoming like God, who is deeply connected to our lives but also able to take stewardship over the entire universe.

What can you do to become more spiritually and temporally independent?

Day 186

Doctrine and Covenants 78:17

How Can I Come to Know the Blessings God Has in Store for Me?

> *Verily, verily, I say unto you, ye are little children, and ye have not as yet understood how great blessings the Father hath in his own hands and prepared for you.*

One of the titles the Lord often uses for the Saints in the scriptures is His children. Here He even refers to them as little children because they are having difficulty seeing the grand nature of the work of the Restoration. This should not be seen as an insult, since the Lord often urges us to be childlike, meaning meek, submissive, and willing to keep His commandments. But it seems here that the Lord is speaking to the inexperience of the Saints and their failure to follow what He is asking them to do.

Children have many wonderful qualities, and this is part of the reason the Lord loves them and holds them up as an ideal for adults to emulate. But children also have short memories. They sometimes lack the ability to see things in the long term or further down the road. I am often reminded of a long road trip with my own children when they ask, "Are we there yet?" We usually give an answer that spells out the time and distance we still have left to travel, but five minutes later they still ask, "Are we there yet?"

There is a map that spells out exactly where we are going and what the blessing are that the Lord has in store for us. It is the scriptures.

If we study and know the blessings God has in store for us, we can appreciate that we really only have begun to comprehend the blessings waiting for us at the end of the road.

How can you be patient while waiting for the blessings of the Lord?

Day 187
Doctrine and Covenants 79:2–3

What Are the Rewards for Faithfulness?

> *And I will send upon him the Comforter, which shall teach him the truth and the way whither he shall go;*
>
> *And inasmuch as he is faithful, I will crown him again with sheaves.*

Jared Carter was a faithful missionary who traveled to Hiram, Ohio, to meet personally with the Prophet Joseph Smith and seek guidance on his life and his service in the Church. He was not disappointed because the Prophet agreed to receive a personal revelation on Jared's behalf, and this short blessing became Doctrine and Covenants 79. Jared was called to serve a mission in the Eastern countries and was told that he would receive blessings for his service.

The Lord promises to "crown" Jared, a word that usually refers to an ascension into a royal family. But the Lord does not promise to crown him with riches, power, or fame. The Lord promises to crown him with sheaves, a word referred to a harvest of wheat. The collecting of sheaves is often used in the Doctrine and Covenants as a metaphor for souls saved. The promise given to Jared is ultimately what the Lord promises to everyone who serves in His kingdom. You won't become the most famous, or the most wealthy, but you will find yourselves crowned with the love and the gratitude of the souls you help along the way. And perhaps the most important sheave you will harvest is your own soul, saved because of your dedication to God.

What rewards have you seen because of your service to God?

Day 188

Doctrine and Covenants 80:3–4

Why Doesn't the Lord Always Give Specific Directions?

Wherefore, go ye and preach my gospel, whether to the north or to the south, to the east or to the west, it mattereth not, for ye cannot go amiss.

Therefore, declare the things which ye have heard, and verily believe, and know to be true.

Stephen Burnett was another young missionary who sought a revelation from Joseph Smith at the beginning of his mission. The message was short and sweet, instructing Stephen to take Eden Smith, another new convert, with him and set out on his mission. The Lord does not provide Stephen or Eden with specific direction but instead exhorts them to set out in any direction and they will find success.

This short section has special significance for me. When I received my mission call, I had dreams of traveling abroad, learning a language and seeing the world. I was a little disappointed when I opened my mission call and learned I was going to Florida. I had already been to Florida twice with my family, and it wasn't as exotic as I had hoped. That Sunday I was asked to speak about getting a mission call to the Primary children in our ward, and I leafed through the scriptures, accidentally turning to this section and reading where the Lord told Stephen Burnett that it didn't matter where he was going; it mattered that he knew the truth and needed to declare it.

That verse hit me like a bolt of lightning. I knew the Lord was speaking to me and giving me a gentle prod to know that the destination was less important than the calling. Like Stephen Burnett, I came to know that the Lord isn't as concerned about the state you serve in as the state of your heart.

Why does the Lord trust His servants enough to allow them to make their own decisions?

Day 189

Doctrine and Covenants 81:1

What Blessings Come with a Calling?

> *Verily, verily, I say unto you my servant Frederick G. Williams: Listen to the voice of him who speaketh, to the word of the Lord your God, and hearken to the calling wherewith you are called, even to be a high priest in my church, and a counselor unto my servant Joseph Smith, Jun.*

This revelation was given to call a new counselor to the First Presidency, establishing the pattern of three presiding high priests serving as the leaders of the Church. The original First Presidency consisted of Joseph Smith, Sidney Rigdon, and Frederick G. Williams. A glance at the earliest manuscript, however, shows that this revelation originally wasn't given to Frederick G. Williams. It was given to a man named Jesse Gause. We don't know much about Jesse Gause, but in the original manuscript of the revelation his name appears in the text and then was crossed out and replaced with Frederick G. Williams' name. Apparently Jesse rejected the call to serve in the First Presidency and shortly after left the Church. Fredrick G. Williams accepted the call and became a close friend of Joseph Smith. Joseph even named his son Frederick in his honor.

At first it can be a little jarring to think that a person's name can be crossed out in a revelation and simply replaced with another. But it should be remembered that this wasn't a revelation for Jesse Gause or Frederick G. Williams. This was a revelation for the second counselor in the First Presidency. The blessings, powers, and authority bestowed in the revelation were given to the calling, not the individual. There is an old saying in the Church that whom the Lord calls, He qualifies. When we are asked to carry out a responsibility it can feel overwhelming, but the Lord will give you the powers and abilities you need to fill the calling. The blessing comes with the calling.

What blessing have you seen as you have served in different ways?

Day 190

Doctrine and Covenants 81:5

How Can I Be Faithful in My office?

Wherefore, be faithful; stand in the office which I have appointed unto you; succor the weak, lift up the hands which hang down, and strengthen the feeble knees.

As Frederick G. Williams was called into the First Presidency, the Lord spelled out the responsibilities of his office but also gave some general counsel to Church leaders. Among the charges given to Frederick, and to everyone who serves in the Church, is to "succor the weak, lift up the hands which hang down, and strengthen the feeble knees."

A large part of why we have a church is that we gain strength from others. Many of us are fighting hard battles on a regular basis and need to know that we have a support system that can help us. Sometimes just a simple act of kindness, like a kind smile or a gentle word of affirmation, can be enough to help us make it to the next day. Sometimes service in the Church is nothing more than just being there for others and helping them know that someone loves them and is looking out for them. Lifting others is the first and most basic responsibility for any members of the Church, whether you are serving in the First Presidency like Frederick G. Williams or in any other calling.

What can you do to lift someone else today?

Day 191

Doctrine and Covenants 82:3

Why Does the Lord Have High Expectations of His Servants?

For of him unto whom much is given much is required; and he who sins against the greater light shall receive the greater condemnation.

One of the principles emphasized in the restored gospel is that when it comes to His expectations for His children, God does not use a one-size-fits-all approach. He deals with each of us individually, working with us on whatever level we might be at. That can be really comforting, especially when we are starting out and need a lot of help. But in order for us to really keep growing, His level of expectation has to grow as well.

As we continue to grow in the gospel, the Lord's expectations for us grow as well. Sometimes our challenges will increase not because we are doing anything wrong but because God knows that we are capable of meeting greater challenges. One of my friends used to say that God loves us just the way we are, but He loves us too much to let us stay the way we are. He gently and carefully increases His expectations for us as we grow and helps us meet greater and greater challenges, gradually molding us into mighty disciples that can do great works in His behalf. So keep in mind that sometimes greater trials mean that you can handle a little bit more and God trusts that you are capable of meeting the challenges He puts before you.

Why is it comforting to know that God has different expectations for different people?

Day 192

Doctrine and Covenants 82:9–10

How Can I Know that the Lord Keeps His Promises?

> *Or, in other words, I give unto you directions how you may act before me, that it may turn to you for your salvation.*
>
> *I, the Lord, am bound when ye do what I say; but when ye do not what I say, ye have no promise.*

In this revelation, the Lord was urging the members of the Literary Firm, a special organization set up to publish the scriptures, to live up to the commitments they had made. This special group was asked to live a higher set of expectations linked to the law of consecration, making a sacrifice to ensure that the revelations could be published to the entire Church. In speaking to them the Lord made a few comments about why He gives us commandments and how He keeps His promises.

A covenant with God is a two-way promise in which He sets the terms. We do not negotiate our covenants with God because He is all-knowing and has already worked out the terms for us. The upside of making covenants with God is that He always keeps His promises. He will work with us, help us, and guide us, and never let us down. We may fail, but God does not fail us. And when we do fail we can approach God and sincerely repent. If we do so, we will find His willingness to help us rise again and succeed.

When have you seen the Lord keep His promises to you?

Day 193

Doctrine and Covenants 82:14

How Can Zion Enlarge Her Borders?

> *For Zion must increase in beauty, and in holiness; her borders must be enlarged; her stakes must be strengthened; yea, verily I say unto you, Zion must arise and put on her beautiful garments.*

Throughout the Doctrine and Covenants, the Lord uses the term "Zion" in several different ways. During this time period Zion referred to the city being built by the Saints on the western frontier of the United States. But passages like Doctrine and Covenants 82 hint that the Lord had something bigger in store for Zion. He wanted Zion to increase and her borders to grow. Zion would start as a city and then grow to become a place where faithful Saints could find refuge from the growing troubles of the world.

Today a little piece of Zion is found in nearly every country on earth. The number of temples is growing, and Saints are building new places of refuge where they can find rest and peace. In the end Zion will fill the entire earth. But from our perspective, Zion is strengthened in small ways each day. We can find ways to make our own homes places of Zion and move the borders just a bit by small acts of devotion. For Zion to fill the whole earth we must do the little things every day that enlarge her borders.

How can you enlarge the borders of Zion today?

Day 194

Doctrine and Covenants 82:18–19

How Can I Seek the Interest of My Neighbor?

> *And all this for the benefit of the church of the living God, that every man may improve upon his talent, that every man may gain other talents, yea, even an hundred fold, to be cast into the Lord's storehouse, to become the common property of the whole church—*
>
> *Every man seeking the interest of his neighbor, and doing all things with an eye single to the glory of God.*

As the Lord urged the early Saints to live the law of consecration and stewardship, He urged them to build upon their talents. The word *talent* appears in the New Testament as a unit of monetary value but by Joseph Smith's time had come to mean any special ability or gift that a person possesses. Here the Lord not only urges the Saints to cast their money but their talents into the storehouse to help lift and bless their neighbors. This suggests that the Lord's storehouse is more than just a building where goods are kept—the real storehouse consists of all the members of the Church, their talents, and their time.

President Thomas S. Monson taught, "The Lord's storehouse includes the time, talents, skills, compassion, consecrated material, and financial means of faithful Church members. These resources are available to the bishop in assisting those in need. Our bishops have the responsibility to learn how to use properly these resources."[35]

Each of us has gifts. Those gifts constitute a way of building the

35. Thomas S. Monson, "Goal beyond Victory," *Ensign*, November 1988, 47.

Lord's storehouse so that it can meet the needs of everyone who is part of our covenant of consecration with the Lord.

What talents do you have that could build the Lord's storehouse?

Day 195
Doctrine and Covenants 83:4

How Can I Help the Children in My Charge?

All children have claim upon their parents for their maintenance until they are of age.

The revelations in the Doctrine and Covenants organize the Church around one fundamental unit: the family. In particular, the Lord seems to be concerned with the welfare of children. Throughout all of the scriptures, the Lord shows great concern for vulnerable groups like children and widows. He urges His disciples to look after these groups, knowing how precious and valuable they are. In this revelation, the Lord commands parents to look after the needs of their children.

Taking care of children is one of the most challenging tasks we are given in this life. Whether you are a parent, teacher, or ministering brother or sister, taking care of children is one of the top priorities the Lord gives to His disciples. "Maintenance" as used in this passage means so much more than just making sure that children have food, clothing, and shelter. They must be maintained spiritually and emotionally as well. Children need to be taught how precious they are in the sight of God. They need to be loved and raised in an environment of warmth and caring.

When we consider that God asks us to call Him "Father," we learn that taking care of children is not just a requirement of this life, but it is also the great task that God carries out in the eternities. To love a child is to experience the joy that God knows.

What can you do to care for the children the Lord has placed in your stewardship?

Day 196

Doctrine and Covenants 83:6

What Is the Purpose of the Lord's Storehouse?

And the storehouse shall be kept by the consecrations of the church; and widows and orphans shall be provided for, as also the poor. Amen.

In the spring of 1832, Joseph Smith and Sidney Rigdon traveled from Kirtland, Ohio, to Independence, Missouri, to conduct Church business with the Saints in the area. During this time Joseph met with the Colesville Branch, who included some of his oldest and dearest friends. Among the members of this branch were at least two widows, Phebe Peck and Anna Rogers. In the rough frontier conditions, Joseph was particularly concerned that these two sisters were being looked after by the members of the branch.

This revelation was received while Joseph was visiting the Colesville Branch. It emphasizes the role the Saints play in creating a surrogate family for those who need it. The Lord emphasizes widows and orphans in this revelation, but in our time other factors like divorce, separation, health, and other challenges create a need for us to consecrate our time and efforts toward families who need help. The family is one of the most basic ways for a person to have their needs met. If a person does not have a complete family, then the family of the Church can step in and help make sure that everyone is provided for.

How can you help the Lord take care of those who need a family?

Day 197

Doctrine and Covenants 84:4–5

Why Hasn't the Temple in Zion Been Built Yet?

Verily this is the word of the Lord, that the city New Jerusalem shall be built by the gathering of the saints, beginning at this place, even the place of the temple, which temple shall be reared in this generation.

For verily this generation shall not all pass away until an house shall be built unto the Lord, and a cloud shall rest upon it, which cloud shall be even the glory of the Lord, which shall fill the house.

Though the location for the first temple was given over a year earlier (see Doctrine and Covenants 57), there were no further mentions of the temple until this revelation. Doctrine and Covenants 84 opens with the command to build the temple in Zion, making it the center of the city. The Lord said the temple would be built within "this generation," but because of persecution the Saints were forced out of Jackson County, the place set aside for the city of Zion. The temple in Zion remains unbuilt.

Does this mean the Lord was wrong when He told the Saints the temple would be built in their generation? Not at all. There are several ways to reconcile the Lord's promise to the Saints. First, the Lord told the Saints, "This generation shall not pass away until an house shall be built unto the Lord." The Saints did not build the temple in Zion, but they did manage to build temples in Kirtland, Ohio, and Nauvoo, Illinois. Some of the Saints of that generation lived long enough to see temples built in St. George, Logan, Manti, and Salt Lake City, Utah. Some Saints even lived long enough to see temples dedicated in Cardston, Alberta, Canada, and Laie, Hawaii. The promise of a temple "reared in this generation" was not fulfilled the way the Saints expected it to be, but it was fulfilled.

It is the same with many of the Lord's promises to us. They can be fulfilled in surprising ways, if we only have the eyes to see it.

When have blessings come to you in an unexpected way?

Day 198
Doctrine and Covenants 84:17–18

What Is the Priesthood?

Which priesthood continueth in the church of God in all generations, and is without beginning of days or end of years.

And the Lord confirmed a priesthood also upon Aaron and his seed, throughout all their generations, which priesthood also continueth and abideth forever with the priesthood which is after the holiest order of God.

Doctrine and Covenants 84 begins by introducing the temple and then branches out to explain the promises and covenants given through the priesthood. The Aaronic and Melchizedek Priesthoods meet together in the temple, where all men and women who make the sacred covenants with God receive authority to serve. This passage mentions one unique aspect of the Aaronic Priesthood, which is that it was passed through the family of Aaron. In the early Church, the offices of the Aaronic Priesthood were primarily given to adult men. Later Church leaders changed the practice so that young men could experience service within the Church. A young man can enter into the offices of the Aaronic Priesthood as early as the age of eleven in the Church today.

While it is true that the family of Aaron had special promises made to them relating to the priesthood, it is incorrect to say that only Aaron's family could hold the priesthood. The priesthood is available to the entire family of God. Those who accept and magnify the priesthood become the heirs of Aaron. Taking the priesthood upon ourselves is another way of not only recognizing God as our Father but taking a step to becoming more like Him.

How does the priesthood help us become more like God?

Day 199
Doctrine and Covenants 84:19–20

How Is the Power of God Made Manifest?

And this greater priesthood administereth the gospel and holdeth the key of the mysteries of the kingdom, even the key of the knowledge of God.

Therefore, in the ordinances thereof, the power of godliness is manifest.

God is the most powerful being in the universe, but He chooses to use His power carefully and thoughtfully. Often when we think of God's power, images come to mind like the parting of the Red Sea through Moses or the pillar of fire that showed the Israelites the way to the promised land. But in Doctrine and Covenants 84, when God points out how His power is made manifest, He points toward the ordinances of the gospel. Ordinances like blessings, baptisms, sacraments, and temple rites demonstrate the power of God on a consistent and daily basis.

A few years ago a young couple living next door to me asked if I would help give a blessing to their baby. It was their first child, and they were worried because her skin was slightly yellow. I explained that a little jaundice is not that unusual for a newborn but remembered that for brand-new parents everything can be a cause for concern. So the new father and I laid our hands on the head of the newborn while her mother held her in her arms. We anointed the baby with consecrated oil, and then the father sealed the blessing with a few inspired words.

Nothing majestic happened, but the power of God was made manifest. The power wasn't just manifested through the baby getting better but in drawing the family closer together. A miracle occurred through the power of the priesthood.

How have you seen the power of God manifested through ordinances?

Day 200
Doctrine and Covenants 84:21–22

What Are the Rewards for Faithfulness?

And without the ordinances thereof, and the authority of the priesthood, the power of godliness is not manifest unto men in the flesh;

For without this no man can see the face of God, even the Father, and live.

One of the most misunderstood passages in all the scriptures is John 1:18, which teaches, "No man hath seen God at any time." Taken simply at face value, this teaching contradicts several other passages which show that prophets can see God. When Joseph Smith translated that passage, he was inspired to change the wording to "no man hath seen God at any time, except he hath borne record of the Son; for except it is through him no man can be saved" (JST, John 1:19). This teaching harmonizes better with passages like Exodus 33:11, which notes that "the Lord spake unto Moses face to face, as a man speaketh unto his friend."

Can only prophets see the face of God? Doctrine and Covenants 84 opens the door by explaining further that anyone can see the face of God as long as they enter into covenants with God. Through the laws and ordinances of the gospel, the natural man—the part of us that would whither in the presence of God—can be overcome. We are sanctified through our acceptance of the gospel and gain the power to live in God's presence. The same promises made to Moses, Peter, John, and Joseph Smith are available to every person as they come to know and enter in the covenants with God.

How have ordinances helped you come closer to the presence of God?

Day 201

Doctrine and Covenants 84:33–34

What Are the Blessings of Obtaining the Priesthood?

For whoso is faithful unto the obtaining these two priesthoods of which I have spoken, and the magnifying their calling, are sanctified by the Spirit unto the renewing of their bodies.

They become the sons of Moses and of Aaron and the seed of Abraham, and the church and kingdom, and the elect of God.

At times the priesthood has been passed down through families. Chosen servants like Abraham, Issac, Jacob, Aaron, and Moses passed the priesthood to their children and created a lineage of dedicated servants of God. But not everyone comes from families who live the gospel. The great chain of priesthood was intended to be passed through families but became broken as people turned away from the promises God made to their fathers.

In Doctrine and Covenants 84 the Lord explains that the chain of priesthood can be reforged when a person chooses to accept the responsibilities that come upon them as part of the family of God. Not only are they promised a renewal of their bodies, but they also become the adopted sons of men like Moses and Aaron. In holy temples, priesthood is used to repair the broken links and forge new ones, creating a great priesthood family that can serve into the eternities.

As the scriptures explain, even great leaders like Abraham, Moses, or Nephi came from complicated families. But the priesthood and its blessings can repair the breaks in our families, help us become part of the great royal family of God, and enter into God's presence to receive all the blessings He has to offer us.

What do you think it means to be faithful in obtaining the priesthood?

Day 202
Doctrine and Covenants 84:35–38

How Can I Receive the Priesthood?

And also all they who receive this priesthood receive me, saith the Lord;

For he that receiveth my servants receiveth me;

And he that receiveth me receiveth my Father;

And he that receiveth my Father receiveth my Father's kingdom; therefore all that my Father hath shall be given unto him.

A key part of the oath and covenant of the priesthood explained in Doctrine and Covenants 84 is the Lord's commandment to "receive" the priesthood. This can be interpreted in several different ways. A person can receive the priesthood by being ordained or receiving the ordinances in the temple. A person can also receive the priesthood in the sense that they sustain those called to priesthood positions in the Church. A person can receive the priesthood by accepting the priesthood authority that comes with any calling in the Church.

The central idea to keep in mind is that receiving the priesthood means receiving Jesus Christ, and receiving Christ means receiving the Father. Those who serve with priesthood authority are not perfect, but they are asked to serve as God's representatives on the earth. How we act toward them shows how we would respond if the Savior or Heavenly Father were before us. If we want to show our devotion to the Father and the Son, then we start by showing our devotion to the men and women chosen to lead and guide us here on earth. If we show humility by listening to those who have been asked to look after us, then we show that we will listen to the Father and the Son. In turn, the Father and the Son promise to give us all that They have.

What do you think it means to receive the priesthood?

Day 203

Doctrine and Covenants 84:39–40

What Is the Oath and Covenant of the Priesthood?

And this is according to the oath and covenant which belongeth to the priesthood.

Therefore, all those who receive the priesthood, receive this oath and covenant of my Father, which he cannot break, neither can it be moved.

The oath and covenant of the priesthood is one of the most profound explanations of how God passes His power to His children and then allows them, step by step, to return to His presence and become like Him. But because "priesthood" is sometimes mistakenly used to only refer to men in the Church, women often misunderstand that the oath and covenant applies to them as well. When Jean B. Bingham was serving as the General Relief Society President, she interviewed President Russell M. Nelson, who explained that the oath and covenant of the priesthood applies to all disciples of Jesus Christ, regardless of their gender. Here is how they described these blessings in their conversation:

> President Nelson: "The oath and covenant of the priesthood means that God's made a promise and He sets the conditions, and if you agree to keep them you make a covenant, and then He also indicates, when you do what I say you will receive the blessings but if you do not what I say you have no promise. So it is clearly a two way conversation, a covenant, two way. He makes the provision and you accept them and keep those covenants and keep the blessings."
>
> Sister Bingham: "So that is just as relevant to women as it is to men?"
>
> President Nelson: "Totally."
>
> Sister Bingham: "All those priesthood blessings from the oath and covenant of the priesthood are enjoyed by both men and women."
>
> President Nelson: "Exactly, exactly."[36]

---

36. "The Oath and Covenant of the Priesthood Is Relevant to Women," interview of

The blessings of the oath and covenant of the priesthood are equally available to both women and men. If we seek God, receive the priesthood, and honor our covenants, all that God has will be given to us.

Why is it important to know that the blessings of the priesthood are open to all people?

Day 204
Doctrine and Covenants 84:57

What Is the New Covenant?

> *And they shall remain under this condemnation until they repent and remember the new covenant, even the Book of Mormon and the former commandments which I have given them, not only to say, but to do according to that which I have written.*

Near the end of this revelation, the Lord delivers a strong warning to the members of the Church to remember the new covenant, meaning the Book of Mormon. The language the Lord uses here suggests that the Book of Mormon is not just another collection of sacred writings but a sign of a new covenant between God and His children in the latter days. When the Lord brought forth the Book of Mormon, He commenced a new phase of His plan. It was beginning of the final phase leading up to the Second Coming of Jesus Christ.

When Ezra Taft Benson was serving as president of the Church, he often quoted this passage, declaring that the Lord's condemnation from this passage has never been lifted. On one occasion President Benson said, "If the early Saints were rebuked for treating the Book of Mormon lightly, are we under any less condemnation if we do the same? The Lord Himself bears testimony that it is of eternal significance. Can a small number of us bring the whole Church under condemnation because we trifle with sacred things? What will we say at the Judgment when we stand before Him and meet

---

Russell M. Nelson by Jean B. Bingham, ChurchofJesusChrist.org.

His probing gaze if we are among those described as forgetting the new covenant?"[37]

No prophet since President Benson has received word that the Lord's condemnation for neglecting the Book of Mormon has been lifted on the Church. But it can be lifted on individuals as we work to diligently study and teach from the Book of Mormon.

How can you use the Book of Mormon more effectively in your life?

Day 205

Doctrine and Covenants 84:85

How Can I Speak by the Spirit?

> *Neither take ye thought beforehand what ye shall say; but treasure up in your minds continually the words of life, and it shall be given you in the very hour that portion that shall be meted unto every man.*

It can be overwhelming to know the right thing to say. We want to show love, provide guidance, and know the best way to help someone else, but we worry about saying the wrong thing. How can we gain confidence that we will say the right thing? The Lord offers this simple counsel: treasure up in your minds continually the words of life, and it shall be given you.

If we are continually filling our minds and hearts with good things, the Spirit will give the right words in the moment we need to speak. Our minds are like a reservoir that needs to be refilled and refreshed through the word of God. When the words the Lord has spoken are in us, the Spirit can speak through us. We can become a conduit for the Lord to deliver the words that His children need to hear in their moments of agony or doubt. We can overcome our doubts and speak the words He needs us to speak.

What have you done recently to treasure up in your mind the words of life?

---

37. Ezra Taft Benson, "The Book of Mormon—The Keystone of Our Religion," *Ensign*, November 1986.

Day 206
Doctrine and Covenants 85:8

What Does It Mean to Steady the Ark?

While that man, who was called of God and appointed, that putteth forth his hand to steady the ark of God, shall fall by the shaft of death, like as a tree that is smitten by the vivid shaft of lightning.

This revelation appeared in a letter sent to the Church in Missouri, where the Lord chastised the members of the Church for their failure to commit to live the law of consecration. Consecration was still relatively new, and Church leaders at times argued over the best way to implement it. The revelation contains a passage where the Lord speaks about sending "one mighty and strong" to set the Church in order. However, since local leaders were able to resolve the difficulty, it seems that the "one mighty and strong" mentioned in the revelation was not needed, or that it referred to Bishop Edward Partridge, who was able to resolve the difficulties.

In the revelation the Lord refers to an incident in the Old Testament where an Israelite named Uzzah saw that the ark of the covenant was about to fall, so he reached forth to steady the ark and was suddenly struck dead (see 2 Samuel 6:6–7). Since that time the phrase "steadying the ark" has become shorthand for interfering in an area where you have no authority. The scriptures don't tell us what Uzzah's intentions were in reaching out to steady the ark but use him as a cautionary tale.

What does it mean to steady the ark in a modern context? In Doctrine and Covenants 85, Church members were ignoring the Lord's counsel about consecration. They were complaining and contending about the promises they made to God when they committed to move to Missouri and build Zion. This kind of murmuring is common in the scriptures and still exists in the Church. It can be difficult for us to see everything from our limited perspective. Sometimes the best act is to trust the Lord, trust His servants, and help others in the stewardship we have been given.

How can you see the good and complain less about the tasks you have been given?

Day 207

Doctrine and Covenants 86:2–3

What Is the Meaning of Wheat And the Tares?

Behold, verily I say, the field was the world, and the apostles were the sowers of the seed;

And after they have fallen asleep the great persecutor of the church, the apostate, the whore, even Babylon, that maketh all nations to drink of her cup, in whose hearts the enemy, even Satan, sitteth to reign—behold he soweth the tares; wherefore, the tares choke the wheat and drive the church into the wilderness.

This revelation gives a clear interpretation of one of the most famous parables of Christ. The Savior often spoke in parables to conceal the true meaning of His words from His adversaries and reveal His meanings to those with the Spirit. The parable of the wheat and tares in Matthew 13:24–30 tells of a lord whose servants planted wheat in their field. During the night, an enemy entered the field and sowed tares, a weed that at first looks like wheat but will eventually choke and destroy the wheat. The lord of the field then instructed his servants to gather all of the wheat and the tares, separate them from each other, and burn the tares.

In this section the Lord explains that the sowers in the parable represent the Apostles called in the New Testament dispensation. The enemy is Satan, and the action of sowing the tares drove the true Church of Jesus Christ into the wilderness. This is one of the clearest places where the Lord speaks about the apostasy of the early Christian church and the need for a Restoration. The Lord also points out that Satan's plan was a cunning attempt to provide a counterfeit for the Church. Just as the tares were similar in appearance to the wheat, a distorted and twisted form of Christianity took hold and committed evil acts in the name of Christ.

We live in a great day of sifting where many still masquerade presenting themselves as disciples of Christ but actually carrying out acts of cruelty, hate, and fear. As in the parable, the Savior asks us to see the marks of true discipleship and seek out those who truly live the teachings of Jesus Christ, not just pretend to follow His name.

What do you think are the signs of those who truly follow the teachings of Jesus Christ?

Day 208

Doctrine and Covenants 86:6–7

Why Does God Allow Evil to Continue?

> *But the Lord saith unto them, pluck not up the tares while the blade is yet tender (for verily your faith is weak), lest you destroy the wheat also.*
>
> *Therefore, let the wheat and the tares grow together until the harvest is fully ripe; then ye shall first gather out the wheat from among the tares, and after the gathering of the wheat, behold and lo, the tares are bound in bundles, and the field remaineth to be burned.*

One of the most challenging questions a person of faith encounters usually follows this line of reasoning. If there is a God, then why is there so much evil in the world? Why does God allow evil people to carry out their actions? The Lord answers these questions in part in this revelation as He expands on the parable of the wheat and the tares. When they are first planted, wheat and tares are difficult to distinguish from one another. Because they look almost exactly the same, it is difficult to separate them at that point without damaging the wheat and keeping it from becoming fully mature. So the Lord teaches that the wheat and the tares must grow together until the harvest is fully ripe. Then they can be gathered, bundled separately from each, and the tares destroyed.

The wheat and the tares represent the children of God on the earth. Everyone who comes to earth gets a fresh start. Another revelation given during this time states that "God having redeemed man from the fall, men became again, in their infant state, innocent before God" (Doctrine and Covenants 93:38). Every person starts out innocent in this life, and God has to allow them to grow, make choices, and become one of the wheat or the tares. God allows us to choose our eternal fate, and that means that He must allow those who will choose evil to do so. He also prepared a way for us to repent of the evil we engage in through the saving grace of Jesus Christ. But choice and agency mean that some people will choose what is wrong, and sometimes others suffer because of it. The Lord helps those who repent and works to help us overcome the actions of those who choose evil. But He has to honor our agency and let us choose.

Some will choose to be wheat. Some will choose to be tares. The important thing is that they choose.

Why do you think God honors our agency even if we choose to do the wrong thing?

Day 209
Doctrine and Covenants 87:1–2

How Did the Millennial Wars Begin?

> *Verily, thus saith the Lord concerning the wars that will shortly come to pass, beginning at the rebellion of South Carolina, which will eventually terminate in the death and misery of many souls;*
>
> *And the time will come that war will be poured out upon all nations, beginning at this place.*

In many of the revelations given to Joseph Smith, the Lord provided clear warnings about the challenges of the last days about to unfold. There is no clearer example of this than the prophecy of the American Civil War, given nearly three decades before the war broke out. Not only does the prophecy offer specifics about how the war would be fought, but it also identifies the place where the war would begin, South Carolina. At the time South Carolina was already seen as the most likely state to begin an insurrection against the United States, so it is possible to write off the prophecy as just an accurate reading of current events. But the prophecy doesn't just end with the rebellion of South Carolina. It predicts the rebellion of all of the Southern States against the Northern States. It even goes so far as to foretell that slaves would be drafted into the war, rising up against their masters to overthrow the system of slavery. With hindsight, the accuracy of this prophecy, given so long before the war started, is astounding.

But the prophecy has not yet been completely fulfilled. It only speaks of the American Civil War as the beginning of the millennial wars leading up to the Second Coming. The wars that have followed, large and small, are fulfillments of the prophecy as well. It can be chilling to look at this revelation and know that it is describing our time. But it is also hopeful. We cannot go from the world of sin and oppression created by men to a millennium of peace and justice without going through some major change. We may live in the best of times and the worst of times, but the Lord is creating a better world for us.

How is it both a blessing and challenge to live in the latter days?

Day 210

Doctrine and Covenants 87:8

How Can I Stand in Holy Places?

> *Wherefore, stand ye in holy places, and be not moved, until the day of the Lord come; for behold, it cometh quickly, saith the Lord. Amen.*

At the end of the prophecy on war, the Lord offers this simple counsel to His disciples: stand ye in holy places. While it can be easy to look on the world we live in and only see the bad, it is also important to note that the number of holy places is increasing. There are more and more temples, more places of refuge, and more people who are entering into covenants with God. The prophecies found in the revelations can be chilling, but we know the story has a happy ending.

In seeking out these holy places, we must also remember that the Lord sees things from an eternal perspective. The Saints will not be entirely spared from the troubles of the last days, but we are promised spiritual safety. Whatever happens, those who have followed the Savior's teachings will find hope, peace, and safety. The gospel teaches us that holy places can be found wherever holy people are found. If we have the courage to hold to the truths we know, we will find ourselves in holy places.

How can you create a holy place to find refuge?

Day 211
Doctrine and Covenants 88:2

What Is the Lord's Message of Peace to Us?

> *Behold, this is pleasing unto your Lord, and the angels rejoice over you; the alms of your prayers have come up into the ears of the Lord of Sabaoth, and are recorded in the book of the names of the sanctified, even them of the celestial world.*

On December 25, 1832, Joseph Smith received a revelation about the coming wars leading up to the Second Coming of Jesus Christ. The revelation on war, Doctrine and Covenants 87, was followed a few days later by a much longer revelation. Contrasting with the revelation on the wars about to commence, Joseph described Doctrine and Covenants 88 as "the olive leaf which we have plucked from the tree of paradise, the Lord's message of peace to us."[38] The revelation on war is eight verses long. The revelation on peace, which was received over several days, is 141 verses long, making it the longest revelation in the Doctrine and Covenants. There is more good ahead of us than bad.

In both revelations the Lord refers to Himself as "the Lord of the Sabaoth," a term that means "the Lord of hosts," referring to His position as the leader of the armies of the righteous. In the revelation on war, the Lord uses the term as a way of saying He has the power to end the contention and strife leading up to the Second Coming. In the revelation on peace, He uses the term to introduce the principles

38. History, 1838–1856, volume A-1 [23 December 1805–30 August 1834], *The Joseph Smith Papers,* 263.

of peace. These contrasting parts of the Savior's mission show that He was willing to speak directly to us about the trials we face, but He will also protect us and guide us through tribulation and into a new era of peace.

How do the Savior's teachings help you find peace in a troubled world?

Day 212
Doctrine and Covenants 88:7

What Is the Light of Christ?

> *Which truth shineth. This is the Light of Christ. As also he is in the sun, and the light of the sun, and the power thereof by which it was made.*

In the revelation on peace, the Savior explains how and why He is able to bring order to chaos in the universe. The Savior's power, here given the simple title of the Light of Christ, is the power that brings life and order to all things. The Savior describes it as "the light which is in all things, which giveth life to all things, which is the law by which all things are governed" (Doctrine and Covenants 88:13). This light makes life physically possible and opens our eyes to understanding.

The Christian writer C. S. Lewis described his belief in Christ by saying, "I believe in Christianity as I believe that the sun has risen: not only because I see it, but because by it I see everything else."[39] This revelation adds that the light of the sun is the Light of Christ. Our life and the ability to appreciate and enjoy our life comes from the light that Christ radiates. One of the greatest contributions of the Restoration is helping us understand the scope of Jesus Christ's mission and powers. He is not only a great moral teacher but also the being at the center of the physical universe. He upholds all things through His power and brings life to everything He touches. If the Savior can handle uphold-

39. https://www.cslewisinstitute.org/resources/reflections-december-2013/, accessed January 5, 2024.

ing the universe, it seems clear that He can handle the daily challenges we face in our lives.

How has the Light of Christ influenced you?

Day 213

Doctrine and Covenants 88:14–16

What Is the Soul of Man?

> *Now, verily I say unto you, that through the redemption which is made for you is brought to pass the resurrection from the dead.*
>
> *And the spirit and the body are the soul of man.*
>
> *And the resurrection from the dead is the redemption of the soul.*

The revelation on peace also introduces some radical new ideas about the nature of our existence. In most places in scripture, the word *soul* is synonymous with *spirit*. But in this revelation, the Lord says that the spirit and the body are the soul of man and that part of His work is to bring the two together eternally. In contrast, most Christian religions see the physical body as a kind of prison that we have to overcome and escape. Latter-day Saints see the body as a precious gift from God and a vital step in becoming more like Him. Rather than seeing God as a kind of ethereal spirit that exists in all things, we see God as an embodied being that has physical form. Through the Light of Christ, God is in all things and can influence all things, but God and Christ are both physical beings that can we can touch, feel, and embrace.

The reuniting of Christ's body and spirit is the central miracle of all of Christian history. His redemption began the process of turning back the ravages of death and time. It opened a way for all of us to be resurrected and enjoy eternal life. Resurrection is a free gift given to all men and women who came to earth and receive a body. Even the most wicked will be resurrected and live forever. Those who truly embrace the Savior and His teachings will not only be resurrected but will come to know the eternal life enjoyed by both the Father and the Son.

How does the Resurrection give you hope in your daily life?

Day 214
Doctrine and Covenants 88:25–26

How Will the Earth Be Sanctified?

And again, verily I say unto you, the earth abideth the law of a celestial kingdom, for it filleth the measure of its creation, and transgresseth not the law—

Wherefore, it shall be sanctified; yea, notwithstanding it shall die, it shall be quickened again, and shall abide the power by which it is quickened, and the righteous shall inherit it.

In the revelation on peace, the Savior explains the infinite nature of His power and influence. He talks about how His light gives life to all of the universe. He also brought about the Resurrection, which provides all women and men with an immortal body, and those who make covenants with God a chance to gain eternal life. But the Doctrine and Covenants expands our understanding of Christ by showing us that He not only came to redeem the children of God but to also redeem all of creation. The revelation talks about how the earth keeps the celestial law and it will be sanctified, die, and be resurrected as well. Just as the Savior promised, the righteous will inherit the earth, and the earth will become the celestial kingdom.

How does a planet keep the laws of the celestial kingdom? The Savior explains this as well: "It filleth the measure of its creation." This is a simple way of saying that the earth does what it was designed to do. The same principle applies to all of us. We were created and designed to become like God. We were built to love one another, find joy, and serve the Lord. When we fill the measure of our creation, we are doing what we were designed to do. In this sense living the celestial law is just carrying out the purposes our Creator gave us. If we follow His designs, we can gain eternal life.

What do you think it means to fill the measure of your creation?

Day 215
Doctrine and Covenants 88:41

How Does God Experience Time?

He comprehendeth all things, and all things are before him, and all things are round about him; and he is above all things, and in all things, and is through all things, and is round about all things; and all things are by him, and of him, even God, forever and ever.

God does not experience time the same way we do. We live in a linear world where we experience the past, present, and future. This passage is just one of many that suggest that God experiences the past, present, and future all at the same time. In the Book of Mormon Alma taught, "All is as one day with God, and time only is measured unto men" (Alma 40:8). Trying to understand the way God experiences time is like trying to describe color to a person who is blind. We just don't have the means to comprehend it fully right now. But God can assure us of one thing: He knows the end from the beginning and is doing all He can to guide us into peace and happiness. We can trust Him because He knows the way.

Just because God is aware of the future does not mean that we can't make our own choices. Knowing something is going to happen does not mean that you are the cause of it happening. God upholds the sacred principle of agency and allows us to make our own decisions. He doesn't always give us every answer because the purpose of life is for us to grow. But it is helpful to know that we have an all-knowing friend who wants to help us along the way.

How have you learned to trust the Lord to guide you?

Day 216
Doctrine and Covenants 88:63

How Can I Draw Nearer to God?

Draw near unto me and I will draw near unto you; seek me diligently and ye shall find me; ask, and ye shall receive; knock, and it shall be opened unto you.

The Savior continually offers this invitation: draw near unto me and I will draw near unto you. In the midst of a revelation filled with wonderful doctrines and complicated theology, the Savior points out the real key to knowledge: seeking Him. We spend much of our time stumbling through life and trying to find the right thing to do, when in reality the answers usually are right in front of us. The message from the scriptures, over and over again, is that the Savior wants to help us; we just have to ask.

Being willing to ask takes time and humility. It also takes patience to wait for the answers to come at the right moment. Our timing does not always line up with God's timing. But when we seek Him out we will find the answers that we need. Sometimes the answer comes in a prompting. Sometimes it comes in the voice of a good friend. But the answers will come if we seek them.

What answers do you need from the Lord right now?

Day 217
Doctrine and Covenants 88:77–78

Why Does the Lord Command Us to Teach Each Other?

And I give unto you a commandment that you shall teach one another the doctrine of the kingdom.

Teach ye diligently and my grace shall attend you, that you may be instructed more perfectly in theory, in principle, in doctrine, in the law of the gospel, in all things that pertain unto the kingdom of God, that are expedient for you to understand.

After teaching a number of profound truths about the nature of existence, the latter part of this revelation directs the disciples to organize a school to teach each other. This became known as the School of the Prophets. If the Savior is the most profound teacher in the history of the world, then why does He organize His disciples to teach each other? In part, He commands us to teach because there is so much gained in teaching. Usually the person most profoundly changed when the gospel is taught is the teacher himself. When we dive deeply into the words of God, we cannot help but be changed.

Each of Christ's disciples is a teacher. We often visualize a teacher as someone standing at the front of a classroom, but in reality teaching moments take place everywhere and appear at unexpected times. They can happen when we are in a car with a loved one, sitting down to a family meal, or any number of places. The Lord provides us with opportunities to teach the gospel every day. We just have to learn to recognize them. The kingdom of God has always been and will always be a kingdom of teachers.

How can you be more aware of teaching moments throughout the day?

Day 218

Doctrine and Covenants 88:124–125

How Can I Be Physically Healthy?

Cease to be idle; cease to be unclean; cease to find fault one with another; cease to sleep longer than is needful; retire to thy bed early, that ye may not be weary; arise early, that your bodies and your minds may be invigorated.

And above all things, clothe yourselves with the bond of charity, as with a mantle, which is the bond of perfectness and peace.

In providing His instructions to the School of the Prophets, the Savior also provided a helping of practical advice. You may not expect advice on getting enough sleep to be found in a scriptural text, but this revelation reflects the Savior's teaching that our spiritual and physical health are connected. If we don't take the time to take care of ourselves, we will not be able to take care of others. It isn't surprising that in the same section where the Savior stresses the importance of having a physical body, He also gives a few instructions on how to take care of it.

At the same time, while the Savior asks us to treat our physical body with care, He also points out that developing charity is "above all things." As much as we try to care for them, our bodies are mortal and will be subject to breakdowns from time to time. We are subject to wear and tear that comes from regular use. But if we can develop the gift of charity, or the ability to love the way the Savior loves, we can weather the ups and downs that come with having a physical body with grace and purpose.

What are some things you can do to show your gratitude for a physical body?

Day 219
Doctrine and Covenants 89:4

Why Did the Lord Give the Word of Wisdom?

> *Behold, verily, thus saith the Lord unto you: In consequence of evils and designs which do and will exist in the hearts of conspiring men in the last days, I have warned you, and forewarn you, by giving unto you this word of wisdom by revelation.*

The fact that Latter-day Saints are asked to abstain from alcohol, tobacco, coffee, tea, and harmful drugs is one of the more well-known things people know about our faith. Guidelines for health are found in all of the scriptures, including the Old Testament, where the Israelites were instructed to only eat certain kinds of animals and avoid other substances. The mistake we sometimes make in explaining the Word of Wisdom is in presenting it as an ancient code of health, when it is stated right in the revelation that it is not ancient. The introduction to the Word of Wisdom actually states that the Lord was instituting a new code of health "in consequence of evils and designs which do and will exist in the hearts of conspiring men in the last days." We don't have to defend why the Savior, Noah, or the Nephites possibly drank wine because they didn't live under the same code of health that we do.

The revelation called the Word of Wisdom is only the beginning as well. As new dangers come along, the modern prophets of the Church will receive revelation directing us toward safety. For example, Joseph Smith probably was not given information about e-cigarettes or vaping, but his prophetic successors have warned against them. As a modern, living revelation, it is possible that the Word of Wisdom will look different a century from now. We do not know what new things will came along that may harm body and spirit. But we do know that the Lord will always direct His prophets to look out for our well-being.

How has the Word of Wisdom been a blessing in your life?

Day 220
Doctrine and Covenants 89:18–21

What Are the Promises of the Word of Wisdom?

> *And all saints who remember to keep and do these sayings, walking in obedience to the commandments, shall receive health in their navel and marrow to their bones;*
>
> *And shall find wisdom and great treasures of knowledge, even hidden treasures;*
>
> *And shall run and not be weary, and shall walk and not faint.*
>
> *And I, the Lord, give unto them a promise, that the destroying angel shall pass by them, as the children of Israel, and not slay them. Amen.*

After explaining substances to avoid and others to use wisely, the Lord ends the brief revelation on the Word of Wisdom with a promise. Some of the promises of the Word of Wisdom, like better health from not using tobacco or alcohol, have become self-evident. The blessings of other promises may be less obvious but are just as real. One of the most prominent blessings given by the Lord is that "the destroying angel shall pass by them, as the children of Israel." The phrasing here ties back to the exodus of the children of Israel from Egypt. The Israelites were asked to smear lamb's blood over their doorways, and when the destroying angel came to take the firstborn of the land, the Israelites who followed this commandment were passed over.

There is a passing over that happens when modern Israel obeys the Word of Wisdom. It happens not just through the obvious health benefits from following this commandment. Think of how many relationships, careers, or opportunities are ruined through the abuse of drugs or alcohol. How many lives are destroyed by abuse of these substances? A lifetime of living the Word of Wisdom shows that not only will the destroyer pass by, but because of our faith and trust, the Lord will bless us in ways we cannot yet imagine.

How has living the Word of Wisdom helped you be more free?

Day 221
Doctrine and Covenants 90:3–4

How Do Prophets Serve as the Oracles of God?

> *Verily I say unto you, the keys of this kingdom shall never be taken from you, while thou art in the world, neither in the world to come;*
> *Nevertheless, through you shall the oracles be given to another, yea, even unto the church.*

This revelation shows another step toward creating the First Presidency as we know it in the Church today. Sidney Rigdon and Frederick G. Williams were called earlier to act as counselors in the First Presidency (see Doctrine and Covenants 81). In this revelation the Lord blessed both of them and instructed that they were to receive the keys given to Joseph Smith and Oliver Cowdery. This was the first step in creating a process of succession, showing that other prophets would eventually be called to succeed Joseph Smith. Later in Nauvoo, the keys of the kingdom were given to the members of the Quorum of the Twelve as well.

When Joseph Smith passed away, Brigham Young, the leader of the Twelve, was called to succeed Joseph Smith as president of the Church. Since that time, the pattern has remained consistent.

Today all members of the First Presidency and the Quorum of the Twelve are given all of the priesthood keys necessary to lead the Church. Only the president of the Church may direct the use of the keys, but all possess them. As important as Joseph Smith, Brigham Young, or any of the other modern prophets are in the work of the Lord, individual leaders are less important to the work than the power the Lord has delegated to His servants. They act as oracles and spokespeople for the Savior, but these leaders serve their time and are released when they leave this life. The true consistent head of the Church has always been and will always be the Savior Jesus Christ.

How have the leaders of the Church helped you know Jesus Christ better?

Day 222

Doctrine and Covenants 90:11

How Will the Gospel Be Spread in the Latter Days?

> *For it shall come to pass in that day, that every man shall hear the fulness of the gospel in his own tongue, and in his own language, through those who are ordained unto this power, by the administration of the Comforter, shed forth upon them for the revelation of Jesus Christ.*

Near the end of this revelation the Lord includes a prophecy about the spread of the gospel. He states that the time will come when every person will hear the gospel in their own tongue and in their own language through those who are ordained unto this power. This implies that the gospel will eventually spread to all cultures, countries, and people. This was a bold statement to make in 1833, but nearly two centuries later the gospel has grown in remarkable ways. The Church has been established in hundreds of countries, and nearly every major city has a congregation of Latter-day Saints.

We have already witnessed the spread of the gospel in new countries and how this beautiful blend of cultures makes for new and fascinating cultural expressions of faith. The gospel is the same, but the Church looks a little different as it blends in with the cultures in countries like Tonga, Thailand, Sweden, Ghana, and a multitude of other locations. Eventually the gospel will not only be established in all nations, but ministers from those cultures will find new ways to interpret and apply the teachings of Jesus Christ. One of the things established early on in the Restoration is that this is a gospel for all people, and from the cultures where the Church is established a new culture of the gospel will emerge.

How has the gospel helped you understand new cultures and people?

Day 223

Doctrine and Covenants 91:4–5

How Can I Find Truth in Other Sources?

> *Therefore, whoso readeth it, let him understand, for the Spirit manifesteth truth;*
>
> *And whoso is enlightened by the Spirit shall obtain benefit therefrom.*

The Bible Joseph Smith used in his biblical translation project was different from the Bibles used in our church. It had a collection of books not normally used by Protestant Christians but often found in the Bibles used by Catholic and Orthodox Christians. A quick perusal of the titles of these books shows interesting names like Tobit, The Wisdom of Solomon, and Bel and the Dragon. Some of these books contain vital history, like 1 and 2 Maccabees, which contains the story of Hanukkah, still celebrated by millions of Jews today. This collection of books is commonly called the Apocrypha, which is associated with works that are of doubtful authorship or authenticity. When Joseph Smith came across these books in the Bible he was using, it was natural for him to ask if these books should be translated as well.

In response to this question, the Lord explained that there were many "things contained therein that are true, and it is mostly translated correctly" but added that "there are many things contained therein that are not true" (Doctrine and Covenants 91:2). He therefore told Joseph that it was not necessary to translate the Apocrypha and that he should use the Spirit to guide him as he read the books. This remains the standard for any text that we encounter. In the years since this revelation was given, other apocryphal works have emerged, such as the Dead Sea Scrolls and the Nag Hammadi library. With each of these texts, the words of the Lord are still our best guide. They contain truth, but we must use the Spirit to discern truth from error.

The same is true with all material outside of the standard works. There is a lot of truth and beauty in works outside the scriptures. But there is also erroneous and misleading material. The Spirit can guide us to know what is uplifting and what might be harmful to our spirits.

Where have you found uplifting truths outside of the scriptures?

Day 224

Doctrine and Covenants 92:2

How Can I Be a Lively Member of the Church?

> *And again, I say unto you my servant Frederick G. Williams, you shall be a lively member in this order; and inasmuch as you are faithful in keeping all former commandments you shall be blessed forever. Amen.*

After Frederick G. Williams was called as a member of the First Presidency of the Church, he was also called to join the United Firm. The United Firm was a special extension of the law of consecration, where several Church leaders were asked to devote their goods toward the publication of the scriptures (see Doctrine and Covenants 78 and 82). In bringing Frederick into the United Firm, the Lord commanded him to be a lively member of the group. This is good counsel for Frederick then and good counsel for us today.

There are many members of the Church but few lively members. In 1833 the word *lively* meant "brisk, vigorous, and active." Many of us go through the motions, carrying out our Church responsibilities without much life to our efforts. A lively member doesn't just do what is expected; they also look for opportunities to bring new life to the work and find new ways to serve. Being a lively member in part entails following the Lord's commandment to be "anxiously engaged" (Doctrine and Covenants 58:27). Instead of sleepwalking through our work in our families and in the Church, we find ways to bring life to them and inspire others to do the same.

What can you do to be a lively member of the Church?

Day 225
Doctrine and Covenants 93:1

How Do I Come to Know the Savior?

> *Verily, thus saith the Lord: It shall come to pass that every soul who forsaketh his sins and cometh unto me, and calleth on my name, and obeyeth my voice, and keepeth my commandments, shall see my face and know that I am.*

We have almost no context for Doctrine and Covenants 93. Where Joseph Smith usually went out of his way to provide the circumstances or questions that prompted each revelation in the Doctrine and Covenants, he provides no background for this revelation. From the text itself, the Savior introduces the truths in the revelation by explaining a simple formula to come to see Him and come to know Him. The clue from the revelation comes from the latter part of it, found in verses 41–53, where the Lord counsels the members of the First Presidency to look after their families.

The section contains some of the most profound philosophical truths found anywhere in scripture. Truman Madsen, a professor of philosophy, wrote, "Section 93 was received in May 1833, where Joseph was twenty-seven years old. It defines beginningless, beginnings, the interrelationships of truth, of light, of intelligence, of agency, of element, of embodiment, of joy. Every sentence, every word, is freighted with meaning. In one fell swoop it cuts many Gordian knots."[40] Perhaps the greatest statement of purpose for the section comes in verse 17, where the Savior states, "I give unto you these sayings that you may understand and know how to worship, and know what you worship" (Doctrine and Covenants 93:17).

The Savior wants us to know what He is like because the promise of the gospel is that if we keep our covenants we can become like Him. Further, after the section lays out these profound truths about the nature of God and man, it ends with a command to take special care with children. Part of the aim of the section might be to realize how precious other people, especially those in our family, are in God's eyes.

How can knowing the Savior help you know yourself better?

Day 226

Doctrine and Covenants 93:12–14

How Did Jesus Become the Son of God?

> *And I, John, saw that he received not of the fulness at the first, but received grace for grace;*
>
> *And he received not of the fulness at first, but continued from grace to grace, until he received a fulness;*
>
> *And thus he was called the Son of God, because he received not of the fulness at the first.*

One of the largest gaps in our understanding about Jesus Christ is what happened during His childhood and adolescence. The beautiful story of the Nativity is covered in Matthew 1–2 and Luke 1–2. Luke provides one more story about how Jesus was accidentally left in the temple when He was twelve years old. After that all of the Gospels pick up the story when Jesus goes to John the Baptist to be baptized when He was thirty years old.

40. Truman G. Madsen, *Joseph Smith the Prophet* (Salt Lake City: Bookcraft, 1989), 140–41.

Doctrine and Covenants 93 does not provide us with specifics about the Savior's childhood, but it does provide us with a few valuable insights.

The author of the passages in section 93 refers to himself as John. One might assume that because of the similarities in the language this is author of the Gospel of John. Others have speculated that because the John being quoted in Doctrine and Covenants 93 mentions that he witnessed the Savior's baptism that this is John the Baptist (see Doctrine and Covenants 93:15). Whichever John it is, he mentions that the Savior received not of the fulness at first but received grace for grace. He became the Son of God because of this.

While we believe Jesus was perfect, we also need to explore what we mean by perfect. We believe that Jesus was morally perfect, that He didn't commit any sin. But John seems to be teaching that outside of this moral perfection, Jesus was a lot more like us than we sometimes assume He was. He came to earth and lost all of His knowledge just like we do. And just like us, He had to relearn everything and grow from grace to grace. The Savior even exhorts His disciples, "You shall receive grace for grace" (Doctrine and Covenants 93:20) just like He did. Jesus is the best of us, but here He seems to be saying that what He did isn't impossible and that we too can learn and grow grace for grace until we become like Him. Asking us to become like Him isn't an unrealistic goal. It is something we can accomplish, grace for grace.

How can you become more like Christ today?

Day 227

Doctrine and Covenants 93:19

How Do I Worship Jesus Christ?

> *I give unto you these sayings that you may understand and know how to worship, and know what you worship, that you may come unto the Father in my name, and in due time receive of his fulness.*

After sharing portions of the record of John designed to help us understand His nature, the Savior openly states His purpose in teaching these truths. "I give unto you these sayings that you may understand and know how to worship and know what you worship." How do we worship Jesus Christ? Bruce R. McConkie explained, "Perfect worship is emulation. We honor those whom we imitate. The most perfect way of worship is to be holy as Jehovah is holy. It is to be pure as Christ is pure. It is to do the things that enable us to become like the Father."[41]

We worship Christ by emulating Him. He emphasizes this by using the same words to describe our journey that John used to describe how He became the Son of God. John said that the Savior grew "from grace to grace." The Savior asks us to follow a similar course, teaching, "You shall receive grace for grace" (Doctrine and Covenants 93:20). The Savior then teaches, "I was in the beginning with the Father," and explains, "Ye were also in the beginning with the Father" (Doctrine and Covenants 93:21, 23). Essentially, the Savior is asking us to do what He has already done. He is the kind of leader who not only explains our journey of faith but experiences it Himself and now stands ready to guide us on the same course.

What can you do today to emulate the Savior?

Day 228
Doctrine and Covenants 93:29–30

How Long Have I Existed?

> *Man was also in the beginning with God. Intelligence, or the light of truth, was not created or made, neither indeed can be.*
>
> *All truth is independent in that sphere in which God has placed it, to act for itself, as all intelligence also; otherwise there is no existence.*

In explaining our journey to become like Him, the Savior also provides us knowledge about what we really are and where we came from. He states, "Man was also in the beginning with God." God is eternal and

41. Bruce R. McConkie, *The Promised Messiah* (Salt Lake City: Deseret Book, 1978), 568.

has always existed; therefore so have we. The Savior labels the eternal part of men and women "intelligence" and then explains that intelligence "was not created or made, neither indeed can be." He also explains that intelligence can act for itself, meaning it has agency. The two things we know about intelligence are that it has always existed and it has the ability to choose for itself.

This raises a few more interesting questions. If intelligence always existed, why do the scriptures describe God as our Father and creator? God created all of us in the sense that He gave us a spirit body (see Hebrews 12:9). He created this world and a way for us to come to earth and gain a physical body. But there is a part of you that God did not create. That part of you has always existed and will always exist. The revelation also teaches that agency is eternal, that you have always had the power to make your own decisions. God nurtures us, gives us more power and agency as we qualify for it, and helps us to grow and achieve our potential, just like any good Father would.

How does it change your daily perspective to know that you have always existed and will always exist?

Day 229

Doctrine and Covenants 93:40

How Can I Bring Up Children in Light and Truth?

> *But I have commanded you to bring up your children in light and truth.*

After the Savior reveals some of the most grand concepts about His nature and the nature of the sons and daughters of God, He brings the concepts down to earth. Knowing what a person really is should change how we act. The revelation explains that a human being is an eternal intelligence that has always existed and that has the potential to become like Jesus Christ and then like Heavenly Father. It makes sense that in emphasizing the fatherhood of God, the Lord points out how important fathers and mothers are here on earth.

The remainder of the revelation is a sincere exhortation to the members of the First Presidency to know how important it is to look after their families and raise their children in the gospel. Once we know how precious a child is, we will make the care and nurture of our children a top priority. This begins with the people closest to us and extends to all the people around us. Everyone we see is an eternal being with the potential to become like God. If we keep that truth in our hearts, it will change all of our interactions with the people around us.

What can you do to teach light and truth to the people you love?

Day 230

Doctrine and Covenants 94:2

How Can I Follow the Lord's Pattern for Me?

> *And behold, it must be done according to the pattern which I have given unto you.*

In a revelation given in January 1833, the Saints were commanded to build a "house of glory" in Kirtland, Ohio (see Doctrine and Covenants 88:119). This building became the first temple built and dedicated by the Saints in this dispensation. In this revelation, the Lord provided further guidance about how the House of the Lord should be built and advised the Saints to follow the pattern provided by the Lord. The revelation called the building of the temple the "foundation of the city of the stake of Zion, here in the land of Kirtland" (Doctrine and Covenants 94:2).

The construction of the temple in Kirtland shows how the Lord provides a pattern but then leaves room for us to use our own gifts to create beauty and meaning. The pattern given in the revelation establishes the size and dimensions of the temple but leaves room for the craftsmen who build the temple to make the space their own. The Kirtland Temple still stands today and is filled with some of the most intricate and attractive woodwork of any building from its era.

In a similar fashion, the Lord has laid out a general pattern for our lives. He gives commandments designed to help us look toward exaltation but leaves room for us to pursue our own desires and improve the talents we have been given. If we follow the Lord's pattern and learn to develop the gifts we have been given, we can establish a life as wonderful and uplifting as the temple that still stands in Kirtland.

What do you think are the most important parts of the pattern the Lord has laid out for your life?

Day 231

Doctrine and Covenants 94:15

What Is the Purpose of the House of God?

> *That they may do the work which I have appointed unto them, to be a committee to build mine houses, according to the commandment, which I, the Lord God, have given unto you.*

If everything had gone according to plan, there would have been three houses of identical size built next to each in the center of Kirtland. One house was for the First Presidency and other Church officers, one was a house to print the scriptures, and the final one was the House of the Lord, the first temple built by the Saints. When persecution and financial challenges arose, the Saints correctly prioritized the construction of the House of the Lord. They were not able to complete the other two houses. Joseph Smith's nearby home functioned as a makeshift Church administration building, and the Saints completed a much smaller building as a temporary place to print the scriptures. Today the Kirtland Temple and Joseph Smith's home still stand, though the printing house was burned down during persecutions in 1838.

Even if the three houses were never built, they reflect three things the Lord expected to provide for His people. The house for the scriptures emphasized the importance of studying the words of ancient prophets to find comfort, guidance, and revelation. The house for the presidency reflected the importance of having living prophets in our midst to provide revelation to guide us in our world. Finally, the House of the Lord shows the way for us to connect with God through ordinances and eternal covenants. These three houses formed the center of the city, and their priorities reflect the ways God can provide us with guidance.

What can you do to place the scriptures, the prophets, and the Lord at the center of your life?

Day 232

Doctrine and Covenants 95:1

Why Does the Lord Chasten His Servants?

> *Verily, thus saith the Lord unto you whom I love, and whom I love I also chasten that their sins may be forgiven, for with the chastisement I prepare a way for their deliverance in all things out of temptation, and I have loved you.*

This revelation opens with a chastisement for the members of the Church for neglecting their duties in building the three houses explained in earlier revelations. The Lord often chastens His servants for their sins, but in this revelation He explains that correcting someone has to come from a place of love and not as a form of punishment. In the New Testament, the Savior could be very direct in the way He dealt with His disciples. The phrase "get thee behind me Satan" was said to Peter, one of the Savior's closest friends, on several occasions (Matthew 16:23).

If we really love people, we will sometimes have to offer correction. There is an old saying that "God loves you just the way you are, but He loves you too much to let you stay that way." Sometimes the Lord chastens us, and sometimes we're are called upon to correct others. But we have to be careful in how we do it. Brigham Young taught, "If you are ever called upon to chasten a person, never chasten beyond the balm you have within you to bind up."[42] We need to remember that chastening is a way of teaching and must be done with love.

When have you felt chastened by the Lord? Did you see it as a sign of His love?

Day 233
Doctrine and Covenants 96:5

How Does Scripture Soften Hearts?

> *For behold, verily I say unto you, this is the most expedient in me, that my word should go forth unto the children of men, for the purpose of subduing the hearts of the children of men for your good. Even so. Amen.*

On the surface, Doctrine and Covenants 96 looks like a revelation about buying a farm. Known as the Peter French farm, Church members in the Kirtland area sought guidance about purchasing the farm, and the Lord provided guidance to them. The farm was purchased and went on to become some of the most important real estate in the history of the Church. Eventually land from the farm was divided into individual inheritances. Joseph Smith built a home on one of these inheritances that became a gathering place for the leadership of the Church. In addition, a printing house for the scriptures was built on land from the French farm. Perhaps most important, land from the French farm was used as the site for the first temple built by the Church.

The Lord saw the larger purpose for the land and urged the Saints to purchase it, knowing the importance of printing the scriptures. In just a few years, the first copies of the Doctrine and Covenants were printed on the land. In counseling the Saints, the Lord declares that one of the functions of His words is to "subdue the hearts of the children of men for your good." The word of God softens hearts. When we find ourselves troubled or in need of guidance, if we turn to the

42. *Journal of Discourses,* 9:124–125.

scriptures we will find that the soothing words of God can help heal us, cool our tempers, or help us find the right thing to say. If we keep the scriptures in our hearts and minds, we will find gentle ways to subdue the challenges we face.

How have the scriptures helped you to soften hearts and help other people?

Day 234
Doctrine and Covenants 97:7–8

How Can I Be Accepted of the Lord?

> *The ax is laid at the root of the trees; and every tree that bringeth not forth good fruit shall be hewn down and cast into the fire. I, the Lord, have spoken it.*
>
> *Verily I say unto you, all among them who know their hearts are honest, and are broken, and their spirits contrite, and are willing to observe their covenants by sacrifice—yea, every sacrifice which I, the Lord, shall command—they are accepted of me.*

This revelation was received during great difficulty for the Saints. Tensions were rising with their neighbors in Missouri. In July 1833 tensions reached a boiling point, and an armed mob attacked the Church printing office in Independence and tarred and feathered Bishop Edward Partridge. The Saints in Missouri found themselves in serious peril and sent for Joseph Smith, who was in Kirtland, Ohio, nearly eight hundred miles away. Before word of the persecutions against the Saints in Missouri arrived, Joseph received this revelation, warning the Saints in Zion of grave danger. The revelation also outlined how the Saints could endure the coming storm and how the Lord would provide help for those caught up in the troubles of Missouri.

Using the language of John the Baptist in the New Testament, the Lord warned the Saints that the "ax is laid at the root of the trees; and every tree that bringeth not forth good fruit shall be hewn down and cast into the fire." He then pleaded with the Saints who needed to repent and offered comfort to those who were striving to keep the commandments, knowing they would be swept up in the coming persecutions as well. We sometimes find ourselves in a situation similar to these faithful Saints. At times we have done nothing wrong but must suffer because of the sins of others. To these faithful Saints the Lord offers His acceptance and help, preparing the way for them to find safety in the coming storm.

When you face challenges, how does it help to know that you are accepted of the Lord?

Day 235
Doctrine and Covenants 97:21

What Is Zion?

> *Therefore, verily, thus saith the Lord, let Zion rejoice, for this is Zion—the pure in heart; therefore, let Zion rejoice, while all the wicked shall mourn.*

Before this revelation, Zion was always spoken of as a place. Members of the Church often referred to the Church settlement in Missouri as Zion. The Lord designated the land where the city of Zion would be built, and the Saints began to settle there. Many of the Saints began to see the building of the city as inevitable, something that was going to happen because it was their divine right. While the Saints were not to blame for the intolerance and aggression shown by their neighbors in Missouri, they were guilty of being arrogant about their right to build the city. Some of the Missourians accused the Saints of unneighborly conduct, including telling the original settlers that they would either join the Church or be swept off the land by divine vengeance.

This isn't true of all of the early Saints, but it does appear that at least part of the Church community missed the point of Zion. They saw Zion as a place, not a people. In this revelation, the Lord corrected them by teaching them the true nature of Zion, the pure in heart. A city is more than just buildings, roads, and trees. What really makes a community is the people. The Lord was trying to warn the Saints that becoming a people who are pure in heart is more important than the location of the city. We are nearly two centuries removed from these problems, and we have yet to build the city of Zion. The real question of Zion has never been about where it will be built but if we will become a pure people ready to live there.

What can you do to become more pure in heart

Day 236

Doctrine and Covenants 98:4–5

How Do I Observe the Laws of the Land?

> *And now, verily I say unto you concerning the laws of the land, it is my will that my people should observe to do all things whatsoever I command them.*
>
> *And that law of the land which is constitutional, supporting that principle of freedom in maintaining rights and privileges, belongs to all mankind, and is justifiable before me.*

In the summer of 1833 the Saints began to experience severe persecution in Jackson County, Missouri. The Church press was destroyed by a mob, Church leaders were publicly tarred and feathered, and many Saints began to fear they would lose their homes. Faced with this hostility, many of the Saints wanted to fight back, even if it meant resorting to the unlawful methods used by the mob. When Church leaders in Missouri asked Joseph Smith how to respond to the persecutions, the Prophet approached the Lord. The Lord responded with this revelation, instructing the Saints to do all they could to avoid violence and resolve the issues peacefully.

The Lord also emphasized the importance of following the laws of the land and working to legally resolve problems. When faced with challenges it can be tempting to fight fire with fire and resort to illegal or immoral means to get what we want. But the Lord asks His followers to take a higher road. This does not mean we can't stand up for ourselves when faced with a challenge. But if we throw our principles out the window, we lose the high ground and fail to be the light the Savior expects us to be to others.

Why is it important to follow lawful principles when we are confronted with challenges?

Day 237

Doctrine and Covenants 98:16

How Can I Renounce War And Proclaim Peace?

> *Therefore, renounce war and proclaim peace, and seek diligently to turn the hearts of the children to their fathers, and the hearts of the fathers to the children.*

In response to the provocations of the mob in Jackson County, the Lord instructed the Saints to "renounce war and proclaim peace." Under threat from their enemies, the Lord asked the Saints to avoid violence and instead seek to make peace with their neighbors. Bishop Edward Partridge, one of the key leaders of the Saints in Missouri, was forcibly taken and tarred and feathered. But under the threat of death from the mob, his quiet response showed how a disciple of Christ can still proclaim peace. He later wrote:

"I was taken from my house by the Mob, George Simpson being their leader, who escorted me about half a mile, to the Court house, on the public square in Independence; and then and there, a few rods from said court house, surrounded by hundreds of the mob. . . . Before tarring and feathering me, I was permitted to speak. I told them that the saints had had to suffer persecution in all ages of the world. That I had done nothing which ought to offend any one. That if they abused me they would abuse an innocent person. That I was willing to suffer for the sake of Christ. . . . Until after I had spoken, I knew not what they intended to do with me, whether to kill me, to whip me, or what else I knew not. I bore my abuse with so much resignation and meekness, that it appeared to astound the multitude, who permitted me to retire in silence, many looking very solemn, their sympathies having been touched as I thought; and, as to myself, I was so filled with the Spirit and Love of God, that I had no hatred towards my persecutors, or anyone else."[43]

Bishop Partridge's actions in the face of the mob showed that if we stay true to our principles, the Lord will soften the hearts of the people around us. His Christlike example saved the Saints from further persecution at that time. In the same way, if we respond to challenges by proclaiming peace, the Lord will prepare a way for us to overcome them.

How can you respond in a Christlike way to those who persecute you?

Day 238

Doctrine and Covenants 98:34

How Do I Lift a Standard of Peace?

> *And if any nation, tongue, or people should proclaim war against them, they should first lift a standard of peace unto that people, nation, or tongue.*

In the face of serious persecutions in Jackson County, the Saints sought advice on if they were justified in striking back against the mobs persecuting them. The Book of Mormon spoke of the need of defending homes and families from attack (see Alma 46:12), but were the Saints justified in going on the offensive against their enemies? The Lord commanded the Saints that they should first raise a standard of peace and be patient in the face of persecution. He promised the Saints that if they bore their burdens, even after multiple offenses they would receive blessings. Eventually if the attacks continued, the Saints would be justified in defending themselves and their families but only after all peaceful options were exhausted.

While we rarely find ourselves under physical threat, we still face persecution for our beliefs from those who are hostile against our faith.

43. History, 1838–1856, volume A-1 [23 December 1805–30 August 1834], *The Joseph Smith Papers*, 327.

In these situations it is still best to follow the Lord's counsel and raise a standard of peace toward our persecutors. Most of the time this will soften their hearts and cause our antagonists to move on. If they do not, we should take every opportunity to respond peacefully or leave the situation. There is a time and a place to defend the faith and to stand up for what is right, but as disciples of Jesus Christ we have an obligation to seek a peaceful solution before we attack in return. If we are forced to defend ourselves, we need to be careful that there is no hatred in our hearts toward the people we fight. This can be difficult, but the path of discipleship is never easy. We have chosen a higher road.

How can you offer a standard of peace to the people who have attacked you in the past?

Day 239

Doctrine and Covenants 99:3

How Can I Receive the Kingdom of God?

> *And who receiveth you as a little child, receiveth my kingdom; and blessed are they, for they shall obtain mercy.*

This revelation was given to one of the great but lesser known Saints of early Church history, a man named John Murdock. John's name is found throughout the Doctrine and Covenants. He served numerous missions of the Church, often at great sacrifice. Shortly after he joined the Church, his wife, Julia, died while giving birth to twins, a little boy and a little girl, who both survived. The same day his wife died, Emma Smith gave birth to twins, both of whom died. Filled with grief, John asked Joseph and Emma if they would raise the twins as their own. They were both adopted into the Smith family. A few months later, one of the adopted twins died as a result of a mob attack on the home where Joseph and Emma were living. John had several other children and spent months arranging for their care before he left on his mission. Some of his children moved to Missouri with the families caring for them, and several years passed before John was reunited with them.

When he finally arrived in Missouri in 1834, he found his daughter Phebe deathly ill from cholera. John was able to care for her during her final days before she passed away at just six years old.

How was John able to endure such severe trials? He followed the same counsel the Savior gave him to receive the gospel "as a little child." John trusted the Savior and at one point even had a vision of Jesus Christ. John recorded, "The visions of my mind were opened, and the eyes of my understanding were enlightened and I saw the form of a man [the Savior] most lovely. The visage of his face was sound and fair as the sun. His hair a bright silver gray, curled in the most majestic form. His eyes a keen, penetrating blue, and the skin of his neck a most beautiful white. And he was covered from the neck to the feet with a loose garment, pure white, whiter than any garment I have ever before seen. His countenance was most penetrating, and yet most lovely."[44]

A few years ago I found John's headstone in the cemetery in Beaver, Utah. It is a simple, plain monument, but it marks the resting place of a person who literally saw Jesus Christ. John's childlike faith led him to have a greater hope for his children and for himself.

What do you think it means to receive Christ like a little child?

Day 240

Doctrine and Covenants 100:1

How Can I Seek Safety in the Lord?

> *Verily, thus saith the Lord unto you, my friends Sidney and Joseph, your families are well; they are in mine hands, and I will do with them as seemeth me good; for in me there is all power.*

This brief revelation was given to Joseph Smith and Sidney Rigdon during a particularly trying time. A few members of the Church asked them to travel to Perrysburg, New York, to preach the gospel. Just before they left, several apostate members of the Church in Kirtland

44. John Murdock Journal, BYU Special Collections, 13.

threatened Joseph and Sidney and their families. Joseph wrote in his journal, "I feel very well in my mind the Lord is with us but [I] have much anxiety about my family."[45] So great was their worry for their families that Joseph and Sidney sought the Lord in revelation to receive some comfort. In response, the Lord told them, "Your families are well; they are in my hands."

There is a constant pull between our responsibilities to our loved ones, our work, and God. At times because of Church callings I spent long hours away from my family and wondered if they were okay. Anxiety is common when we deal with church, work, and family because we care so much, and there is so little we can control. But just like the Lord promised Joseph and Sidney, He has all power and will keep an eye on the people we love while we serve. The Lord sees everything and will take care of our families while we are away from them.

How has the Lord blessed your family when you have had to be absent?

Day 241

Doctrine and Covenants 100:13

When Will Zion Be Redeemed?

> *And now I give unto you a word concerning Zion. Zion shall be redeemed, although she is chastened for a little season.*

As Joseph Smith and Sidney Rigdon traveled to Perrysburg, New York, two great worries weighed on their minds. First, they worried about their families in Kirtland, Ohio. Second, they worried over the Saints in Missouri, who faced an increasingly serious series of persecutions. The early members of the Church saw building the city of Zion as a critical part of the mission of the Church and were only beginning to grasp how challenging it would be to carry out the Lord's will. Joseph and Sidney inquired about Zion, and the Lord assured them that Zion would be redeemed, "although she is chastened for a little season."

---

45. JS Journal 1832–1834, 6–12 October 6–12,1833, *The Joseph Smith Papers*, 7.

The Lord's time is different from ours, and it can be difficult to know how long "a little season" is from His perspective. Depending on how you view things, Zion may still be going through this little season of chastening. We still have not built the city as the Saints saw it. At the same time there are hundreds of little Zions growing in communities all over the world. The Lord keeps His promises on His own timetable, but we can trust that He will keep His promises. The redemption of Zion, like all of the Lord's promises, will eventually come, but we must be patient.

How can you show patience when waiting for promised blessings?

Day 242

Doctrine and Covenants 101:4–5

Why Must the Saints Endure Chastening?

> *Therefore, they must needs be chastened and tried, even as Abraham, who was commanded to offer up his only son.*
>
> *For all those who will not endure chastening, but deny me, cannot be sanctified.*

In the fall of 1833, mob persecutions in Jackson County, Missouri, forced the Saints from their homes. When Joseph Smith and Oliver Cowdery heard of the fall of Zion, they were devastated and sought the Lord in prayer. Oliver was particularly worried because his wife was with the Saints in Missouri and he didn't know if she was alive. In response, the Lord gave one of the lengthiest revelations in the Doctrine and Covenants, explaining why Zion had fallen and how it could be redeemed.

Before the Lord answered the questions about why Zion fell, He taught a simple principle. Chastening and trials are part of being a disciple of Jesus Christ. The Lord uses our times of trouble to refine us and make us into better disciples. Being a disciple doesn't mean you will be free from all trouble. But it does mean that when trials come, they will be more meaningful. Trials have a way of sanding the sharp edges off our character and making us more tender and caring toward those in need.

Trials also have a way of clarifying what we really believe. The Lord told the Saints that "all those who will not endure chastening, but deny me, cannot be sanctified." Often in the midst of our trials we really find God and our testimony. Trials have a way of burning away the impure parts of our nature and leaving behind the most refined and pure parts of who were are.

How have your trials helped your testimony and faith grow?

Day 243
Doctrine and Covenants 101:7–8

How Can I Be Quick to Hearken to God's Word?

> *They were slow to hearken unto the voice of the Lord their God; therefore, the Lord their God is slow to hearken unto their prayers, to answer them in the day of their trouble.*
>
> *In the day of their peace they esteemed lightly my counsel; but, in the day of their trouble, of necessity they feel after me.*

In addressing the reasons the Saints faced such serious opposition in Missouri, the Lord first acknowledges that experiencing challenges is part of being a disciple. But He also addresses some serious sins among the Saints as well. The Lord declares that among the Saints in Missouri "there were jarrings, and contentions, and envyings, and strifes, and lustful and covetous desires among them; therefore by these things they polluted their inheritances" (Doctrine and Covenants 101:6). He further offers that "in the day of their peace, they esteemed lightly my counsel, but, in the day of their trouble, of necessity they feel after me."

This a common problem among all of God's disciples in all ages of the world. When things are going well for us we forget to listen to God's counsel, but we immediately run to Him for help when trouble arises. Adversity is often the bullhorn that arouses us from our spiritual sleep and points us back to God. The key is to remember to always keep God in our hearts whether things are good or bad. This doesn't mean that we won't find ourselves in challenging circumstances from time to time. But when those challenges come, we will find ourselves stronger and more prepared to handle them.

How can you work to keep God near in good times and bad times?

Day 244

Doctrine and Covenants 101:17–18

How Will Zion Be Built?

> *Zion shall not be moved out of her place, notwithstanding her children are scattered.*
>
> *They that remain, and are pure in heart, shall return, and come to their inheritances, they and their children, with songs of everlasting joy, to build up the waste places of Zion.*

This revelation to the Saints in Missouri addressed both their current and future concerns. In the fall of 1833 it seemed impossible that the Saints could ever build Zion in the place the Lord designated for them. To help calm their fears, the Lord assured them that "Zion shall not be moved out of her place." It must have been difficult for the weary Saints, struggling to find new homes for their families, to have seen how Zion could ever be built in the chosen spot. Even today, it is difficult to imagine that Zion will rise in the Lord's chosen place. But it also appears that the Saints' view then, as well as now, is more limited than the Lord's view of what Zion really is.

In describing the return of the Saints to Zion, the Lord says that "they that remain, and are pure in heart, shall return, and come to their inheritances, they are their children." He directly makes reference back to His earlier teaching that Zion is the pure in heart (Doctrine and Covenants 97:21). While this passage in Doctrine and Covenants 101 shows that the location matters, the Lord emphasizes at the same time that the people who will build Zion will be the pure in heart. The way will be opened for those who are ready. We cannot know the miracles that will open the door for the Saints to build the city of Zion, but we know that miracles come to those who are ready to receive them. The question of Zion has always been less about where you live than the purity of your heart.

Elder Robert D. Hales explained, "This promised Zion always seems to be a little beyond our reach. We need to understand that as much virtue can be gained in progressing toward Zion as in dwelling there. It is a process as well as a destination."[46]

What can you do to make sure that you are progressing on the road to Zion?

Day 245
Doctrine and Covenants 101:32

When Will the Lord Reveal All Things?

> *Yea, verily I say unto you, in that day when the Lord shall come, he shall reveal all things.*

In the midst of helping the Saints work through the persecutions forcing them to leave their homes in Jackson County, the Lord also takes the time to point them toward the Millennium. Doctrine and Covenants 101:23–35 contains one of the most extensive descriptions of the conditions that will exist in the one thousand years of peace following the coming of Jesus Christ. Part of what the Savior describes is that life will go on, though without many of the challenges we face right now. The Savior teaches that "an infant shall not die until he is old" and that rather than dying a person will be changed into a resurrected being without facing death (Doctrine and Covenants 101:32).

The Lord also promises that during the Millennium He will reveal all things. He promises a flood of knowledge concerning "things which have passed, and hidden things which no man knew, things of the

46. Robert D. Hales, "Welfare Principles to Guide Our Lives: An Eternal Plan for the Welfare of Men's Souls," *Ensign*, May 1986.

earth, by which it was made, and the purpose and the end thereof" (Doctrine and Covenants 101:33).

It can be difficult for us to have patience until that time. But the Saints back then and the Saints today still need to know that if we can be patient, the answers will come.

What do you most look forward to being revealed during the Millennium?

Day 246
Doctrine and Covenants 101:39

How Are the Saints the Salt of the Earth?

> *When men are called unto mine everlasting gospel, and covenant with an everlasting covenant, they are accounted as the salt of the earth and the savor of men.*

In the New Testament, the Book of Mormon, and the Doctrine and Covenants, the Lord refers to His disciples as "the salt of the earth" (Matthew 5:13; 3 Nephi 12:13). In Israelite culture, salt was often seen as a sign of the covenant and was mixed in with sacrificial offerings (see Leviticus 2:13; Numbers 18:19). Beyond this, there are practical reasons the Savior often compares His disciples to salt. Salt enhances the natural flavor of food. Salt is a preservative that allows food to be stored longer without spoiling. Salt itself will never spoil with age, only if it is contaminated by some other substance.

There is perhaps one application linked to the troubles the Saints had in Missouri that ties into salt. Most dishes that use salt only use a dash. It only takes a sprinkling of salt to make a meal much better. Likewise, the Saints will probably always be a small part of the general population until Christ returns to the earth. There are prophecies about the Church filling the whole earth, but these must be carefully measured against other prophecies that say the Saints will be only a small number among the people of the earth. Nephi saw the Church of the Lamb "upon all the face of the earth; and their dominions upon the face of the earth were small" (1 Nephi 14:12).

The Saints may be few in number, but like salt, they have an immense impact on the world around them. We don't have to be the largest group out there to effect change. We can be the salt of the earth and make everything around us better through the goodness and light that Christ has given us.

How can you have an impact on the people you come into contact with?

Day 247

Doctrine and Covenants 101:79–80

Who Are the Laws Meant to Protect?

> *Therefore, it is not right that any man should be in bondage one to another.*
>
> *And for this purpose have I established the Constitution of this land, by the hands of wise men whom I raised up unto this very purpose, and redeemed the land by the shedding of blood.*

As He did in earlier revelations, the Lord urges the Saints not to respond to their enemies with violence. Instead He asks the Saints to use the law to seek reparations for the damage done by their enemies. The persecutions against the early Saints remain a blot on the history of the United States, a country set up with the intent to provide religious freedom to all citizens. The Lord doesn't condemn the principles the country was set up on. In fact, He explains that He raised up wise men to establish the Constitution of the United States and redeemed the land by the shedding of blood.

This does not mean that the citizens of the county have always lived up to the ideals the country was founded on. One of the reasons the Saints were evicted from their homes in Jackson County was that the Church newspaper published an editorial inviting all people to gather with the Saints. The old settlers of Missouri, many of whom owned slaves, accused the Saints of "tampering with our slaves. . . . To sow dissensions and to raise seditions among them."[47] Despite the anger of the mobs, the Lord spoke against the evils of slavery, telling the Saints, "It is not right that any many should be in bondage to another."

Captured here is one of the paradoxes of discipleship. The Lord asked the Saints to avoid violence but also told them they could not compromise with an evil like slavery. The Saints must live lawfully among society but can still recognize the flaws in the lawful societies they are part of and work to put an end to injustice.

How can you respect the law, but also work to change laws that are unjust?

Day 248
Doctrine and Covenants 102:2

How Do Councils Help Us Make Wise Decisions?

> *The high council was appointed by revelation for the purpose of settling important difficulties which might arise in the church, which could not be settled by the church or the bishop's council to the satisfaction of the parties.*

Doctrine and Covenants 102 looks a lot different than the rest of the sections in the book because section 102 consists of the minutes of the first stake high council held in Kirtland, Ohio. It was not only the first high council meeting but also one of the first council meetings in the Church. The meeting marked the beginning of a new phase of development for the Church, where councils were created at all levels to help meet the needs of the Saints. In the months following, the Quorums of the Twelve, Seventy, and in time Relief Society and other organizational councils were added to the Church. Eventually councils were organized at every level of the Church, beginning with family councils and leading all the way up to the council of the First Presidency.

Why do we use so many councils? One member of the First Presidency stated, "The genius of our Church government is government

47. Letter from John Whitmer, 29 July 1833, *The Joseph Smith Papers*, 53.

through councils. . . . I have no hesitancy in giving you the assurance, if you will confer in council as you are expected to do, God will give you solutions to the problems that confront you."[48] Sometimes revelation comes to God's children in a pillar or light, but usually God meets our needs through another person. A group of people in tune with the Spirit are much less likely to make a bad decision than a single individual. Councils allow us to receive wisdom and guidance, and to train new leaders up so they can learn by example. Even our Heavenly Father, who knows all things, held a council before sending us to earth!

How can you use councils more effectively at home and in your church work?

Day 249
Doctrine and Covenants 103:12

How Can I See the Blessings in Tribulation?

> *For after much tribulation, as I have said unto you in a former commandment, cometh the blessing.*

When this revelation was received, the Saints were still reeling from the persecutions they suffered in Missouri. Daily reports poured into Church headquarters about the suffering Saints, thrown out of their homes by the mob and forced to live as refugees. Church leaders in Kirtland felt helpless and sought the Lord to know how they could help their friends in Zion. Parley P. Pratt described the tribulations of the Missouri Saints when he wrote, "Hundreds of people were seen in every direction, some in tents and some in the open air around their fires, while the rain descended in torrents. Husbands were inquiring for their wives, wives for their husbands; parents for children, and children for parents. Some had the good fortune to escape with their families, household goods, and some provisions; while others knew not the fate of their friends, and had lost all their goods."[49]

---

48. Stephen L. Richards, Conference Report, October 1953, 86.
49. *Autobiography of Parley P. Pratt* (1985), 82.

Like the early Saints, we often find ourselves in tribulation with no end in sight to our troubles. We can feel weak and hopeless in the face of opposition. But there is always hope. The Lord allows us to experience tribulation because it has a way of burning away the impure parts of our personalities and learning behind the most valuable parts of our testimony. In addition, tribulation gives us empathy for others who are experiencing trials. Like the early Saints, we struggle and stumble, but if we keep moving forward we will find that the Lord has a blessing waiting for us on the other side of our trials.

Is there someone struggling with trials right now that you could reach out to?

Day 250
Doctrine and Covenants 103:22

How Can Everyone Contribute to the Work?

> *Therefore let my servant Joseph Smith, Jun., say unto the strength of my house, my young men and the middle aged—Gather yourselves together unto the land of Zion, upon the land which I have bought with money that has been consecrated unto me.*

In response to the suffering of the Saints in Missouri, the Lord instructed Church leaders in Ohio to organize a relief mission. It was initially known as the Camp of Israel but later came to be known as Zion's Camp. Eventually Zion's Camp consisted of 230 men, women, and children who marched over eight hundred miles from Ohio to Missouri to assist the Saints in Zion. The call of Zion's Camp came at a challenging time for Church members in Ohio, and finding enough men to accompany the expedition was difficult. Most of the Saints already lived in Missouri, but the Lord instructed Church leaders in Ohio to recruit men of all ages. Any man, young or old, who could make the journey was asked to travel to Missouri to assist the Saints there. The Saints who marched with Zion's Camp traveled over three months in the spring of 1834. Some of the participants went on to become some of the most important leaders of the Church. Brigham Young, Heber C. Kimball, Parley P. Pratt, Wilford Woodruff, and Hyrum Smith all served in Zion's Camp.

We see a similar call among the Saints today. One of the wonderful things about how the Lord operates His Church is that people of any age, whether nine or ninety-nine, can serve in the kingdom. At ages long after retirement, the Lord calls us to serve in any capacity we can. For some of us, this means the rigorous work full-time missionary service. For others, serving might mean doing family history work at home. Everyone has value and can be useful regardless of our age and health. Just like the men and women who served with Zion's Camp, we can find a place to serve others and find joy in the work!

In what ways can you serve, or help others to serve?

Day 251

Doctrine and Covenants 103:27

How Can I Find My Life in the Service of God?

> *Let no man be afraid to lay down his life for my sake; for whoso layeth down his life for my sake shall find it again.*

The men and women leaving with Zion's Camp knew they were heading into hazardous territory. The mob leaders in Jackson County had threatened further violence if any attempt was made to assist the refugee Saints. The aim of Zion's Camp was to restore the Missouri Saints to their homes, and the mob was dead set against this goal. Justice, not violence, was the hope for Zion's Camp, but as the Saints set out on their journey they did not know what lay ahead. However, the Lord assured them that if they were willing to offer up their lives, they would find eternal life. In the end, Zion's Camp was not called on to fight the mob, though they did suffer hardship and death because of a cholera epidemic that swept through the camp.

The Lord rarely calls on His disciples to lay down their life for the cause, but He often asks people to give up their life for the gospel. More often than not, this has nothing to do with giving up our actual life but giving up our lives of selfishness and sin. When we do so we find that the Savior wasn't asking us to give up our life at all. Instead He was offering us a completely new life of peace and happiness. Asking us to give up our lives is a way of testing our commitment to the gospel. We often try to think we can change one little thing here or there. But the Savior asks us for mighty change, a complete commitment to His cause. Then we find a more fulfilling and richer life waiting for us.

How can you more fully commit to live the gospel?

Day 252

Doctrine and Covenants 104:13

How Can I Be a Good Steward?

> *For it is expedient that I, the Lord, should make every man accountable, as a steward over earthly blessings, which I have made and prepared for my creatures.*

This revelation was given in the aftermath of the persecutions that afflicted the Saints in Missouri. With the Saints in Zion left as refugees and robbed of many of their earthly possessions, the system of consecration followed by the Saints needed to be reordered. In response to this, the Savior combined the resources of the consecrated order in Kirtland and the order in Missouri into one, allowing the Saints to pool their resources and help Church members in Missouri to survive the current crisis. In the revelation the Lord asked the Saints in Kirtland to sacrifice to help their brothers and sisters in Missouri but also asked them to be good stewards over the limited resources in their possession.

Stewardship is a central principle in how the Lord asks us to live the law of consecration. We are given stewardships in our callings, in our work, and most importantly in our families. The Lord holds us accountable for how we manage these stewardships, but He also gives us tools to help us make good decisions. We can seek and receive revelation for how we manage our stewardships. We can seek out the help of wise and experienced people in knowing how to order our priorities.

Finally, it we prove to be wise stewards in this life, the Lord promises us an infinite stewardship in the eternities.

What are the priorities in your stewardship? Do you need to make adjustments to manage them better?

Day 253

Doctrine and Covenants 104:17

How Can Use the Blessings I Have to Help Others?

> *For the earth is full, and there is enough and to spare; yea, I prepared all things, and have given unto the children of men to be agents unto themselves.*

In this revelation on stewardship, the Lord encourages the Saints by explaining that "the earth is full, and there is enough and to spare." This is not to say that we can be wasteful and the Lord will continually provide for us, but if we are careful and cautious with what we have, the Lord will bless us and help us to make ends meet. Life is full of challenges and can seem overwhelming, but in telling us "I have prepared all things," the Lord is reminding us that He wants us to be successful and will do all in his power to help us achieve those our goals.

At the same time the Lord reminds us that His intention is not to make every decision for us. Instead, He teaches that He "has given unto the children of men to be agents unto themselves." At times He will allow us to stumble and make mistakes because that is how we grow. The goal of the plan of salvation was never to have God completely control our lives by telling us in exact detail everything that we need to do. God wants us to grow and become independent, to learn to make our own decisions and to counsel with Him, not be dominated by Him. He gently guides us and helps us through our challenges, reminding us that He has prepared the way and we must walk the path prepared for us.

How is it helpful to know the Lord has prepared all things for you?

Day 254

Doctrine and Covenants 104:58–59

What Was the Purpose of the Sacred Treasury?

And for this purpose I have commanded you to organize yourselves, even to print my words, the fulness of my scriptures, the revelations which I have given unto you, and which I shall, hereafter, from time to time give unto you—

For the purpose of building up my church and kingdom on the earth, and to prepare my people for the time when I shall dwell with them, which is nigh at hand.

As part of the financial reorganization of the Church commanded in this revelation, the Lord asked Church leaders to set apart some of their funds in a sacred treasury intended to facilitate the printing of the scriptures. The Lord explained that it was necessary to get the scriptures into the hands of the people "for the purpose of building up my church and kingdom on the earth, and to prepare my people for the time when I shall dwell with them, which is nigh at hand." This priority to get the information from the scriptures into the minds and hearts of the people remains a high priority for the Church today. A large part of Church resources goes toward getting the sacred words of the scriptures into any form possible where the messages can be received and studied. The Church has put the scriptures into electronic form, made films based on the scriptures, and searched for every means of getting the word of God into the hands of the people.

The priorities reflected here show how important the Lord saw the scriptures. Yet in spite of the fact that the scriptures are now more widely available than they have ever been, Church leaders have warned of a growing scriptural illiteracy. Sometimes our approach to the scriptures is like a student who has been given their teacher's answer book but hasn't bothered to look at it. In the scriptures are found the words that provide us with hope, uplift us, and help us draw nearer to Jesus Christ. So much work has gone into putting them into our hands, but are we truly using them?

What can you do to engage more deeply in your study of the scriptures?

Day 255
Doctrine and Covenants 104:67–68

How Can I Improve on My Stewardship?

And again, there shall be another treasury prepared, and a treasurer appointed to keep the treasury, and a seal shall be placed upon it;

And all moneys that you receive in your stewardships, by improving upon the properties which I have appointed unto you, in houses, or in lands, or in cattle, or in all things save it be the holy and sacred writings, which I have reserved unto myself for holy and sacred purposes, shall be cast into the treasury as fast as you receive moneys, by hundreds, or by fifties, or by twenties, or by tens, or by fives.

In this revelation, the Lord reorganized the finances of the Church to deal with the crisis in Missouri and to reflect the priorities of the Church. With this aim in mind, the Lord first asked the Saints to put their money into a sacred treasury with the aim of printing the scriptures and building up the kingdom of God (see Doctrine and Covenants 104:58–59). Then the Lord asked the Saints to prepare another treasury where the money taken from the stewardship of the Church could be kept with the aim of improving on the properties owned by the Church and its membership.

These priorities remain in place in the Church today. The Church first aims to build up the kingdom by sharing the truths in the scriptures but also to be wise stewards by improving the communities where the Church is found. If we have our financial house in order, we can follow the same priorities. It is important to make sure that your family is taken care of, but after that, our time, talents, and resources can do a lot toward improving our communities. Latter-day Saints don't believe in a "prosperity gospel" where greater righteousness is linked to greater wealth. But the Lord has been clear that we should share the blessings we receive with those around us. In the Book of Mormon the prophet Jacob counseled, "But before ye seek for riches, seek ye for the kingdom of God. And after ye have obtained a hope in Christ ye shall obtain riches, if ye seek them; and ye will seek them for the intent to do good—to clothe the naked, and to feed the hungry, and to liberate the captive, and administer relief to the sick and the afflicted" (Jacob 2:18–19).

We can do a lot of good in the world. If we have the resources, we can help our communities.

What can you do to contribute to the community that you live in?

Day 256

Doctrine and Covenants 105:5

What Are the Principles of the Celestial Kingdom?

And Zion cannot be built up unless it is by the principles of the law of the celestial kingdom; otherwise I cannot receive her unto myself.

After a trying journey of several weeks, the weary men and women of Zion's Camp arrived in Missouri. They immediately began to offer assistance to the Saints there but also worried about an attack from the mobs in Jackson County. On June 19, 1834, five men rode into the camp of Israel, threatening them with an attack from a group of four hundred men and telling them they would "see hell before morning."[50] However, that night a huge storm arose seemingly out of nowhere, raising the river between the camp and the mob to nearly forty feet deep. Seeing the storm as a sign of divine protection, some of the men in Zion's Camp began to prepare for battle. Joseph Smith asked the Lord what to do next and received Doctrine and Covenants 105.

The revelation was a rebuke of those in the camp who thought bloodshed would allow them to take back Zion. Instead, the Lord told them that "Zion cannot be built up unless it is by the principle of the law of the celestial kingdom." God was not going to build the new Jerusalem on a foundation of blood. Even though the Lord had protected them from the dangers of the mob, He asked them to follow

50. See "Zion's Camp," https://www.churchofjesuschrist.org/study/history/topics/zions-camp-camp-of-israel?lang=eng

a higher path and seek a higher way to resolve the conflict. He urged the Saints to work toward a peaceful solution, find a way to love their enemies, and not engage in further violence.

During our challenges we sometimes face a similar dilemma. There are worldly ways of solving problems that usually can hurt ourselves and others in the long run. But the Lord asks us to live by the law of the celestial kingdom even if we aren't living there yet. If we learn to "think celestial,"[51] it may be more difficult at first, but will ultimately lead us to a higher and happier way of living.

What can you do to "think celestial" in your dealings with others today?

Day 257

Doctrine and Covenants 105:18

How Can I Receive a Change in Direction in My Life?

> *But inasmuch as there are those who have hearkened unto my words, I have prepared a blessing and an endowment for them, if they continue faithful.*

This revelation came at the end of a long and difficult journey for the men and women of Zion's Camp. They had traveled all the way from Ohio to Missouri and endured many hardships along the way. Just when they were on the borders of Jackson County, they were told to disband the camp and travel home. Instead of redeeming Zion, the Lord told them to return to Ohio, where He had prepared "a blessing and an endowment for them." This was a difficult request for some. They had traveled all the way to Zion, and they wanted to see it redeemed. But as the Lord told them it was not yet time for that to happen.

Often we think we are working toward something only to discover that the Lord has a different path in mind for us. It can be difficult to accept this, but if we embrace the new path we will find a different, but perhaps better, reward there. When Brigham Young arrived back

51. Russell M. Nelson, "Think Celestial!" *Liahona*, November 2023.

in Kirtland, he recalled someone asking him, "What did you gain from this journey?" Brigham replied, "Just what we went for; but I would not exchange the knowledge I have received this season for the whole of Geauga County [the county he lived in]; for property and mines of wealth are not to be compared to the worth of knowledge."[52]

If we can have an attitude like Brigham Young's, we can see that the twists and turns of our lives can be opportunities for us to grow and learn new things. The goal we have in mind for ourselves is not always the goal that the Savior has in store for us.

How can you recognize the blessings that came when the Lord asks you to change direction?

Day 258

Doctrine and Covenants 105:39–40

How Can I forgive Those Who Have Wronged Me?

> *And lift up an ensign of peace, and make a proclamation of peace unto the ends of the earth;*
>
> *And make proposals for peace unto those who have smitten you, according to the voice of the Spirit which is in you, and all things shall work together for your good.*

In this revelation the Lord instructed Zion's Camp to disband and return to Ohio without returning the Saints to their homes in Jackson County. The dispersal of the camp was hastened when an outbreak of cholera swept through the camp, taking the lives of thirteen people. Joseph Smith was taken ill but recovered, though several important stalwarts among the Saints lost their lives, including A. Sidney Gilbert (see Doctrine and Covenants 53). Many of the Saints wanted vengeance on their enemies for the persecutions they had endured.

Instead, the Lord asked the Saints to make peace with their enemies and to find ways to build Zion on the principles of the celestial

52. *Journal of Discourses,* 2:10

kingdom, which includes being a peacemaker in a world of contention. At times we are genuinely wronged and are within our rights to seek recompense for what we have endured. However, even in times when we are in the right, we must find a way to forgive those who have wronged us. The Savior's promise is that if we make this effort "all things shall work together for your good." This isn't an easy teaching to follow, but if we can let go of our anger and bitterness, we might even find a lesson or two that we can learn from the challenges we've faced.

How have you encountered a challenge but saw that "all things worked together for your good"?

Day 259

Doctrine and Covenants 106:3

How Can I Be Worthy of the Callings I Have Been Given?

> *And devote his whole time to this high and holy calling, which I now give unto him, seeking diligently the kingdom of heaven and its righteousness, and all things necessary shall be added thereunto; for the laborer is worthy of his hire.*

Warren Cowdery was the older brother of Oliver Cowdery. He lived in Freedom, New York, and for a long time refused to join the Church his brother was so instrumental in founding. In the spring of 1834, Joseph Smith stayed in Warren's home during a drive to recruit men to serve in Zion's Camp. Warren was moved by the suffering of the Saints in Missouri, and in the months following his visit with Joseph, he was baptized and appointed as the head of a branch in Freedom. That fall he visited Kirtland and requested a revelation, which the Prophet granted to him. Warren was called at that time to serve as the presiding officer and was told to "devote his whole time to this high and holy calling."

Being appointed as a presiding leader of a branch must have been a little overwhelming for Warren. At times we feel the same way, especially if we are given a large responsibility at home or at work. But the Lord only asks that "the laborer is worthy of his hire." It can be difficult to measure success when it comes to spiritual things, which can't be measured in dollars or cents. But the Lord only asks us to do our best and promises to make up the difference. If we serve diligently and seek to help others, then we are worthy of our hire. We may not always be profitable servants, but all the Lord asks is that we are sincere servants.

What can you do to be more diligent in the responsibilities you have been given?

Day 260

Doctrine and Covenants 106:5

How Can I Be One of the Children of Light?

> *Therefore, gird up your loins, that you may be the children of light, and that day shall not overtake you as a thief.*

In calling Warren Cowdery to serve in the Church, the Lord also called him to be one of the "children of light." The name "children of light" was used in the New Testament by both Jesus and Paul to describe the Saints (see Luke 16:8; John 12:36; 1 Thessalonians 5:5; Ephesians 5:8). Calling Warren and the Saints the children of light was another way of reinforcing the Savior's request to His disciples to let their light shine. The Savior also called the Saints the "light of the world" (Matthew 5:14–15). This teaching could be misunderstood to imply that the Saints are better than others. Instead, the Savior is giving the Saints a responsibility to lead others and use their light to show them the way.

Most of us tend to shy away from opportunities to share our light. We need to remember that the light is not us holding ourselves up as an example to the world. Christ taught the Nephites, "Behold, I am the light; I have set an example for you" (3 Nephi 18:16). The light we hold up is the teachings, life, and salvation offered by the Savior. The light we possess is just reflected from His glory. When we live our lives the way He taught, we can take comfort in knowing the we are offering a new way of seeing the world around us and a better way of living.

What can you do to live up to the name "the children of light" today?

Day 261

Doctrine and Covenants 107:2–4

What Is the Melchizedek Priesthood?

Why the first is called the Melchizedek Priesthood is because Melchizedek was such a great high priest.

Before his day it was called the Holy Priesthood, after the Order of the Son of God.

But out of respect or reverence to the name of the Supreme Being, to avoid the too frequent repetition of his name, they, the church, in ancient days, called that priesthood after Melchizedek, or the Melchizedek Priesthood.

Doctrine and Covenants 107 defines how priesthood works on every level of the Church. It lays out the Melchizedek and Aaronic Priesthoods, defines their areas of authority, and establishes the presiding quorums of the Church. But before it goes into specifics about the roles and functions of the priesthood, it defines what priesthood is all about. The revelation explains that the Melchizedek Priesthood is not the original name of the priesthood. The original name is actually the Holy Priesthood, after the Order of the Son of God. It is the authority of Jesus Christ.

In one sense, this priesthood is an order, an organization that men and women enter into as they are ordained to priesthood office or enter the temple. In another sense, priesthood consists of the authority that is given to anyone to act in the name of Jesus Christ. In this sense, everyone who serves in the Church is given the authority to act on behalf of Jesus Christ. President Dallin H. Oaks explained, "We are not accustomed to speaking of women having the authority of the priesthood in their Church callings, but what other authority can it be? When a woman—young or old—is set apart to preach the gospel as a full-time missionary, she is given priesthood authority to perform a priesthood function. The same is true when a woman is set apart to function as an officer or teacher in a Church organization under the direction of one who holds the keys of the priesthood. Whoever functions in an office or calling received from one who holds priesthood keys exercises priesthood authority in performing her or his assigned duties."[53]

How does knowing you are an authorized representative of Jesus Christ help you carry out your responsibilities?

Day 262

Doctrine and Covenants 107:13–14

What Is the Aaronic Priesthood?

> *The second priesthood is called the Priesthood of Aaron, because it was conferred upon Aaron and his seed, throughout all their generations.*
>
> *Why it is called the lesser priesthood is because it is an appendage to the greater, or the Melchizedek Priesthood, and has power in administering outward ordinances.*

The revelation also lays out a second priesthood, the Aaronic Priesthood, which was restored in May 1829 when John the Baptist conferred this authority on Joseph Smith and Oliver Cowdery (see Doctrine and Covenants 13). While it is common to speak of the Aaronic Priesthood as a separate order, the revelation also clarifies that in reality it is an appendage, or a part of the Melchizedek Priesthood. On another occasion, Joseph Smith taught, "All priesthood is Melchizedek; but there are different portions or degrees of it. . . . All the prophets had the Melchizedek Priesthood."[54]

Why do we have a separate order if they are the same thing? Later in the revelation, the Lord specifies that the Aaronic Priesthood is designed to "administer in outward ordinances." It has become common practice to speak of the Aaronic Priesthood as administering in temporal things, while the Melchizedek Priesthood administers in spiritu-

---

53. Dallin H. Oaks, "The Keys and Authority of the Priesthood," *Ensign*, May 2014.
54. Discourse, 5 January 1841, as reported by William Clayton, *The Joseph Smith Papers*, 5.

al things. The Aaronic Priesthood was built for service. When an act of service is needed, Church leaders often call on the young men of the Aaronic Priesthood. In part, because of this practice, the Aaronic Priesthood often serves as the "training priesthood" for the young men of the Church. Both young men and young women need to be introduced to a life of service. These outward acts of goodness lead to real inward changes, helping them to grow into disciples of Jesus Christ.

How can you help others learn the value of service?

Day 263

Doctrine and Covenants 107:18–19

What Are the Powers of the Melchizedek Priesthood?

> *The power and authority of the higher, or Melchizedek Priesthood, is to hold the keys of all the spiritual blessings of the church—*
>
> *To have the privilege of receiving the mysteries of the kingdom of heaven, to have the heavens opened unto them, to commune with the general assembly and church of the Firstborn, and to enjoy the communion and presence of God the Father, and Jesus the mediator of the new covenant.*

After defining the two primary branches of the priesthood, the Lord explains that the Melchizedek Priesthood holds the "keys of all the spiritual blessings of the church." This priesthood is the same authority that God the Father and Jesus Christ possess, and it allows us to commune with Them and exist in Their presence. Since the entire purpose of the gospel of Jesus Christ is to help us become more like Him, the power of the priesthood allows us to have His authority to carry out His work.

The Savior is not jealous about sharing His power to help others. In the New Testament the Savior promised His disciples, "He that believeth on me, the works that I do shall he do also; and greater works than these shall he do; because I go unto my Father" (John 14:12). True to His word, the record later attests that while Jesus could heal with touch, even the touch of Peter's shadow healed people (see Acts 5:15). This is the power that Jesus Christ gives to His servants. If we want to become like Him, we qualify for priesthood ordination and the ordinances of the temple, and then we can inherit all that He has.

How does the priesthood help us understand the Father and the Son?

Day 264

Doctrine and Covenants 107:20

What Are the Powers of the Aaronic Priesthood?

> *The power and authority of the lesser, or Aaronic Priesthood, is to hold the keys of the ministering of angels, and to administer in outward ordinances, the letter of the gospel, the baptism of repentance for the remission of sins, agreeable to the covenants and commandments.*

After explaining the powers of the Melchizedek Priesthood, the Lord explains the primary purpose of the priesthood of Aaron, which is to "hold the keys of the ministering of angels, and to administer in outward ordinances, the letter of the gospel." There was much discussion at the time about the letter of the law and the spirit of the law. We need to remember that those two terms are not always in conflict. If we understand the spirit of the gospel, in most cases we will also live the letter of the gospel as precisely as we can.

Aaronic Priesthood holders are asked to administer the letter of the gospel. It is no surprise that this is part of this priesthood, since it was the Aaronic Priesthood that ministered during the time of Moses. In Moses's time, the Israelites lived a strict law of performances designed to teach them the deeper meaning of the law. The Savior often does the same thing with younger or newer members of the Church, emphasizing the simple, outward commandments designed to teach deeper principles. The daily ordinances and performances of the law of Moses lead us to understand and appreciate the profound truths behind the higher law. Both the higher law and the lesser law have their place in leading us to the Savior. At times, when we are wandering, focusing on the simple acts of the gospel can help us reconnect and lead us back to a more nuanced understanding of the gospel.

What little daily acts can help you appreciate the higher principles of the gospel?

Day 265
Doctrine and Covenants 107:23

What Is an Apostle?

> *The twelve traveling councilors are called to be the Twelve Apostles, or special witnesses of the name of Christ in all the world—thus differing from other officers in the church in the duties of their calling.*

The word *apostle* in the New Testament simply means "one sent forth." Scripture scholars have debated over whether the Apostles called by Jesus Christ were filling an official office within the Church or just acting as witnesses of Christ. The Book of Mormon reveals that there is much more to being an Apostle than just being one sent forth. Nephi saw in vision that the Twelve Apostles called at Jerusalem would assist the Savior in judging the house of Israel (see 1 Nephi 12:9). It was later revealed that the twelve called among the Nephites would assist in judging the people they served (see 1 Nephi 12:10). From this we can assume that the Twelve Apostles in our time will also play a role in our final judgment.

But in another sense, an Apostle's most important role is testifying of Jesus Christ. Doctrine and Covenants 107 teaches that the Twelve Apostles are called to be "special witnesses of Christ in all the world." Apostles travel and serve for as long as their health allows, teaching and witnessing of Jesus Christ. In this sense, every member of the Church can claim to be an apostle, one sent forth to share their witness of Jesus Christ.

How can you share your witness of Jesus Christ with others?

Day 266

Doctrine and Covenants 107:53–54

What Is a Patriarchal Blessing?

Three years previous to the death of Adam, he called Seth, Enos, Cainan, Mahalaleel, Jared, Enoch, and Methuselah, who were all high priests, with the residue of his posterity who were righteous, into the valley of Adam-ondi-Ahman, and there bestowed upon them his last blessing.

And the Lord appeared unto them, and they rose up and blessed Adam, and called him Michael, the prince, the archangel.

A careful examination of Doctrine and Covenants 107 shows that it consists of several different revelations on Church government that were combined to create a single document. This segment of the revelation is originally part of a blessing that Joseph Smith gave to his father and mother on December 18, 1833. In the blessing, Joseph mentioned the original patriarch, Adam, and revealed that his father was given the keys of the patriarchal priesthood. After this Joseph Smith Sr. became the first patriarch in the Church and was given the charge to provide Church members with patriarchal blessings. Because this role was so important in the structure of the Church, the blessing was included in the revelation.

Today stake patriarchs provide blessings to every member of the Church who requests them and is worthy. These communications from God are a way of providing a personal revelation to everyone who seeks them. My patriarchal blessing has been a comfort and guide through some of the most difficult moments of my life. God, as our loving Father, uses personal revelation given through His servants to help us know of His love for us.

If you already have a patriarchal blessing, when was the last time you looked at it? If you don't yet have a patriarchal blessing, have you thought about receiving one?

Day 267
Doctrine and Covenants 107:84

How Does Hierarchy Work in the Church?

Thus, none shall be exempted from the justice and the laws of God, that all things may be done in order and in solemnity before him, according to truth and righteousness.

Part of the purpose of Doctrine and Covenants 107 is to explain the hierarchy of the Church. It is necessary to understand the hierarchy to know how decisions are made in the Church. At the same time, the revelation stresses that though there has to be a hierarchy for administrative purposes, placement in the hierarchy is not a measure of righteousness. President Dallin H. Oaks emphasized this when he taught, "There is no 'up or down' in the service of the Lord. There is only 'forward or backward,' and that difference depends on how we accept and act upon our releases and our callings. I once presided at the release of a young stake president who had given fine service for nine years and was now rejoicing in his release and in the new calling he and his wife had just received. They were called to be the nursery leaders in their ward. Only in this Church would that be seen as equally honorable!"[55]

The revelation also sets up a series of checks and balances in the Church. The highest council in the Church is the First Presidency. What happens if a member of the First Presidency is found in transgression? The revelation states that a hearing will be held, led by the Presiding Bishop of the Church, assisted by twelve high priests. "Thus, none shall be exempted from the justice and laws of God," the revelation explains. The inclusion of this rule is further evidence that everyone is seen as equal in the Lord's Church regardless of their position.

Why do you think the Lord saw it important to include checks and balances in the Church?

---

55. Dallin H. Oaks, "The Keys and Authority of the Priesthood," *Ensign*, May 2014.

Day 268

Doctrine and Covenants 108:2

How Can I Know My Spiritual Standing?

Therefore, let your soul be at rest concerning your spiritual standing, and resist no more my voice.

This revelation was given to one of the lesser-known but valiant figures in Church history, a man known as Lyman Sherman. Lyman was a member of the Quorum of the Seventy who showed great loyalty to the gospel even in the face of fierce opposition. A few years after this revelation was given, a severe apostasy broke out in Kirtland, Ohio, and Lyman was one of the few defenders of the Prophet Joseph Smith during this time. While several members of the Quorum of the Twelve and even a member of the First Presidency were excommunicated, Lyman stayed on the Prophet's side. Even when it meant leaving behind the home he built in Kirtland, Lyman never hesitated to follow the Lord's call.

From the revelation it appears clear that Lyman felt some anxiety about his spiritual standing before the Lord. In response to these concerns, the Lord assured him that he didn't need to worry. In the wake of the Kirtland apostasy, Lyman was called to serve as an Apostle, stepping into the role of the members of the Quorum of the Twelve who had apostatized. Unfortunately, he passed away before he was notified of the call. But his call to serve as a special witness of the Savior finally confirmed Lyman Sherman's spiritual standing before the Lord.

Have you ever prayed to know your spiritual standing before the Lord?

Day 269
Doctrine and Covenants 109:5

What Is the Purpose of Temples?

For thou knowest that we have done this work through great tribulation; and out of our poverty we have given of our substance to build a house to thy name, that the Son of Man might have a place to manifest himself to his people.

Doctrine and Covenants 109 is a revealed prayer and coincides with a number of firsts in the Church. It was given at the dedication of the first temple in the Church, the House of the Lord at Kirtland, Ohio. It was read in the first temple dedication, where for the first time the hosanna shout was performed and "The Spirit of God" was sung as part of the services. These practices set the standards still followed for dedicatory services for temples to this day. The Kirtland Temple still stands today, though its purpose is different than those of modern temples. Those who tour the Kirtland Temple may be surprised to find that there is no baptismal font, endowment rooms, or sealing rooms. The primary purpose of this temple is spelled out in its dedicatory prayer. It was meant to provide a sacred space "that the Son of Man might have place to manifest himself to his people."

The Kirtland Temple was built after nearly two thousand years without a dedicated temple on the earth. Today there are hundreds of temples being built around the world in locations undreamed of by the early Saints. Every time one of these sacred edifices is built, the Lord has a new place to manifest Himself. More importantly, these holy houses are places where we can go to commune with the Lord.

Have you had a sacred experience in a temple?

Day 270
Doctrine and Covenants 109:13

How Can I Seek Places of Holiness?

And that all people who shall enter upon the threshold of the Lord's house may feel thy power, and feel constrained to acknowledge that thou hast sanctified it, and that it is thy house, a place of thy holiness.

What makes temples special? While we do our best to make sure that the architecture is inspiring, the people are friendly, and the grounds are well-maintained, none of those things are what make temples special. The early Saints who built the Kirtland Temple barely had the work force or the skills to build a structure like the temple. Though the temple still stands today and is a beautiful monument to their sacrifice, a closer look at the temple shows signs that its construction was more of a labor of love than a labor of skill. When the stucco that gives the temple its white walls is removed, the stones of the temple walls are shown to be of random shapes and sizes. Whereas later structures such as the Salt Lake Temple were built of stone precisely cut, polished, and measured, the Kirtland Temple was built of a motley collection of stones cemented and held together by nothing more than mortar and prayer. Looking closely at some of the woodwork, one can see places that don't exactly match. But it is a temple nonetheless.

What makes a temple special is holiness. We strive to make temples as beautiful as possible, but it is not the beauty of the place that makes it holy. Holiness comes from the way we worship within the temple. It comes from our attitude toward God, our love for Him, and our respect for His creations. On every temple next to the phrase "the House of the Lord" is the phrase "Holiness to the Lord." We can create these holy spaces through our love and devotion to the Savior. A holy place can be anywhere; it just depends on us making it a holy place.

How can you make the places you visit into holy places?

Day 271
Doctrine and Covenants 109:21

How Can I Speedily Repent?

And when thy people transgress, any of them, they may speedily repent and return unto thee, and find favor in thy sight, and be restored to the blessings which thou hast ordained to be poured out upon those who shall reverence thee in thy house.

In the dedicatory prayer of the Kirtland Temple it is assumed that those who attend the temple will transgress and sin. That is part of life. The Apostle Paul wrote, "All have sinned, and come short of the glory of God" (Romans 3:23). King Benjamin declared that we are all "unprofitable servants" (Mosiah 2:21). Modern Apostles have taught that "a saint is just a sinner who keeps on trying."[56] Because none of us are without sin, Joseph Smith asked in the dedicatory prayer of the Kirtland Temple for the Lord to help us "speedily repent."

We need to remember that the people who enter temples are all sinners. Whatever brings us to the temple, to the sacrament table, or to our knees in prayer matters less than how quickly we realize our sins and seek to repent. J. Golden Kimball was a General Authority in the early twentieth century who struggled with swearing. He used to joke, "I won't go to hell for swearing because I repent too damn fast!" Being a saint isn't about being perfect; it is about sincerely striving to do our best. Blessings are poured out upon the sincere who quickly realize their mistakes and work to become better.

When you sin, how speedily do you repent?

---

56. Dale G. Renlund, "Latter-day Saints Keep On Trying," *Ensign*, May 2015.

Day 272

Doctrine and Covenants 109:36–37

How Can Spiritual Manifestations Help Me Draw Closer to God?

Let it be fulfilled upon them, as upon those on the day of Pentecost; let the gift of tongues be poured out upon thy people, even cloven tongues as of fire, and the interpretation thereof.

And let thy house be filled, as with a rushing mighty wind, with thy glory.

The dedication of the Kirtland Temple brought a spiritual Pentecost unmatched in any other time in Church history. Joseph Smith's history later noted that during a meeting in the temple, "a voice was heard like the sound of a rushing mighty wind which filled the Temple and all the congregation simultaneously arose being moved upon by an invisible power many began to speak in Tongues and prophecy others saw glorious visions and I beheld the Temple was filled with angels which fact I declared to the to the congregation. The people in the neighborhood came running together (hearing an unusual sound within and seeing a bright light like a pillar of Fire resting upon— the Temple) and were astonished at what was transpiring."[57]

This season of spiritual outpouring was a great blessing to the Saints in Kirtland, but we must also remember that the Lord taught earlier in the Doctrine and Covenants that "faith cometh not by signs, but signs follow those that believe" (Doctrine and Covenants 63:9). One of the paradoxes of the Kirtland Temple is that the one of the richest outpourings of the Spirit was followed less than two years later by one of the worst seasons of apostasy in the history of the Church.

Signs can be a blessing for our faith, but they come from faith, not the other way around. We must nourish our faith every day through small acts of devotion, and then signs will come if they are needed.

What can you do today to nourish your faith?

---

57. History, 1838–1856, volume B-1 [1 September 1834–2 November 1838], *The Joseph Smith Papers,* 4 [addenda].

Day 273
Doctrine and Covenants 104:59

What Will the Gathering in the Latter Days Look Like?

> *We ask thee to appoint unto Zion other stakes besides this one which thou hast appointed, that the gathering of thy people may roll on in great power and majesty, that thy work may be cut short in righteousness.*

In the early days of the Church, the Saints were laser-focused on building Zion. They saw the construction of the New Jerusalem on the American continent as their great work and the best way to prepare the earth for the Second Coming. But as persecutions forced the Saints in Zion to flee from their homes, they searched for answers about how Zion would rise in the latter days. Many of the Saints began to look toward the prophet Isaiah's description of Zion, where Zion is likened to a great tent with many stakes to strengthen its stability. Isaiah wrote, "Enlarge the place of thy tent, and let them stretch forth the curtains of thine habitations: spare not, lengthen thy cords, and strengthen thy stakes" (Isaiah 54:2).

At this time there were only two stakes in the Church, one in Kirtland, Ohio, and the other among the refugee Saints in Missouri. When the Kirtland Temple was dedicated, Joseph Smith prayed that the Lord would appoint other stakes. Today we are witnesses to the answer to this prayer, with stakes now in diverse places around the globe. As new stakes are formed in places such as Chile, Finland, Kiribati, and a host of other locations, the tent of Zion is enlarged. New cultures are welcomed into Zion, and the tapestry of the Restoration becomes richer. We do our part in enlarging Zion by welcoming other people and cultures into this great work among the human family.

How has the gospel helped you learn about and appreciate other cultures?

Day 274
Doctrine and Covenants 110:2–3

How Does the Savior Accept His House?

We saw the Lord standing upon the breastwork of the pulpit, before us; and under his feet was a paved work of pure gold, in color like amber.

His eyes were as a flame of fire; the hair of his head was white like the pure snow; his countenance shone above the brightness of the sun; and his voice was as the sound of the rushing of great waters.

In late March of 1836 the Kirtland Temple was dedicated in Pentecostal outpouring where thousands of people witnessed spiritual manifestations. But the greatest of all these manifestations occurred on Sunday, April 3, 1836. Joseph Smith and Oliver Cowdery returned to the temple and lowered the veils around the Melchizedek Priesthood pulpits and offered a prayer to give thanks for the blessings they had received during the temple dedication. As they prayed, the resurrected Savior appeared to them and accepted the house. His presence caused even the wooden pulpits to take on the appearance of gold. Whatever the Savior touches becomes priceless in the hearts of His disciples.

I have seen this illustrated in trips I have made leading tour groups to the Holy Land. There are a few places in Israel where you can say with a high degree of certainty that Jesus walked there. Among these is the Valley of the Doves in Galilee, the Caiphas steps in Jerusalem, and the steps leading up to the place where the temple stood in the time of Christ. But even in these sacred spaces, we are just guessing that Jesus stood there. There is only one place on earth that I know of where you can say that the Savior stood and narrow it down to just a few feet. That is in the Kirtland Temple.

Joseph and Oliver said that the appearance of the pulpits became like gold. Likewise, the Savior's appearance made this crude pioneer temple a sacred space like none other on the face of earth. Just as His presence transformed the Kirtland Temple into a holy house, His presence in our lives can transform us into beings of holiness and light.

When have you felt the presence of the Savior in your life?

Day 275
Doctrine and Covenants 110:11

What Were the Keys Brought by Moses?

After this vision closed, the heavens were again opened unto us; and Moses appeared before us, and committed unto us the keys of the gathering of Israel from the four parts of the earth, and the leading of the ten tribes from the land of the north.

Jesus was only the first divine visitor to the temple in Kirtland. After the Savior gave His acceptance of the house, Moses appeared and gave Joseph Smith and Oliver Cowdery the keys of the gathering of Israel. He was followed by Elias and Elijah, who brought other keys. There are obvious parallels here to the events on the Mount of Transfiguration described in the New Testament gospels (see Matthew 16:13–19; 17:1–9). There, Peter, James, and John, the heads of the ancient church, were taken to a high mountain. The Savior was transformed before them into a being that shone like the sun, and they saw Moses and Elias (Elijah). Doctrine and Covenants 63 adds that the Apostles also saw the transfiguration of the earth that will take place during the Millennium (see Doctrine and Covenants 63:20–21).

The New Testament accounts describe the appearance of Moses but not his purpose in appearing on the mount. Joseph and Oliver recorded that when Moses appeared in the Kirtland Temple, he brought with him the keys of the gathering of Israel. A lot of attention is sometimes given to the wording that the lost tribes will be gathered "from the north," but this is likely a reference to a return from sin and wickedness. Ancient Israel was often threatened by neighboring empires from the north. The "lost" tribes were also taken away to the north by the Assyrian Empire, so their return symbolically comes from the north. But on a deeper level, the Book of Mormon describes the latter-day gathering as a physical and spiritual gathering (see 2 Nephi 9:1–2). In the Kirtland Temple, Moses, the great gatherer of the house of Israel, bestowed the keys to gather Israel in their physical and spiritual wanderings.

How can you assist in the gathering of Israel?

Day 276
Doctrine and Covenants 110:12

What Are the Keys Brought by Elias?

After this, Elias appeared, and committed the dispensation of the gospel of Abraham, saying that in us and our seed all generations after us should be blessed.

The second of the three visitors introduced by the Savior in the Kirtland Temple is the most mysterious. The name Elias appears several times in the New Testament, but it is the Greek version of the name Elijah and appears to always refer to that Old Testament figure. Joseph would have been well aware of this, but he identified a second visitor to the temple in Kirtland who identified himself as Elias.

Who is Elias? The scriptures provide several possible answers. In Doctrine and Covenants 27:6, Elias is identified as the angel Gabriel, who in turn was later identified by Joseph Smith as the ancient prophet Noah.[58] Later, in Doctrine and Covenants 77:9 and 14, John the Revelator is identified as an Elias who was commanded to "gather the tribes of Israel" (Doctrine and Covenants 77:14).

Different uses of the name indicate that Elias is a title. Other scholars have speculated that Elias was a prophet from the Old Testament era that is currently not in the scriptural record. Another theory is that since this prophet brought "the dispensation of the gospel of Abraham" it may have been Abraham himself. Whatever the identity was of this messenger, the keys that he restored seem to be tied to the covenant God made with Abraham. The Lord promised Abraham and his wife, Sarah, an innumerable posterity, telling them, "Look now toward heaven, and tell the stars, if thou be able to number them: and he said unto him, So shall thy seed be" (Genesis 15:5).

Because of what happened in the Kirtland Temple, the promises made to Abraham are now available to everyone who is willing to qual-

58. Letter to the Church, 7 September 1842 [D&C 128], *The Joseph Smith Papers,* 7; see also Discourse, between circa 26 June and circa 2 July 1839, as reported by Wilford Woodruff, *The Joseph Smith Papers*, 26.

ify themselves to receive them. The door is open to becoming a father of multitudes, just as Abraham became.

What is your understanding of the promises made to Abraham? You might want to take quick look at Abraham 2:8–11.

Day 277

Doctrine and Covenants 110:13–15

What Are the Keys Brought by Elijah?

> *After this vision had closed, another great and glorious vision burst upon us; for Elijah the prophet, who was taken to heaven without tasting death, stood before us, and said:*
>
> *Behold, the time has fully come, which was spoken of by the mouth of Malachi—testifying that he [Elijah] should be sent, before the great and dreadful day of the Lord come—*
>
> *To turn the hearts of the fathers to the children, and the children to the fathers, lest the whole earth be smitten with a curse.*

April 3, 1836, was an Easter Sunday and coincided with the Jewish celebration of the Passover. For hundreds of years observant Jews have gathered together for Passover celebrations, eating unique foods to remind them of their ancestors' freedom from slavery in Egypt. Among the customs that are part of the Passover is the practice of setting an extra place at the table and leaving the door open in case Elijah returns. This custom grew out of the haunting prophecy found in the book of Malachi, which reads, "Behold, I will send you Elijah the prophet before the coming of the great and dreadful day of the Lord: And he shall turn the heart of the fathers to the children, and the heart of the children to their fathers, lest I come and smite the earth with a curse" (Malachi 4:5–6).

Elijah did return during the Passover, but instead of going to a family home, he went to the House of the Lord in Kirtland. He was the final messenger to appear to Joseph Smith and Oliver Cowdery, committing to them the keys of this dispensation. In time, Joseph came to realize that the sealing keys given by Elijah allowed faithful Saints to carry out work for their loved ones on both sides of the veil. Elijah's coming began the process of turning the hearts of the children to their fathers, a work that will eventually bring billions into the presence of God.

When have you felt the spirit of Elijah, and how has it inspired you?

Day 278

Doctrine and Covenants 111:1–2

How Can the Lord Turn Our Follies into Blessings?

> *I, the Lord your God, am not displeased with your coming this journey, notwithstanding your follies.*
>
> *I have much treasure in this city for you, for the benefit of Zion, and many people in this city, whom I will gather out in due time for the benefit of Zion, through your instrumentality.*

This revelation was received during a trying time for the Saints. The costs of the construction of the Kirtland Temple, combined with the need to help the refugee Saints in Missouri, caused immense financial strain on the Church. Joseph Smith and other Church leaders became desperate to find a way to raise funds to alleviate the debts of the Church. According to several sources, a member of the Church suggested to Church leaders that there was a house in Salem, Massachusetts, with a large store of money inside if they could just access it. Joseph Smith led a group of Church leaders to Salem, but they were unable to access the home. Seeking guidance from the Lord, they received this revelation.

In the revelation the Lord gently chides the leaders for their follies. It seems that they were absolutely sincere in seeing the treasure as a way of helping the Church but may have been misguided. In a similar way we sometimes pursue paths with dead ends. More than a few times I have become enthusiastic about something that wasn't the best use of my time. But the Lord can take our follies and direct us to more productive pursuits. The treasure the Lord had in mind likely consisted of the men and women that Joseph and the other leaders preached to during their time in Salem. Eventually a healthy branch of the Church was established there, and many faithful Saints were converted from the local population. It can be the same with us, if we humble ourselves, even in the midst of our follies.

How has the Lord helped you turn your follies into blessings?

Day 279

Doctrine and Covenants 111:5–6

How Can the Lord Help Me Overcome My Fears?

> *Concern not yourselves about your debts, for I will give you power to pay them. Concern not yourselves about Zion, for I will deal mercifully with her.*

From the revelation it appears that at least part of the reason that Joseph Smith and the other Church leaders traveled to Salem was because of the fears they felt over the debts of the Church and the struggles of Church members in Missouri. In response to both of these fears, the Lord offered a calm assurance that He would give them power to pay their debts, and that He would deal mercifully with the Saints in Zion. In saying this, the Lord didn't magically solve their problems. It still took years of hard work and sacrifice to pay off the debts of the Church, and the problems surrounding Zion are still being dealt with today.

But we can have the assurance from the Lord that He will help us with our problems. There are many nights when we stay up late with only our anxiety to keep us company. There might be difficult days ahead, but if the Lord is on our side we don't need to concern ourselves too much with the worries we have. When we live the gospel we have the assurance of better things to come. The Lord will help us overcome our challenges.

How do the teachings of the gospel help you manage your worries?

Day 280
Doctrine and Covenants 112:10

How Can I Choose to Be Humble?

Be thou humble; and the Lord thy God shall lead thee by the hand, and give thee answer to thy prayers.

The financial problems in Kirtland continued to fester, resulting in the disaffection of many Church members. The problems worsened when Church leaders opened the Kirtland Safety Society, a bank intended to help the poor of the Church, in January of 1837. The bank was subject to a number of challenges, including attempts from the enemies of the Saints to bankrupt the institution, and it soon began failing. In this moment of crisis several key leaders of the Church, including several members of the Quorum of the Twelve, began to publicly criticize Joseph Smith. Doctrine and Covenants 112 was a revelation given to Thomas B. Marsh, the president of the Quorum of the Twelve, who was also struggling with issues related to pride. The Lord counseled Thomas to humble himself and seek the Lord in prayer.

It is easy to relate to Thomas B. Marsh because each of us struggles with pride. Pride often stems from negative comparisons we make with other people. We can look down on others, thinking we are better than them. We can also experience pride from the bottom looking up, where we feel jealousy for others who we see as having more than us. This is a universal sin that everyone experiences. But in response to this sin we can choose to be humble. Humility allows us to see the blessings we have and appreciate the blessings others have been given. It doesn't harm us when someone else receives a blessing. Humility doesn't come easily, but if we choose to be humble, the Lord will lead us to better things.

How can you choose to be humble today?

Day 281
Doctrine and Covenants 112:15

How Can I Rid Myself of a Spirit of Rebellion?

Exalt not yourselves; rebel not against my servant Joseph; for verily I say unto you, I am with him, and my hand shall be over him; and the keys which I have given unto him, and also to youward, shall not be taken from him till I come.

The Apostasy in Kirtland is among the most severe in Church history. Because of the failure of the Kirtland Safety Society, many Church members turned against Joseph Smith, seeing him as a fallen prophet. Some of Joseph's oldest and dearest friends openly criticized him in public settings. Several Apostles, as well as one member of the First Presidency, were excommunicated. As the president of the Quorum of the Twelve, Thomas B. Marsh was given the charge to assist in bringing back the lost Apostles of his quorum. Thomas stayed true during the trials of Kirtland but apostatized the following year.

In contrast to the rebellious apostles, Brigham Young stayed true to the prophet. He was invited to attend a meeting held in the Kirtland Temple where a faction sought to remove Joseph Smith as Church president and replace him with David Whitmer. When Brigham was asked to share his thoughts he said, "I rose up, and in a plain and forcible manner told them that Joseph was a Prophet, and I knew it, and they might rail and slander him as much as they pleased, they could not destroy the appointment of the Prophet of God, they could only destroy their own authority, cut the thread that bound them to the Prophet and to God and sink themselves to hell."[59]

In the face of personal opposition, Brigham, demonstrated his belief in the Lord's statement that the Prophet holds the keys and acts as the Savior's representative on earth.

What do you think it means to sustain the prophet?

---

59. "History of Brigham Young," *Deseret News Weekly*, February 10 1858, 386.

Day 282

Doctrine and Covenants 112:32

Who Is Allowed to Receive Priesthood Keys?

For verily I say unto you, the keys of the dispensation, which ye have received, have come down from the fathers, and last of all, being sent down from heaven unto you.

This revelation was given just over a year after Moses, Elias, and Elijah appeared in the Kirtland Temple and gave Joseph Smith and Oliver Cowdery the "keys of this dispensation" (Doctrine and Covenants 110:16). At the time many members of the Church were in rebellion over the failure of the Kirtland Safety Society, including several Apostles and prominent Church leaders. Thomas B. Marsh was among those who were wavering in their support of the Prophet. The Lord admonished Thomas to turn away from his criticisms and remember the keys of leadership he was given as president of the Quorum of the Twelve. Unfortunately, Thomas left the Church the following year, leading to David W. Patten becoming the president of the quorum. When David Patten was killed in Missouri, Brigham Young took over as leader of the quorum and was the eventual successor to Joseph Smith.

This passage in Doctrine and Covenants 112 indicates that the keys of the priesthood could have been passed to Thomas B. Marsh if he had proven faithful. Because he left the Church the keys were passed on to Brigham Young, and they remain operative in the Church today. Priesthood keys operate regularly in the lives of men and women who serve in the Church. They also act as a reminder to us of God's power, present in our lives through the priesthood. If we are faithful, God will eventually pass on all that He has to us.

How has your life been affected by the power of the priesthood?

Day 283
Doctrine and Covenants 113:1–2

Who Is the Stem of Jesse?

Who is the Stem of Jesse spoken of in the 1st, 2d, 3d, 4th, and 5th verses of the 11th chapter of Isaiah?
Verily thus saith the Lord: It is Christ.

In January 1838 Joseph Smith fled Kirtland, Ohio, because of the severe apostasy growing there. He arrived in the Church community of Far West, Missouri, a few weeks later. The Saints in Missouri were excited to have the Prophet in their midst and anxious to seek his guidance. The Saints in Missouri sought the Prophet's answers on interpreting several verses in the book of Isaiah that mention the "stem of Jesse." Joseph sought the Lord in revelation and received answers that become Doctrine and Covenants 113.

The revelation declares that the "stem of Jesse" is Jesus Christ. Jesse was the father of David, the founder of the royal house of Israel. Identifying the stem of Jesse as Christ points to the fact that the mission of Jesus marked the return of the royal house of David and fulfilled its true mission to the Messiah to earth. The Hebrew word from Isaiah translated as "stem" in the King James Version of the Bible is actually closer to "stump." The implication is that when Christ was born, the royal house of David was like a dead stump, the remnant of a once great tree, now cut down and destroyed. But Christ showed that life remained in the House of David. Through His Atonement and Resurrection, Christ brought life back to a family that was thought of as dead.

Christ brings life to all things. He restored life to the royal house of Israel by bringing to light its real mission, to bring life and salvation to women and men everywhere.

How have you seen the power of Christ bring life to things in your life?

Day 284

Doctrine and Covenants 113:3–4

Who Is the Rod of Jesse?

What is the rod spoken of in the first verse of the 11th chapter of Isaiah, that should come of the Stem of Jesse?

Behold, thus saith the Lord: It is a servant in the hands of Christ, who is partly a descendant of Jesse as well as of Ephraim, or of the house of Joseph, on whom there is laid much power.

The second part of the Isaiah's prophecy is that a "rod" would come out of the "stem of Jesse." Isaiah 11:1 reads, "And there shall come forth a rod out of the stem of Jesse, and a Branch shall grow out of his roots." The Hebrew word translated as "rod" in the King James translation is usually translated as "shoot" or "branch" in more modern translations. It suggests that out of the stem of Jesse will come new life. Many non-Latter-day Saint Christians have interpreted the rod to be Jesus Christ, but Doctrine and Covenants 113:1 says that the stem of Jesse is Christ. So who is the rod?

The revelation only identifies the rod as "a servant in the hands of Christ, who is partly a descendant of Jesse as well as of Ephraim." While the scriptures never directly identify who the rod is, the person who most closely fits the description is Joseph Smith. This scripture was among the passages that Moroni quoted to Joseph the first night he appeared (see Joseph Smith—History 1:40). Joseph Smith was also told in another revelation that "the priesthood hath continued through the lineage of your fathers—for ye are lawful heirs, according to the flesh, and have been hid from the world with Christ in God" (see Doctrine and Covenants 86:8–10).

Whether this prophecy refers to Joseph Smith or another prophet yet to come, it is clear that the Lord watches over families and keeps His promises to them. When we keep our covenants with God we can become like Jesse or Ephraim and secure the blessings of God not only for ourselves but for our descendants in future generations.

What blessings do you think have come to you because of the righteousness of your ancestors?

Day 285
Doctrine and Covenants 113:7–8

How Does Zion Put on Its Strength?

Questions by Elias Higbee: What is meant by the command in Isaiah, 52d chapter, 1st verse, which saith: Put on thy strength, O Zion—and what people had Isaiah reference to?

He had reference to those whom God should call in the last days, who should hold the power of priesthood to bring again Zion, and the redemption of Israel; and to put on her strength is to put on the authority of the priesthood, which she, Zion, has a right to by lineage; also to return to that power which she had lost.

The revelation also contains two questions asked by Elias Higbee, a Church member living in Missouri. Elias asked about Isaiah 52, which contains this prophecy, "Awake, awake; put on thy strength, O Zion; put on thy beautiful garments, O Jerusalem, the holy city: for henceforth there shall no more come into thee the uncircumcised and the unclean" (Isaiah 52:1).

The Lord replied that the "beautiful garments" Isaiah talked about represent the authority of the priesthood, which was lost to the ancient Israelites because of their wickedness. Then the Lord explains that righteous people called in the last days "should hold the power of priesthood to bring again Zion, and the redemption of Israel" (Doctrine and Covenants 113:8).

This is another prophecy that underlines the fact that Zion is more than just a place, it is a people (see Doctrine and Covenants 97:21). Zion will rise and become powerful as its people grow in their power in the priesthood and their righteousness. Every time a Church member makes covenants, lives up to them, and works to do good, Zion grows and comes closer to meeting her potential.

How can you help Zion put on her strength?

Day 286

Doctrine and Covenants 114:2

How Does the Lord Reward the Faithful?

For verily thus saith the Lord, that inasmuch as there are those among you who deny my name, others shall be planted in their stead and receive their bishopric. Amen.

This revelation acknowledges the service of David W. Patten, the second president of the Quorum of the Twelve Apostles. David became the leader of the quorum when Thomas B. Marsh, the original quorum president, apostatized in 1838. David was described by those who knew him as tall and strong and was affectionately known among the Saints as "Captain Fear-not" because of his immense physical courage. During his brief time leading the Quorum of the Twelve, he headed the efforts to defend the Saints in Missouri from the unruly mobs attacking their settlements.

This was a time of severe testing. Several Apostles left the Church, while others were excommunicated. Even David questioned the leadership of Joseph Smith, but he repented and returned to full fellowship. Wilford Woodruff recalled a conversation between David Patten and Joseph Smith, where "David made known to the Prophet that he has asked the Lord to let him die the death of a martyr, at which the Prophet, greatly moved, expressed extreme sorrow, 'for,' he said to David, 'when a man of your faith asks the Lord for anything, he generally gets it.'"[60]

A few months later David was involved in a mission to rescue three hostages captured by a mob. During a battle with the mobbers, David was fatally wounded. He survived long enough affirm his faith to his wife, Phoebe Ann, telling her "Whatever you do else, O, do not deny the faith!" After his passing, the Prophet Joseph Smith spoke at his funeral, saying, "There lies a man that has done just as he said he would—he has laid down his life for his friends."[61]

Do you think you would be willing to make a sacrifice like David Patten?

---

60. Lycurgus A. Wilson, *The Life of David W. Patten,* 53.
61. Wilson, *The Life of David W. Patten,* 70–71.

Day 287
Doctrine and Covenants 115:4–5

Why Is It Important to Use the Correct Name of the Church?

For thus shall my church be called in the last days, even The Church of Jesus Christ of Latter-day Saints.

Verily I say unto you all: Arise and shine forth, that thy light may be a standard for the nations.

In this revelation the Lord revealed the full name of the Church. When the Church was first organized, it was simply referred to as "the Church of Christ" (Doctrine and Covenants 20:1). A few years later, possibly because there were several other churches know as the Church of Christ, a conference of Church leaders voted to change the name to "The Church of the Latter-day Saints." In the following two years, the two names were occasionally combined. Finally, in 1838, the Lord established the full name of the Church through revelation as "The Church of Jesus Christ of Latter-day Saints."

Throughout the history of the Church, members have been called by many names. The most widely known name was Mormons because of our belief in the Book of Mormon. In 2018, Russell M. Nelson, newly called as the president of the Church, emphasized the importance of using the proper name of the Church. "The Lord has impressed upon my mind the importance of the name He has revealed for His Church, even The Church of Jesus Christ of Latter-day Saints. We have work before us to bring ourselves in harmony with His will."[62] Just a few weeks later in general conference, President Nelson gave an even more forceful address, particularly to those critical of attempts to emphasize the name of the Church. "It is not a name change. It is not rebranding. It is not cosmetic. It is not a whim. And it is not inconsequential. Instead, it is a correction. It

62. Russell M. Nelson in "The Name of the Church," official statement, August 16, 2018, https://newsroom.churchofjesuschrist.org/article/name-of-the-church.

is the command of the Lord. . . . The name of the Church is not negotiable."[63]

Why do you think the Lord has emphasized the need to use the correct name of the Church?

Day 288
Doctrine and Covenants 115:6

How Can I Create Places of Refuge?

> *And that the gathering together upon the land of Zion, and upon her stakes, may be for a defense, and for a refuge from the storm, and from wrath when it shall be poured out without mixture upon the whole earth.*

Many of the early Saints believed that in the last days all of the righteous would gather to Zion, the New Jerusalem built on the American continent. But as the challenges of building Zion became clearer, the Lord expanded the Saints' perspective, pointing out that Zion is a people as much as a place, and it can exist anywhere. The Lord also likened Zion to a great tent, supported by many stakes. In Doctrine and Covenants 115 the Lord addresses the concept of stakes and their purpose.

The Lord speaks of stakes as a place for defense and "for a refuge from the storm." Today thousands of stakes are found all over the world. They serve as places where faithful Saints can find others who have made covenants with God, and means for defending their faith. But stakes are also spoken of as a refuge. They are meant to be a place where anyone can go and find safety from the terrible trials of the last days. The Lord organized His people into stakes as a way of offering protection, guidance, and solace to those exhausted by the endless conflicts of our time.

When our stakes become places of refuge, we can take comfort in knowing that we will survive the storms of our time. While we cannot

63. Russell M. Nelson, "The Correct Name of the Church," *Ensign*, November 2018.

avoid the challenges of the last days, we can create a haven for all who will join us.

What can you do to make your home a refuge for others?

Day 289

Doctrine and Covenants 116:1

What Is the Meeting at Adam-Ondi-Ahman?

> *Spring Hill is named by the Lord Adam-ondi-Ahman, because, said he, it is the place where Adam shall come to visit his people, or the Ancient of Days shall sit, as spoken of by Daniel the prophet.*

In the spring of 1838, Joseph Smith spent several days scouting through Northwest Missouri in search of proper locations for settling the Saints in the area. One of the places he visited was named Spring Hill, a beautiful little valley situated along the Grand River. During his stay at Spring Hill, Joseph recorded this revelation in his journal. It makes reference to a prophecy of the ancient prophet Daniel, who saw in vision that "one like the Son of man came with the clouds of heaven, and came to the Ancient of days" (Daniel 7:9).

The revelation identifies the "Ancient of Days" to be Adam, the father of the human race. In an 1843 discourse Joseph taught that Adam "will call his children together and hold a council with them to prepare them for the coming of the Saint of Man."[64] This council could possibly include Saints from all ages or given to Christ from out of the world (Doctrine and Covenants 27:14). This mirrors an earlier appearance of Christ in Adam-ondi-Ahman, where the Savior appeared to Adam and his righteous children, three years before the death of Adam (see Doctrine and Covenants 107:53–56). Apostle Orson Pratt later taught that Adam-ondi-Ahman means "the valley of God, where Adam dwelt."[65]

---

64. Discourse, between circa 26 June and circa 4 August 1839–A, as reported by Willard Richards, *Joseph Smith Papers*, 63–64.
65. *Journal of Discourses*, 18:342–43.

We sometimes only think of the last days in negative terms. We only talk about the fire, earthquakes, wars, and rumors or wars. But there are wonderful things ahead as well. Huge trials lay ahead, but so does Adam-ondi-Ahman.

What positive things do you look forward to about the Second Coming?

Day 290

Doctrine and Covenants 117:4

How Can I Avoid Becoming Too Materialistic?

Let them repent of all their sins, and of all their covetous desires, before me, saith the Lord; for what is property unto me? saith the Lord.

After the Church center at Kirtland fell into apostasy, Joseph Smith and most of the remaining faithful Saints there moved to Missouri. But in the months following his move, many Church members remained behind, including Newell K. Whitney, who was serving as the bishop of the Church in Kirtland. Newell was a pillar of the community, and leaving Kirtland meant leaving behind several successful businesses. Leaving Kirtland behind came at a much higher personal cost for Bishop Whitney than for most of the Saints, and he was understandably hesitant. To encourage Bishop Whitney to gather with the Saints, the Lord asked a simple question: "What is property unto me?"

This is a question we still need to ask ourselves on a regular basis. It can be easy for us to be swept up in the greed and materialism that seems to surround us at all times. We sometimes spend a lot of time worrying about things that we can't take with us when we leave this life. While we need to be good providers for ourselves and our families, at times too much focus on material things takes us away from God. In the end, most property is only a passing concern in the grand scheme of things. But if we focus on the things that are truly eternal, like our relationship with God and with our loved ones, we will find things that last into the eternities.

What can you do to avoid becoming too focused on material things?

Day 291
Doctrine and Covenants 117:13

Why Is Our Sacrifice Greater Than Our Increase?

> *Therefore, let him contend earnestly for the redemption of the First Presidency of my Church, saith the Lord; and when he falls he shall rise again, for his sacrifice shall be more sacred unto me than his increase, saith the Lord.*

The revelation also addressed a Church member named Oliver Granger, who was asked to stay behind in Kirtland settle the debts of the Church before gathering with the Saints. Oliver was given a very difficult task. Many of the people who stayed in Kirtland were openly hostile toward the Church, and Oliver was asked to serve as an official representative of the faith. The failure of the Kirtland Safety Society also left behind numerous debts that he was asked to take charge of and find a way to pay off. The Lord know that the task was difficult but urged Oliver to "contend earnestly" and promised him that when he fell he would rise again.

Oliver spent the rest of his life laboring in Kirtland to pay off the debts of the Church. He passed away just a few years after his call to serve. Today his grave is marked by a lonely marker next to the Kirtland Temple. As the Lord prophesied, his sacrifice was more sacred than his increase, and his name will be held "in sacred remembrance from generation to generation, forever and ever, saith the Lord" (Doctrine and Covenants 117:12).

Like Oliver Granger, sometimes our sacrifice is the thing the Lord is looking for from us. We will not always experience increase from the work we do, but the sacrifice refines us, brings us closer to God, and helps us become more like Him.

When have you seen blessings for the sacrifices you have made?

Day 292
Doctrine and Covenants 118:5

How Is Prophecy Fulfilled?

Let them take leave of my saints in the city of Far West, on the twenty-sixth day of April next, on the building-spot of my house, saith the Lord.

When this revelation was given, Far West, Missouri, was a bustling hub of Church activity. The revelation called several new apostles to replace the losses in the Quorum of the Twelve. Among the new apostles were John Taylor and Wilford Woodruff, both future presidents of the Church. The Lord had ambitious plans for the Apostles calling them to travel to Europe to teach the gospel. The revelation declared this plan, then even gave a place and a date when they should leave on their mission. Wilford Woodruff later recalled, "It is the only revelation that has ever been given since the organization of the Church, that I know anything about, that had day and date given with it."[66]

Unfortunately, in the year between the time when the revelation was given and the time it was to be fulfilled, the conditions in Far West changed radically. Joseph Smith and other Church leaders were arrested and thrown into Liberty Jail. The Saints were driven from Missouri under an extermination order issued by the governor of the state. Far West practically became a ghost town, occupied primarily by those who threatened the Saints. Some of the Saints' enemies in Far West swore that this revelation would not be fulfilled, threatening to kill any of the Apostles who came to Far West.

Faced with these threats, the Quorum of the Twelve debated what they should do. A number of Church leaders, including the Prophet's father, felt there was no need to fulfill the revelation if it might cause death or harm to befall them. In the end Brigham Young decided to fulfill the revelation. In the dead of night on April 26, 1839, they quietly came to the temple lot in Far West. Wilford Woodruff was ordained an apostle on the spot. They quietly began their mission, fulfilled the

66. *Journal of Discourses,* 13:59.

prophecy, and left Far West before anyone was aware of their presence.

What role do we have in fulfilling prophecy? Like the Apostles, we cannot just sit back and wait for prophecy to be fulfilled without effort on our part. Prophecy is fulfilled when the faithful take action. If the Lord has given you a task through a Church leader, a blessing, or a prompting, you can go and fulfill it.

How do you respond when you receive a prompting?

Day 293
Doctrine and Covenants 119:1–3

Did the Law of Tithing Replace the Law of Consecration?

> *Verily, thus saith the Lord, I require all their surplus property to be put into the hands of the bishop of my church in Zion,*
>
> *For the building of mine house, and for the laying of the foundation of Zion and for the priesthood, and for the debts of the Presidency of my Church.*
>
> *And this shall be the beginning of the tithing of my people.*

Doctrine and Covenants 119 is short but critical. With the Saints still recovering from the loss of Kirtland, Ohio, as a meaningful Church center and their forcible eviction from Jackson County, they were struggling to live the law of consecration. Joseph Smith sought the Lord in revelation and received a the law of tithing, first revealed in this revelation.

Did the law of tithing replace the law of consecration? The revelation does not say this. In fact it asked all of the Saints to adhere to the law by bringing their surplus to the bishop. Only after they had done this were they asked to begin to tithe. Even after this there was no revelation that declared an end to consecration. Consecration remains a vital principle to the Church, though the way we live consecration is based on a set of principles and not a fixed system. Tithing may be a subset of the law of consecration, but it did not replace it.

Consecration is a holistic law. It involves more than just money.

To consecrate means to make sacred, and the Lord asks us to make everything in our lives sacred. Our time, gifts, and talents can all be used by the Lord to help those around us lead better lives. In a letter written just a few months after this revelation, Joseph Smith emphasized the law of consecration, explaining, "For a man to consecrate his property . . . is nothing more nor less than to feed the hungry, clothe the naked, visit the widow and the fatherless, the sick, and the afflicted, and do all he can to administer to their relief in their afflictions, and for him and his house to serve the Lord."[67]

What can you do to more fully live the law of consecration in the way Joseph Smith described it?

Day 294
Doctrine and Covenants 119:4

What Is the Law of Tithing?

> *And after that, those who have thus been tithed shall pay one-tenth of all their interest annually; and this shall be a standing law unto them forever, for my holy priesthood, saith the Lord.*

Tithing has been mentioned in numerous places in scripture since ancient times. The book of Genesis speaks of Abraham offering tithes to Melchizedek, the king of Salem (Genesis 14:18–20). Speaking to Moses, the Lord commanded that "all the tithe of the land, whether of the seed of the land, or of the fruit of the tree, is the Lord's: it is holy unto the Lord" (Leviticus 27:30). Tithing has been defined in different ways over time, but the Lord has always required a sacrifice from His people.

Church leaders today interpret the word *interest* in the revelation to mean income.[68] The particulars of how a person measure their tithing, and what they pay tithing for, are usually left up to the individual.

---

67. Letter to the Church in Caldwell County, Missouri, 16 December 1838, *The Joseph Smith Papers*,5.
68. *General Handbook*, 2020, 34.3.1.

When Church leaders ask if you are a full tithe payer it is a test of integrity.

When I was serving as a Church leader, I used to hesitate when I asked a family who was struggling to pay their tithing. But after a little time and experience I learned it was usually the best way to solve their financial challenges. Tithing is the Lord's way of encouraging us to keep a budget and be wise in our expenditures. I also found that if people had the faith to make this sacrifice, the Lord would usually open the way for them to make ends meet. This simple law asks the same sacrifice of everyone, whether you are well-off or struggling. It is our way of giving something back to the person who gave us everything.

What blessings have you seen from living the law of tithing?

Day 295

Doctrine and Covenants 120:1

How Is Tithing Managed?

> *Verily, thus saith the Lord, the time is now come, that it shall be disposed of by a council, composed of the First Presidency of my Church, and of the bishop and his council, and by my high council; and by mine own voice unto them, saith the Lord. Even so. Amen.*

The law of tithing is explained in these two brief revelations to the Church. Doctrine and Covenants 119 established the basics of the law of tithing for each Church member, and section 120 explains how the offerings are managed by the Church. The revelation established the Council on the Disposition of the Tithes, which consists of the First Presidency, the Presiding Bishopric (referred to as "the bishop and his council" in the revelation), and the Quorum of the Twelve Apostles (referred to as "my high council" in the revelation).

Elder David A. Bednar commented on how these revelations work in everyday life, saying, "I marvel at the clarity and brevity of these two revelations in comparison to the complicated financial guidelines and administrative procedures used in so many organizations and governments around the world. How can the temporal affairs of an organization as large as the restored Church of Jesus Christ possibly operate throughout the entire world using such succinct instructions? To me the answer is quite straightforward: this is the Lord's work, He is able to do His own work and the Savior inspires and directs His servants as they apply His directions and labor in His cause."[69]

Church leaders faced difficult choices over the best way to use the resources they have to help people around the world. Tithing funds can be used for sacred purposes such as building temples and meetinghouses, helping the poor, or delivering humanitarian aid. While Church leaders follow principles of thrift and self-reliance, we are asked to do the same with the resources we have. We too make difficult choices over how to support ourselves, help others, and build the kingdom of God on earth.

What principles from the scriptures do you use to manage your finances?

Day 296

Doctrine and Covenants 121:1

What Can I Do When I Feel God Is Distant?

> *O God, where art thou? And where is the pavilion that covereth thy hiding place?*

The winter of 1838–39 was one of the most challenging times in the life of the Prophet Joseph Smith. Conflict with their neighbors in Missouri led to a series of terrible persecutions, climaxing with the slaughter of eighteen men and boys at Hawn's Mill. In the aftermath, Lilburn Boggs, the governor of the state, issued an extermination order, declaring that the Saints "must be treated as enemies and must be exterminated or driven from the state."[70] In the persecutions that followed,

69. David A. Bednar, "The Windows of Heaven," *Ensign*, November 2013.
70. "A History, of the Persecution, of the Church of Jesus Christ, of Latter Day Saints in Missouri," December 1839–October 1840, *The Joseph Smith Papers*, 129.

Joseph Smith was illegally arrested, sentenced to be executed, and then saved from execution and placed in a series of prisons.

He finally found himself in the jail in Liberty, Missouri, along with several other Church leaders, including his brother Hyrum Smith and Sidney Rigdon. During their stay in the jail the men were subject to extreme cold, awful food, and anxiety over the fate of their families. They also felt helpless, knowing the Saints were forced out of Missouri in the middle of winter. In the midst of this severe trial, Joseph and his companions wrote a letter to the Church. Part of the letter made up Doctrine and Covenants 121, 122, and 123.

Admitting his fears, Joseph wrote in the letter that at times he was led to ask, "O God, where art thou?" That is a question that each of us asks at some point in our lives. When we experience trials for whatever reason, it can be easy to feel abandoned and alone. But we must remember that we are never alone. When Joseph asked where God was, the Savior answered. The words of God that came to Joseph Smith transformed a lonely prison into a sacred temple, a place where God dwelt with His servants and provided comfort. It can be the same in our lives. When we feel God is distant, we can reach out to Him, and He will hear us. He is always there for us.

How can you reach out to God when you feel He is distant?

Day 297

Doctrine and Covenants 121:7–8

How Can I Endure Adversity Well?

> *My son, peace be unto thy soul; thine adversity and thine afflictions shall be but a small moment;*
>
> *And then, if thou endure it well, God shall exalt thee on high; thou shalt triumph over all thy foes.*

Joseph Smith's plea to God from Liberty Jail prompted a reply from on high. The Savior did not remove Joseph from his trials but told him that his season of adversity would "be but a small moment." He also gave Joseph the assurance that his "friends do stand by thee, and they shall hail thee again with warm hearts and friendly hands" (Doctrine and Covenants 121:9). Joseph spent five months in Liberty Jail. This is not a "small moment" in the way most of us view things, but it is in the way God views things. In the grand view of eternity, our entire mortal lives are just a small moment.

It is also telling that the Savior does not collapse the prison walls and free Joseph and his friends, as he did on at least two occasions in scripture (Alma 14:26–29; Acts 16:25–27). Most of the time, the Lord does not free us from our trials. Instead He gives us the strength to endure them. Trials have a way of burning away the superficial things in our lives and leaving behind what really matters. The question is not *if* we will endure trials but *how* we will endure them. If we endure our trials well, they can become some of the most instructive and powerful experiences of our lives. Rather than driving us away from God, they can bring us closer to God.

What trials are you facing right now? How can you find a way to allow them to bring you closer to God?

Day 298
Doctrine and Covenants 121:33

What Power Can Stay the Heavens?

> *How long can rolling waters remain impure? What power shall stay the heavens? As well might man stretch forth his puny arm to stop the Missouri river in its decreed course, or to turn it up stream, as to hinder the Almighty from pouring down knowledge from heaven upon the heads of the Latter-day Saints.*

Just a few miles away from Liberty Jail lies the Missouri River. The river is one of the longest and most powerful rivers in North America, running over 2,341 miles from Southwest Montana until it flows into the Mississippi River just north of St. Louis, Missouri. Today massive bridges span the Missouri River near where Liberty Jail was located.

In speaking to Joseph Smith and his companions in the jail, the Lord compared an attempt of a single person to stop the Missouri River from flowing to anyone stopping the Savior from "pouring knowledge from heaven upon the heads of the Latter-day Saints."

The Lord wants us to learn. He wants to teach us about the wonders of eternity. It is no surprise that the Lord spoke about His desire to teach His Saints while Joseph and his companions were going through severe trials. Trials have a way of softening our hearts and helping us be more receptive to being taught. When we allow the challenges of our lives to make us more humble and help us, the Lord can instruct us. The only thing that can really stop God from pouring out knowledge on us is our own pride and unwillingness to learn. But if we can humble ourselves and align our will with God's, we can find untold wisdom waiting to be bestowed upon us.

What can you do to be more teachable today?

Day 299
Doctrine and Covenants 121:36

What Is the Key to Power in the Priesthood?

> *That the rights of the priesthood are inseparably connected with the powers of heaven, and that the powers of heaven cannot be controlled nor handled only upon the principles of righteousness.*

During his incarceration in Liberty Jail, Joseph Smith and his companions may have pondered over the situation of similar prophets held in prison for their beliefs. In the Bible, Paul and Silas were freed from their incarceration when an earthquake destroyed the prison they were kept in (see Acts 16:25–27). In the Book of Mormon, Alma and Amulek were freed when the Lord collapsed the walls of the building where they were imprisoned (see Alma 14:26–29). This must have prompted Joseph and his friends to ask if the Lord would grant a similar blessing, free them from Liberty Jail, and avenge the Saints of the wrongs they endured at the hands of their persecutors. They may have also been prompted to ask if they could use their priesthood to call upon the powers of heaven and destroy their enemies.

Instead of granting them power to seek vengeance, the Lord delivered a profound set of instructions on how to gain power in the priesthood. "Behold, there are many called, but few are chosen, the Lord declared. "And why are they not chosen? Because their hearts are set so much upon the things of this world, and aspire to the honors of men, that they do not learn this one lesson—That the rights of the priesthood are inseparably connected with the powers of heaven, and that the powers of heaven cannot be controlled nor handled only upon the principles of righteousness" (Doctrine and Covenants 121:34–36).

The power of heaven cannot be used for selfish or unrighteous purposes. We can use them to bless others, to heal, and to build. But we cannot use them for our own self-aggrandizement. The power of God is given to us to bless others. When our hearts are aligned with God amazing things can happen, but if we are not aligned with God we have no power and are left to our own devices.

What can you do or change about your life to draw more fully on the powers of heaven?

Day 300

Doctrine and Covenants 121:41–42

How Can I Lead in a Christlike Way?

> *No power or influence can or ought to be maintained by virtue of the priesthood, only by persuasion, by long-suffering, by gentleness and meekness, and by love unfeigned;*
>
> *By kindness, and pure knowledge, which shall greatly enlarge the soul without hypocrisy, and without guile.*

The Lord's instructions to Joseph Smith and his companions in Liberty Jail first explain how to lose power in the priesthood and then how to gain it. The power dynamic in the gospel of Jesus Christ is flipped from how most people see leadership in worldly settings. In the world, the leader is seen as the greatest figure, someone who others bow down to or pay homage. In the gospel, the leader is a servant who works to take care of others. In another revelation to Joseph Smith, the Lord explained, "He that is ordained of God and sent forth, the same is appointed to be the greatest, notwithstanding he is the least and the servant of all" (Doctrine and Covenants 50:26).

Instead of leadership being a call to dominate, the Lord's call to leadership asks us to use long-suffering, gentleness, meekness, and love unfeigned. We are asked to help persuade those we lead to do the right thing through Christlike means. We lead with love and service. These words, spoken to the prisoners of Liberty Jail, show that power from heaven comes to those who are meek and lowly. When we aim to use divine power not to dominate but to serve, we truly unlock the powers of heaven.

How can you follow the Lord's counsel in these verses in your relationships?

Day 301
Doctrine and Covenants 121:45

How Can I Have Charity towards All People?

> *Let thy bowels also be full of charity towards all men, and to the household of faith, and let virtue garnish thy thoughts unceasingly; then shall thy confidence wax strong in the presence of God; and the doctrine of the priesthood shall distill upon thy soul as the dews from heaven.*

After counseling the Saints to use persuasion, gentleness, kindness, and love unfeigned, the Lord summarizes His expectations for His servants by asking them to "be full of charity towards all men." In the New Testament, the Greek word translated as charity is agape. Agape was generally thought of as the highest form of love, generally meaning love of God for His children and love of God's children for Him. The Greek language had other forms of love, such as eros (romantic love), philia (friendship), and storge (family love). Of all these loves, agape, or charity, was considered the highest. This was in part because it is relatively natural to feel love for someone you are in love with, a close friend, or a family member. But charity was considered to be supernatural, a gift from God given to those who seek it. Paul spoke of charity as the highest of the gifts, saying, "Though I speak with the tongues of men and of angels, and have not charity, I am become as sounding brass, or a tinkling cymbal" (1 Corinthians 13:1).

Charity is unique because you can feel it for a complete stranger. It allows us to see the world around us the way God sees all of us, as His children who need love and respect. It can even allow us to love those who may have wronged or hurt us. The Savior asked Joseph Smith and his associates in Liberty Jail to have charity towards all men, even those who were responsible for them ending up in a decrepit jail. Developing this form of love qualifies us and prepares us to enter the presence of God. The revelation even says that with it our confidence will wax strong in the presence of God. When we can love the way that God loves us, then we can live in the way God lives.

What can you do to have greater charity today?

Day 302
Doctrine and Covenants 122:7

Why Does God Give Us Trials?

And if thou shouldst be cast into the pit, or into the hands of murderers, and the sentence of death passed upon thee; if thou be cast into the deep; if the billowing surge conspire against thee; if fierce winds become thine enemy; if the heavens gather blackness, and all the elements combine to hedge up the way; and above all, if the very jaws of hell shall gape open the mouth wide after thee, know thou, my son, that all these things shall give thee experience, and shall be for thy good.

Doctrine and Covenants 122 was taken from another part of the Liberty Jail letter where the Lord describes the harrowing experiences Joseph

Smith and his companions went through during the Missouri persecutions. The list is not hypothetical. Everything described in section 122 actually happened to Joseph. This included being separated from his young son who was pleading to know his father's fate. Lyman Wight described the scene of Joseph Smith's arrest at Far West as follows: "When passing his own house [Joseph] was taken out of the wagon and permitted to go into the house but not with out a strong guard, and not permitted to speak with his family but in the presence of his guard his eldest son Joseph, about 6 or 7 years old, hanging to the tail of his coat crying, "Father is the mob going to kill you?"

The guard said to him "You damned little brat, go back, you will see your father no more."[71]

After listing the trials Joseph endured, the Savior tenderly counseled, "All these things shall give thee experience, and shall be for thy good." While most of us will not experience trials on the level Joseph Smith endured, we will still experience them. We can choose to have them make us more tender and kind, or bitter and hollow. Joseph's trials in Missouri softened him and made him appreciate more deeply the relationships in his life. While in Liberty Jail he wrote to another friend, "No tongue can tell what inexpressible Joy it gives a man to see the face of one who has been a friend after having been enclosed in the walls of a prison for five months it seems to me that my heart will always be more tender after this than ever it was before."[72]

How have your trials made your heart more tender?

Day 303
Doctrine and Covenants 122:8

How Does the Savior Know My Trials?

The Son of Man hath descended below them all. Art thou greater than he?

71. Lyman Wight, Testimony, 1 July 1843 [Extradition of JS for Treason], *The Joseph Smith Papers, 26.*
72. Letter to Presendia Huntington Buell, 15 March 1839, *The Joseph Smith Papers,* 1.

The Savior concludes His assurances to Joseph Smith and his companions in Liberty Jail with one of the most empathetic and powerful statements He has ever made about His atoning sacrifice. "The Son of Man hath descended below them all. Are thou greater than he?"

We can feel very lonely in our suffering. At times we may feel like no one understands what we are going through. But one person always understands our suffering and can offer us empathy. In the Book of Mormon, Alma taught, "And he shall go forth, suffering pains and afflictions and temptations of every kind; and this that the word might be fulfilled which saith he will take upon him the pains and the sicknesses of his people. And he will take upon him death, that he may loose the bands of death which bind his people; and he will take upon him their infirmities, that his bowels may be filled with mercy, according to the flesh, that he may know according to the flesh how to succor his people according to their infirmities" (Alma 7:11–12).

The Savior knows you and understands your suffering. His love is there in the midst of all of your trials. If you can remember that, you are never truly alone.

How does a knowledge of the Savior's suffering help you endure your trials?

Day 304

Doctrine and Covenants 123:12

How Can I Help Others Find the Truth?

For there are many yet on the earth among all sects, parties, and denominations, who are blinded by the subtle craftiness of men, whereby they lie in wait to deceive, and who are only kept from the truth because they know not where to find it.

The final section taken from the Liberty Jail letter shows how Joseph Smith and his friends in the jail planned to spend their time once they were freed. They did not look for revenge from their captors and tormentors. Instead they planned to use their time once they left the jail to continue the work of bringing the good news of the gospel to as many people as possible. After all their suffering, they still believed that most people are basically good and would respond to the truth if it was presented to them.

While there is more than a fair share of evil in the world, this view basically holds true. Most of Heavenly Father's children are striving to live according to the light and truth they know. While we need to recognize that there is genuine evil in the world that tries to extinguish the light of the gospel, most people are not part of that evil. Latter-day Saints have endured horrible persecutions like those in Missouri, but we are still optimistic about human nature. Most people will repent and accept the gospel, whether in this life or the next. For now our purpose is to bring as many people to Christ as we can and help them escape the "subtle craftiness of men."

What can you do to help bring light to others?

Day 305
Doctrine and Covenants 123:17

How Can I Face My Trials with Cheerfulness?

> *Therefore, dearly beloved brethren, let us cheerfully do all things that lie in our power; and then may we stand still, with the utmost assurance, to see the salvation of God, and for his arm to be revealed.*

In April 1838, Joseph Smith and his companions in Liberty Jail were allowed to escape. In the months following Joseph's arrest, public opinion began turning against the leaders of the state of Missouri. Seeking a way to escape the controversy, the men in Liberty Jail were taken in a wagon out into the country and allowed to go free. Over the next few days they made their way across the state to Quincy, Illinois, where the Saints had gathered as refugees.

Dimick Huntington, who was at the docks when Joseph Smith arrived, later vividly described Joseph's appearance after months of confinement in Liberty Jail. The Prophet "was dressed in an old pair of boots, full of holes, pants torn [and] tucked inside of boots." He "had not been shaved for some time" and wore a "blue cloak with collar turned up, wide brim black hat, rim sopped down." Huntington finished his description by adding that Joseph "looked pale and haggard."[73]

Joseph was tired but cheerful. Having lost nearly everything but his faith, friends, and family, he began the process of rebuilding the Church and his life. He did so cheerfully. Cheerfulness is an under-appreciated virtue. We will face trials; in this we have no choice. But we can choose to face them cheerfully and with a smile, and we will usually find a way through them.

What can you do to face your trials more cheerfully?

Day 306
Doctrine and Covenants 124:23

How Can I Be More Inclusive?

> *And it shall be for a house for boarding, a house that strangers may come from afar to lodge therein; therefore let it be a good house, worthy of all acceptation, that the weary traveler may find health and safety while he shall contemplate the word of the Lord; and the cornerstone I have appointed for Zion.*

After the trials of Missouri, the Saints found themselves as refugees on the banks of the Mississippi River. The citizens of Quincy, a small Illinois town, welcomed the Saints and did their best to accommodate them. In the meantime, the Saints began looking for a new place to settle. The only land they could afford was a swampy peninsula jutting out into the Mississippi River called Commerce, Illinois. The Saints purchased the land, and Joseph Smith renamed the settlement Nauvoo, a Hebrew word meaning "beautiful place or situation."

As the Saints settled in Nauvoo, they reflected on the persecutions they experienced in Missouri and what they could do to prevent such

73. Quoted in Anthony Sweat, *Repicturing the Restoration* (Salt Lake City: Deseret Book, 2020), 134–35.

attacks in the future. Some Church members wondered if they could have done a better job reaching out to their neighbors. Soon after the Lord gave a revelation, Doctrine and Covenants 124, that laid out the blueprint for the city of Nauvoo. The Lord instructed the Saints to build two houses. As was expected, one of the houses was a temple, a place for sacred ordinances. But the other was "a house that strangers may come from afar to lodge therein." The second house, which became known as the Nauvoo House, was to be built right by the river, where most travelers would arrive in the city.

The civic life of Nauvoo was to revolve around these two houses, the House of the Lord and the house for strangers. It was a direct way of letting the Saints know they needed to be more inclusive of other people. Today there is a wonderful fellowship found among the Saints. We need to make the Church a welcoming place for all people. How we treat the strangers among us says a lot about our relationship with Jesus Christ.

What can you do to make the Church more inclusive?

Day 307

Doctrine and Covenants 124:31

How Can I Place the Temple at the Center of My Life?

> *But I command you, all ye my saints, to build a house unto me; and I grant unto you a sufficient time to build a house unto me; and during this time your baptisms shall be acceptable unto me.*

The plans laid out by the Lord for Nauvoo called for the heart of the city to be a majestic temple built on the bluff overlooking the settlement. Plans for the new temple called for a structure much larger and more impressive than the previous temple built in Kirtland and the one planned for Far West. This temple had large meeting spaces like the Kirtland Temple but also rooms set apart for specific ordinances. The Lord commanded the Saints to build a baptismal font in the basement of the temple for the purposes of performing baptisms for the dead, a new practice introduced in Nauvoo.

It is not an exaggeration to say that everything in Nauvoo revolved around the temple. The men and women of the city sacrificed their time and resources to complete the House of the Lord. In the end it took six years of hard labor to complete the structure. By the time it was finished, Joseph and Hyrum Smith had been martyred in Carthage Jail. Shortly after completing the temple, the Saints were forced to abandon it and leave their homes in Nauvoo for an uncertain future in the West. In 1848 the temple was destroyed by an arsonist, and its remaining walls were leveled by a tornado a few years later. But over a century later the Saints returned to Nauvoo and rebuilt the temple.

The sacrifice the Saints in Nauvoo made to build the temple was not in vain. By placing the temple at the center of their city and their lives they showed their devotion to God and to the gospel of Jesus Christ. Today hundreds of communities of Saints exist with temples where covenants can be made with God. Because of the sacrifices of the Saints in Nauvoo, millions can receive the blessings of temple covenants.

What can you do to place the temple and God at the center of your life?

Day 308

Doctrine and Covenants 124:39

What Is the Purpose of Temples?

> *Therefore, verily I say unto you, that your anointings, and your washings, and your baptisms for the dead, and your solemn assemblies, and your memorials for your sacrifices by the sons of Levi, and for your oracles in your most holy places wherein you receive conversations, and your statutes and judgments, for the beginning of the revelations and foundation of Zion, and for the glory, honor, and endowment of all her municipals, are ordained by the ordinance of my holy house, which my people are always commanded to build unto my holy name.*

The temple in Nauvoo was going to be different than the temple in Kirtland. The temple in Kirtland was a beautiful meetinghouse with large open spaces. It had no ordinance rooms, no baptismal font, and no sealing rooms like we are accustomed to seeing in modern temples. The primary purpose for the temple in Kirtland was to create a sacred space where the Savior could manifest Himself and for Moses, Elias, and Elijah to appear and restore important priesthood keys.

In the revelation commanding the Saints to build the temple in Nauvoo, it is clear the Savior had different purposes in mind for this temple. The temple was to be a place "that your anointings, and your washings, and your baptisms for the dead, and your solemn assemblies" might be conducted, along with a number of other things. While the Kirtland Temple took on the appearance of a stately meetinghouse, the exterior of the Nauvoo temple was covered in rich symbolism. Stones with stars, moons, and sunstones adorned the outside of the temple.

The complexity on the outside of the Nauvoo temple was only the beginning. Inside the temple a more complicated collection of teachings were intended to introduce the Saints to the higher ordinances of the gospel and the mysteries of eternal life. Today each temple built by the Saints has its own unique set of symbols on the outside, but the symbolic teaching on the inside of the temple is the same in every holy house. When we enter that setting, the Lord prepares us for higher things.

What are some meaningful experiences you have had with the temple?

Day 309

Doctrine and Covenants 124:49

What Does the Lord Require of His Servants?

Verily, verily, I say unto you, that when I give a commandment to any of the sons of men to do a work unto my name, and those sons of men go with all their might and with all they have to perform that work, and cease not their diligence, and their enemies come upon them and hinder them from performing that work, behold, it behooveth me to require that work no more at the hands of those sons of men, but to accept of their offerings.

The first temple built in this dispensation was not supposed to be built in Kirtland, Nauvoo, or Salt Lake City. The first temple was intended to be built in Zion, the New Jerusalem planned by the Saints in Jackson County, Missouri. The Lord gave the command to build the temple in an 1832 revelation (see Doctrine and Covenants 84:1–5). The Saints committed themselves to build the temple and went to work. Unfortunately, horrific persecution from the other settlers in Jackson County forced the Saints to leave under the threat of their lives in the fall of 1833. In the years following, the Saints found themselves as refugees in Missouri, driven from place to place until they were forcibly evicted from the state under the threat of an extermination order.

After the Saints arrived in Nauvoo and began to rebuild their lives, the Lord addressed the question of His command to build the temple in Zion. Recognizing the terrible suffering of the Saints and their sincere desire to build the temple, the Lord declared, "It behooveth me to require that work no more at the hand of those sons of men, but to accept their offering." The temple would still be built, but for this time, the Savior was relieving the Saints of the command to build the temple at that time.

At times the Savior asks us to do hard things. This revelation reveals that the Lord doesn't always expect us to succeed. He expects us to try. He expects to put our whole heart and soul into the work, just like the early Saints in Zion did. But accomplishing the task isn't always the goal. The goal is to be changed by the task. One day the temple in Zion will be built, but for now the offering of the Saints was accepted by the Lord.

Have you ever failed to accomplish a task but felt that your offering was accepted by God?

Day 310

Doctrine and Covenants 125:2

What Can I Do to Be Prepared for the Future?

Verily, thus saith the Lord, I say unto you, if those who call themselves by my name and are essaying to be my saints, if they will do my will and keep my commandments concerning them, let them gather

> *themselves together unto the places which I shall appoint unto them by my servant Joseph, and build up cities unto my name, that they may be prepared for that which is in store for a time to come.*

As the Saints struggled to build their community in the swamps of Nauvoo, Church members also looked to find other places to build. Across the Mississippi River in Iowa territory, land was plentiful and inexpensive. A group of Church members approached Joseph Smith, who sought a revelation from the Lord about founding these cities in Iowa. The Lord instructed the Saints to purchase the land and build up cities "that they may be prepared for that which is in store for a time to come." The time the Lord was referring to came just a few years later when the Saints were forced to flee across the river. The settlements set up in Iowa acted as places of refuge until they were able to gather and begin the long trek west to the Rocky Mountains. Rather than just having all of the Saints settle in Nauvoo, there was wisdom in building up communities in other places.

Often we find ourselves doing things that aren't immediately urgent but will help us further down the road. For instance, Church leaders have long counseled members to keep emergency supplies on hand and food storage in case of emergency. These are the kinds of things that may not seem immediately important but are placed in store for a time to come. Setting aside an emergency fund, getting an education, and a host of other things may not seem like something that has to be done right now, but if you look to the future and not just the present you will find yourself prepared for times to come.

What can you do right now so you are more prepared for the future?

Day 311

Doctrine and Covenants 126:3

How Can I Make My Family My Priority?

> *I therefore command you to send my word abroad, and take especial care of your family from this time, henceforth and forever. Amen.*

In 1838 Brigham Young and the other Apostles were commanded by the Lord to prepare to cross the Atlantic Ocean and serve a mission in the British Isles (see Doctrine and Covenants 118). Brigham and his fellow missionaries left their families during a particularly trying time, when the Saints were still attempting to settle Nauvoo. They left home with assurances that the Church would look after their families, but still filled with anxiety of the fate of their loved ones. Brigham and his close friend Heber C. Kimball felt their hearts might burst at the idea of leaving their families in such a precarious state. Heber later recalled, "I asked the teamster to stop, and said to Brother Brigham, 'This is pretty tough, isn't it; let's ruse up and give them a cheer.' We arose, and swinging our hats three times over our heads, shouted: 'Hurrah, hurrah for Israel." As they rode away their wives came to the door to acknowledge their cheer, easing their fears.[74]

Doctrine and Covenants 126 was received after Brigham arrived home from a successful mission in the British Isles, where he helped bring thousands of new converts into the Church. His sacrifice in leaving his family resulted in a multitude of new families the Church. But now that Brigham was home, he was asked to take "especial care of your family."

In our lives there is a constant tug and pull between different priorities. There may be times when we have to leave our families, like Brigham did, in order to carry out an important task. But as we order the priorities of our lives, we must keep in mind that family relationships are eternal. In the grand scheme of things they matter more than most of the concerns we spend a lot of time and worry with. If we take especial care of our family, we are only taking care of the things that matter most.

How can you make your family a priority?

---

74. Orson F. Whitney, *The Life of Heber C. Kimball,* 266.

Day 312
Doctrine and Covenants 127:2

How Can I Find Joy in Tribulation?

And as for the perils which I am called to pass through, they seem but a small thing to me, as the envy and wrath of man have been my common lot all the days of my life; and for what cause it seems mysterious, unless I was ordained from before the foundation of the world for some good end, or bad, as you may choose to call it. Judge ye for yourselves. God knoweth all these things, whether it be good or bad. But nevertheless, deep water is what I am wont to swim in. It all has become a second nature to me; and I feel, like Paul, to glory in tribulation; for to this day has the God of my fathers delivered me out of them all, and will deliver me from henceforth; for behold, and lo, I shall triumph over all my enemies, for the Lord God hath spoken it.

In May 1842 Joseph Smith was in hiding. An unknown assailant made an assassination attempt on Lilburn W. Boggs, the governor of Missouri who issued the extermination order against the Saints. The former governor, who had plenty of enemies that would have welcomed his demise, survived the attempt. But the Saints began to fear that Joseph would be extradited to Missouri, where his life would be in grave danger. In an attempt to stave off any attempts to forcibly arrest him and take his back to Missouri, Joseph Smith went into hiding. It was during a crucial time when Joseph was implementing the new practice of baptisms for the dead, so the Prophet wrote a letter giving the Saints further instructions.

But before he addressed the questions concerning baptisms for the dead, Joseph took a moment to address the tribulations that never seemed to leave the Saints. Rather than complaining about the inconvenience of going into hiding, Joseph rejoiced that he was persecuted for the cause of Christ. "I feel, like Paul, to glory in tribulation," he wrote. He response to these trials was similar to the ancient apostles, who were taken and beaten by the local Jewish leaders, but "departed from the presence of the council, rejoicing that they were counted worthy to suffer shame for his name" (Acts 5:41).

The response of Joseph and the New Testament apostles reminds us of a valuable principle. We cannot choose whether or not we will experience trials. But we can choose how we respond to those trials.

How do you response when you are faced with tribulation?

Day 313
Doctrine and Covenants 127:7

Why Is It Important Keep a Record of My Life?

> *That in all your recordings it may be recorded in heaven; whatsoever you bind on earth, may be bound in heaven; whatsoever you loose on earth, may be loosed in heaven.*

As the Saints settled in Nauvoo, they reflected on the losses they suffered in Missouri. Even as they mourned those lost in the persecutions, death came among them again, as the malarial swamps of the peninsula took more lives among the refugee Saints. The Saints knew that they would overcome death because of Jesus Christ and His Resurrection, but they also wondered about their loved ones who died without a chance to hear the restored gospel. Joseph Smith wrestled with these issues as well. He lost his father and his brother Don Carlos shortly after their arrival in Nauvoo. Joseph and Emma also lost an infant son during their time in Nauvoo. In addition, Joseph often reflected on the fate of his oldest brother, Alvin, who died before the Book of Mormon was translated and the Church was restored.

Many of these threads came together when Joseph delivered a sermon in the summer of 1840 at the funeral of Seymour Brunson. In his remarks, he read most of 1 Corinthians 15, where the ancient Apostle Paul refers to the practice of baptism for the dead. In the congregation was a woman named Jane Neyman, whose son, Cyrus, had died without baptism. A few days later Jane was baptized in behalf of her son in the Mississippi River. The practice caught on like wildfire among the Saints. Joseph wrote this letter to clarify that when baptisms for the dead were performed there must be a recorder present so the names of those baptized would not be lost.

Joseph taught that those whose names were recorded on earth would be recorded in heaven, remarking that "whatsoever you bind on earth, may be bound in heaven." This was the beginning of the great work of the Saints in family history. It is important for people to be remembered and even more important that everyone be given an invitation to make covenants with God.

How has temple work helped you remember your loved ones who have moved on?

Day 314
Doctrine and Covenants 127:8

How Were the Temple Ordinances Restored?

> *For I am about to restore many things to the earth, pertaining to the priesthood, saith the Lord of Hosts.*

Nauvoo was a great time of innovation in the Church. Joseph Smith began to understand the powers of the priesthood given by the heavenly messengers who visited him in the Kirtland Temple. As he began to understand the power he was given, he was anxious to use it to set a unique system of salvation allowing all people to open the doorway to heaven. In the spring of 1842, Joseph invited the first men to receive their endowments. This was before the completion of the Nauvoo Temple, so Joseph explained and carried out these ordinances in his red brick store in Nauvoo. During the following two years, Joseph performed the endowment for a number of men and women, instructing them to pass on what they had learned when the temple was finished to all the Saints who qualified.

This new system of salvation created a way for families to be together eternally. It looked to the future, but the system of temple ordinances also looked to the past. It aimed to created a new chain of salvation, linking the ancestors of the Saints to their current and future descendants. Doctrine and Covenants 127, a letter Joseph wrote to the Saints, began to outline this system of salvation that would transform the Church and eventually the whole world. In the temples of the last days, men and women, armed with priesthood power, began a work destined to save and influence the entire family of God.

How have the temple ordinances changed the way you see the living and the dead?

Day 315

Doctrine and Covenants 128:9

How Does Temple Work Help People on Both Sides of the Veil?

> *It may seem to some to be a very bold doctrine that we talk of—a power which records or binds on earth and binds in heaven.*

In the fall of 1842, Joseph Smith was still in hiding. He wrote in a letter to the Saints that the subject of baptism for the dead "seems to occupy my mind, and press itself upon my feelings the strongest, since I have been pursued by my enemies" (Doctrine and Covenants 128:1). Anxious to help the Saints understand the doctrine behind the practice, Joseph wrote this letter connecting the threads found in the Old and New Testaments surrounding work for the dead. Joseph in particular zeroed in on a promise the Savior made to the Apostle Peter: "I will give unto thee the keys of the kingdom of heaven: and whatsoever thou shalt bind on earth shall be bound in heaven: and whatsoever thou shalt loose on earth shall be loosed in heaven" (Matthew 16:19).

Joseph explained that the sealing power given to him by the ancient prophets who appeared in the Kirtland Temple gave the Saints priesthood power to reach the other side of the veil and perform work for their loved ones who had passed on to the next life. At the same time, the sealing power allowed God's authorized servants to perform ordinances here on earth that would still be in force after death. This power connects the living and the dead. It allows us a way to reach our loved ones who have passed on but also connect us with our loved ones still with us in a way that will endure beyond death.

How have you seen the sealing power affect you and your perspective on the next life?

Day 316

Doctrine and Covenants 128:13

What Is the Symbolism of Baptism for the Living and the Dead?

> *Consequently, the baptismal font was instituted as a similitude of the grave, and was commanded to be in a place underneath where the living are wont to assemble, to show forth the living and the dead, and that all things may have their likeness, and that they may accord one with another—that which is earthly conforming to that which is heavenly.*

Joseph Smith's letter on baptism for the dead explains the scriptural connections behind doing work on behalf of the deceased. It also shows that all ordinances have a connection in symbolizing the atoning act of Jesus Christ. As the Apostle Paul explained, baptism is a symbol of death, burial, and resurrection. "Therefore we are buried with him by baptism into death: that like as Christ was raised up from the dead by the glory of the Father, even so we also should walk in newness of life" (Romans 6:4). Baptism is symbolic not only of the death and resurrection of Jesus but also of our own death as a creature of sin and birth into a new life in Jesus Christ. The symbolism becomes even more potent when applied in a temple context, where we are baptized on behalf of someone who is literally dead and then given the promise of eternal life by entering into a covenant with God.

Baptism for the dead allows the living to experience their baptism again. We also assist those who have passed on by allowing them this opportunity to enter into a new relationship with Christ. Even if we don't go to the temple, when we take the sacrament in our Sunday services we are given a chance to renew the covenant in a simpler way. Taking the bread and the water of the sacrament allows us to enter into that special relationship all over again. Whether it is through our own baptism, the proxy baptism of another person, or the simple act of taking the sacrament, the end result is the same: a new life in Christ.

How have the ordinances of baptism, baptism for the dead, or the sacrament helped you experience a new life in Christ?

Day 317

Doctrine and Covenants 128:15

How Does Work for the Dead Help Save the Living?

> *And now, my dearly beloved brethren and sisters, let me assure you that these are principles in relation to the dead and the living that cannot be lightly passed over, as pertaining to our salvation. For their salvation is necessary and essential to our salvation, as Paul says concerning the fathers—that they without us cannot be made perfect—neither can we without our dead be made perfect.*

The revelations given in Nauvoo introduced a wonderful new system of bringing the whole human race, both the living and the dead, into a new relationship with God and Jesus Christ. Joseph Smith even went so far as to say that "their salvation is necessary and essential to our salvation." How is work for the dead essential to our salvation? Joseph also quotes another prophecy made in the scriptures about the last days, where the prophet Malachi testified that the proud and the wicked shall be burned and left with "neither root nor branch" (Malachi 4:1). One of the curses on those who deny the gospel is that they are left without a righteous ancestry (the roots) or a righteous posterity (the branch).

Doing work for the dead is one of the ways of connecting the roots and the branches. Some of my relatives, whom I love dearly, have passed on. Some of them were not active Church members. Instead of writing them off, as I grew older I studied their lives and found out that their stories were much more complicated than I first thought. There are a number of reasons the gospel may not connect with a person in this life. Even more important there is hope for everyone to find Christ in this life, or in the next. The hope we feel for our loved ones who have passed allows us to have hope for ourselves. Temple work for the dead allows us to create a wonderful circle of love between children and parents that grows into the eternities.

How do you think work for the dead is essential to your salvation?

Day 318

Doctrine and Covenants 128:21

Who Are the Angels of the Restoration?

> *And again, the voice of God in the chamber of old Father Whitmer, in Fayette, Seneca county, and at sundry times, and in divers places through all the travels and tribulations of this Church of Jesus Christ of Latter-day Saints! And the voice of Michael, the archangel; the voice of Gabriel, and of Raphael, and of divers angels, from Michael or Adam down to the present time, all declaring their dispensation, their rights, their keys, their honors, their majesty and glory, and the power of their priesthood; giving line upon line, precept upon precept; here a little, and there a little; giving us consolation by holding forth that which is to come, confirming our hope!*

Near the end of his letter explaining work for the dead, Joseph Smith allows himself to reflect on the glorious collection of visitors who assisted in bringing about the Restoration of the gospel of Jesus Christ in the last days. He mentions Michael, the archangel, identified in another revelation as Adam, the father of the human race (see Doctrine and Covenants 27:11). Then he speaks of Gabriel, the angel who told Mary that she would be the mother of the Savior (see Luke 1:26–27). He even mentions Raphael, an angel we know very little about but who is mentioned in the apocryphal books of the Bible.

On many Latter-day Saint temples there stands an angel who is identified as Moroni. But Moroni is only a nickname for the angel on temples. The angel was fashioned after the prophecy given by John the Revelator when he saw "another angel fly in the midst of heaven, having the everlasting gospel to preach unto them that dwell on the earth, and to every nation, and kindred, and tongue, and people" (Revelation 14:6). That angel, in turn, symbolizes all of the angels of the Restoration, a group including Moroni, John the Baptist, Peter, James, John, Michael, Gabriel, Raphael, and a host of others.

The work of restoration was the culmination of all of these angels visiting the earth and working in collaboration with mortal men and women to carry out this great work. The work continues today, and angels continue to assist us as we find the faith to serve God and carry out His work.

How does the work of the Church today connect to the work of these ancient prophets?

Day 319
Doctrine and Covenants 128:22

How Can I Have Courage to Go forward?

> *Brethren, shall we not go on in so great a cause? Go forward and not backward. Courage, brethren; and on, on to the victory! Let your hearts rejoice, and be exceedingly glad. Let the earth break forth into singing. Let the dead speak forth anthems of eternal praise to the King Immanuel, who hath ordained, before the world was, that which would enable us to redeem them out of their prison; for the prisoners shall go free.*

Joseph Smith ended his letter on work for the dead with a stirring call for the work to move forward, declaring, "Shall we not go on in so great a cause? Go forward and not backward. Courage, brethren; and on, on to the victory!" His words explain the fundamentally optimistic message of the Restoration. To put it another way, we have seen the end of the story, and we know the good guys win.

It can be difficult when caught up in the day-to-day challenges of our lives to lose sight of the great work that we are participating in. Once I had a visitor from another faith speak with a few of my students and then surprisingly remark, "Why, you really think you are going to save the world!"

That is what we think. We believe that the work begun with the first generation of Saints will continue until the world is prepared for the Second Coming of Christ. And then it will continue until everyone who is willing to be saved will be brought into the presence of God. We know we are going to win, so don't lose sight of that. It takes courage to stand up for what is right in a sinful world, but it helps to know that we are on the winning side.

How does the gospel help you have courage in your everyday life?

Day 320

Doctrine and Covenants 129:1–2

What Is an Angel?

> *There are two kinds of beings in heaven, namely: Angels, who are resurrected personages, having bodies of flesh and bones—*
>
> *For instance, Jesus said: Handle me and see, for a spirit hath not flesh and bones, as ye see me have.*

Angels have always been a central part of the restored gospel. We believe angels still appear in our day, that angels still minister to women and men on earth, and that angels helped restore the priesthood authorities needed to lead the Church. But what is an angel? The Hebrew word translated as angel in the Old Testament means "messenger." In other religions, angels are thought to be higher beings than humans. But in this revelation, we learn the true nature of angels. Angels are human beings in a different phase of their existence. As Joseph clarifies, "There are two kinds of beings in heaven, namely: Angels, who are resurrected personages . . . [and] secondly: the spirits of just men made perfect, they who are not resurrected, but inherit the same glory"

(Doctrine and Covenants 129:1, 3).

If an angels are messengers, their roles could extend beyond these two categories. An angel can be a premortal spirit, such as when the premortal Christ ministered to the brother of Jared in the Book of Mormon (see Ether 3:14–16). Angels can also be mortal men and women given a message or commission by God to share with other mortals. For instance, Joseph Smith's translation of the Bible refers to the messengers who appeared to Lot in the book of Genesis as "holy men" (see JST, Genesis 19:15).

There are angels in heaven, like Joseph described, and angels on earth. We can choose to be angels when we act as God's messengers here. But angels are really only one type of being—the children of God sent to accomplish His works.

Have you ever felt like you were called to serve as an angel of God?

Day 321
Doctrine and Covenants 129:3

How Are Angels Connected to Us?

> *Secondly: the spirits of just men made perfect, they who are not resurrected, but inherit the same glory.*

In his instructions on the nature of angels, Joseph next addresses that angels can be the spirits of just men and women made perfect. One of the earliest revelations given to Joseph Smith identified Michael, the archangel who defeated Satan, as "Adam, the father of all, the prince of all, the ancient of days" (Doctrine and Covenants 27:11). Other revelations identified the angels of the scriptures as mortal men who had returned to minister in angelic form. In a discourse given in Nauvoo, Joseph Smith identified the angel Gabriel as the ancient prophet Noah "who stands next in authority to Adam."[75] Latter-day Saints today take

75. Discourse, between circa 26 June and circa 4 August 1839–A, as reported by William Clayton, *The Joseph Smith Papers*, 11.

this concept for granted, ignoring the fact that in most other religions angels are seen as beings who are wholly separate from humanity.

Joseph's teaching that angels can be mortals not yet resurrected raised another intriguing possibility. Do the angels that minister to us know us? Are they connected to us? President Joseph F. Smith taught, "When messengers are sent to minister to the inhabitants of this earth, they are not strangers, but from the ranks of our kindred, friends, and fellow beings. Our fathers and mothers, brothers, sisters and friends who have passed away from this earth...bringing messages of love, warning, reproof and instruction, to those whom they had learned to love in the flesh."[76]

These angels are not separate from our story. They are a part of our story. They may be the people who loved us the most, and when we pass on we undoubtedly still minister to the people we love the most.

Have you ever felt influenced by the work of loved ones beyond the veil?

Day 322

Doctrine and Covenants 129:8–9

How Do the Laws of God Affect Angels and Devils?

> *If it be the devil as an angel of light, when you ask him to shake hands he will offer you his hand, and you will not feel anything; you may therefore detect him.*
>
> *These are three grand keys whereby you may know whether any administration is from God.*

On the surface, Doctrine and Covenants 129 may seem like the strangest section in the entire book! Most readers skip past what Joseph Smith was trying to teach about angels and go directly to the part where he teaches that if an angel appears you should ask to shake hands with him. If he is a resurrected person, you will feel flesh. If he is the spirit of a just man made perfect, he will decline your offer. But if he is an

76. Joseph F. Smith, *Gospel Doctrine,* 435–436.

evil spirit, "he will offer you his hand, and you will not feel anything; you may therefore detect him."

Listening to this section as a young student, I wondered, "Hasn't Satan read this section? Why does he keep falling for the old handshake trick?" It seems that a being as intelligent as Satan would quickly learn to lie or not shake hands and get past this quite easily. But in asking these questions, I think that I also missed the point of the Prophet's instructions.

Joseph's instructions are not about the gullibility of devils but the nature of eternal law and the balance of power in the universe. Satan and his followers don't decline to shake hands not because they haven't learned this trick yet but because they are still subject to law. They don't have a choice if they want to offer their hand. Joseph was teaching that God and Satan are not equal powers in the universe. He taught this in greater detail in one of his discourses where he declared, "It would seem also that wicked spirits have their bounds, limits, and laws by which they are governed or controlled, and know their future destiny."[77]

The struggle between God and Satan is not a struggle between equal powers. Satan will lose, God will triumph, and even now the powers of evil are only operating on limited time.

How have you found power in obeying the laws of God?

Day 323

Doctrine and Covenants 130:1,3

What Kind of Being Are the Father and the Son?

> *When the Savior shall appear we shall see him as he is. We shall see that he is a man like ourselves . . .*
>
> *John 14:23—The appearing of the Father and the Son, in that verse, is a personal appearance; and the idea that the Father and the Son dwell in a man's heart is an old sectarian notion, and is false.*

77. History, 1838–1856, volume C-1 [2 November 1838–31 July 1842], *The Joseph Smith Papers*, 1308.

In the Spring of 1843, Joseph Smith traveled with several other Church leaders to Ramus, Illinois, a small settlement where his sister, Sophronia McCleary, and a number of other close friends lived. During the stake conference, Orson Hyde, a member of the Quorum of the Twelve, preached a sermon based in part of 1 John 3:2, which reads, "Beloved, now are we the sons of God, and it doth not yet appear what we shall be: but we know that, when he shall appear, we shall be like him; for we shall see him as he is." Elder Hyde then taught, "It is our privilege to have the Father and the Son dwelling in our hearts."

After the meeting Joseph dined with Orson and his sister Sophronia, and offered to provide some corrections to Orson's earlier remarks. Orson replied that "they shall be thankfully received."[78] Joseph's corrections to Orson Hyde's statements largely make up the contents of Doctrine & Covenants 130. Joseph began by addressing the question of whether the Savior could dwell in our hearts. "When the Savior shall appear we shall see him as he is. We shall see that he is a man like ourselves." Joseph wanted to emphasize that Jesus is not a mystical spirit or force, but a person who experienced a mortal life and was resurrected, just like each of us will be.

Because of their great power, it can be easy for us to be overwhelmed in trying to understand who and what the Father and the Son really are. When Joseph Smith taught that Jesus Christ was "a man like ourselves" he was not trying to downplay the divinity of the Savior. He was trying to help us understand our divine potential as sons and daughters of divine parents. Jesus is the best-case scenario for every child of God. We will never attain the perfection that He did, but He can help us to grow, become more like Him, and eventually inherit all the Father has to offer us.

While saying that the Father and Son can dwell in our heart, is a nice notion on a symbolic and sentimental level, it also runs the risk of us losing our sense of our divine identity. We are the same kind of beings as God and Jesus Christ. We can become like them. This is the entire point of the Gospel of Jesus Christ.

How does it help you to know your divine heritage as a child of God?

78. Joseph Smith History, vol. D-1, p. 1510, Joseph Smith Papers.

Day 324

Doctrine and Covenants 130:1–2

What Is Sociality Like in the Next Life?

> *When the Savior shall appear we shall see him as he is. We shall see that he is a man like ourselves.*
>
> *And that same sociality which exists among us here will exist among us there, only it will be coupled with eternal glory, which glory we do not now enjoy.*

After correcting the teaching that the Father and Son can literally dwell in our hearts, Joseph provided one of his most expansive teachings about the nature of sociality in the next life. Joseph shared that "the same sociality which exists among us here will exist among us there, only it will be coupled with eternal glory."

This was revolutionary for the time. Most people of faith, then and now, believe that the next life will be nothing like this one. But Joseph taught that the best things in life, especially our relationships [sociality] will stay with us. There is no reason why a wife or a husband will not still love each other in the next life. Parents and children will still love one another, friendships will still exist, and all of the things that make life worth living can continue into the eternities. By this one simple statement, Joseph effectively doubled our knowledge of the next life, allowing us to see heaven as a real place where the trials of this life will fade from memory, and the joys of this life will be magnified, and we will finally begin our real life in the eternities.

Today we take for granted the notion that when we pass from this life our loved one will be waiting for us. But the idea that our family relationships and friendships will endure beyond this life was not commonly taught in the Christianity of Joseph Smith's day. It is comforting to know that rather than abandoning all earthly things, the best parts of this life come with us into the next life, where our love and relationships can endure and grow forever.

How does it help you to know your relationships will continue into the eternities?

Day 325
Doctrine and Covenants 130:14–17

What Is the Best Way to Approach the Second Coming?

I was once praying very earnestly to know the time of the coming of the Son of Man, when I heard a voice repeat the following:

Joseph, my son, if thou livest until thou art eighty-five years old, thou shalt see the face of the Son of Man; therefore let this suffice, and trouble me no more on this matter.

I was left thus, without being able to decide whether this coming referred to the beginning of the millennium or to some previous appearing, or whether I should die and thus see his face.

I believe the coming of the Son of Man will not be any sooner than that time.

Section 130 is effectively a Q&A in which the congregation asked questions and Joseph Smith gave his responses. Given that format, it is hardly surprising that Joseph eventually approached the question asked by believers in Christ since the earliest days: When will the Second Coming of Jesus Christ take place? Joseph knew more about the subject than most people and even spoke about a revelation he received while praying to know the answer. The way he approached this question is a good model for all of us to follow.

First, Joseph was given an answer. While praying, he was told, "Joseph, my son, if thou livest until thou art eighty-five years old, thou shalt see the face of the Son of Man; therefore let this suffice, and trouble me no more on this matter." Rather than just committing to one interpretation of this answer, Joseph remained flexible on what the meaning could be. Did this refer to the beginning of the Millennium? Was it just an appearance? Would he die at this age and therefore see the Savior? He didn't commit to any option and remained open to further revelation.

This cautious, measured approach is still best when talking about subjects in which we don't fully have the answers yet. Sometimes we can jump the gun when it comes to the signs of the times and the end of the world. But signs can be fulfilled in surprising ways. There is no doubt that the Savior will return, but there may be a good reason we don't know yet.

What did you learn from Joseph Smith's approach toward the Second Coming?

Day 326

Doctrine and Covenants 130:18

What Can I Take with Me to the Next Life?

Whatever principle of intelligence we attain unto in this life, it will rise with us in the resurrection.

There's a saying "you can't take it with you when you die." This is true of the material things we gain in this life. In the discourse Joseph Smith gave in Ramus, he emphasized that there are a few things you can take with you. First, you can take your family relationships. Joseph taught that "the same sociality that exists among us here will exist among us there" (Doctrine and Covenants 130:2). Second, you can take whatever intelligence you obtain in this life. Everything that we have learned in this life is not erased at death. There are untold wonders to learn in the next life.

Joseph was a strong believer in education and had a voracious curiosity for the world around him. But this is also found in the scriptures. The revelations given to Joseph repeatedly emphasized the importance of seeking learning (see Doctrine and Covenants 88:79–80; 93:36, 53). This emphasis on the importance of learning and growing remains an important part of our faith today. Elder Dieter F. Uchtdorf declared, "For members of the Church, education is not merely a good idea—it's a commandment."[79] We can gain intelligence through education and also through our "diligence and obedience" to the commandments. The lessons of this life carry into the next and help us travel further down the road to becoming like God.

What experiences have helped you gain greater intelligence?

---

79. Dieter F. Uchtdorf, "Two Principles for Any Economy," *Ensign*, November 2009.

Day 327
Doctrine and Covenants 130:20–21

What Is the Purpose of Eternal Law?

There is a law, irrevocably decreed in heaven before the foundations of this world, upon which all blessings are predicated—

And when we obtain any blessing from God, it is by obedience to that law upon which it is predicated.

The revelations in the Doctrine and Covenants often speak of law. To God, the moral laws that govern our existence are as unchangeable as the laws of physics we observe every day. God's law oversee all aspects of our existence, from the movement of planets (see Alma 30:44; Doctrine and Covenants 88:42) to to the salvation of His sons and daughters (see 2 Nephi 9:25). Joseph Smith teaches here that our blessings are based on our obedience to God's law. But there is another factor that also affects the way the law governs us, God's love.

Because God loves His children, He gave His Only Begotten Son "to answer the ends of the law, unto all those who have a broken heart and a contrite spirit" (2 Nephi 2:7). Through the work of Jesus Christ, God found a way to obey the law but also offer mercy to His children. When we obey the law, we are simply recognizing the way the universe works. Learning about these laws and mastering them helps us gain mastery over ourselves and eventually gain the kind of mastery God holds over all the universe. Joseph Smith taught on another occasion, "God has made certain decrees which are fixed, and immovable, for instance; God set the sun, the moon, and the stars in the heavens; and gave them their laws, conditions and bounds which they cannot pass, except by his commandments; they all move in perfect harmony in their sphere, and order, and are as lights, wonders, and signs unto us."[80]

When have you seen blessings because you chose to obey God's laws?

80. History, 1838–1856, volume C-1 [2 November 1838–31 July 1842], *The Joseph Smith Papers*, 1296.

Day 328

Doctrine and Covenants 130:22

What Is the Nature of the Godhead?

> *The Father has a body of flesh and bones as tangible as man's; the Son also; but the Holy Ghost has not a body of flesh and bones, but is a personage of Spirit. Were it not so, the Holy Ghost could not dwell in us.*

God the Father has a physical body. You could give Him a hug if you were in His presence. This teaching is taken for granted today by most Church members, but it was a radical departure from Christian thought in Joseph Smith's time. This teaching comes from direct revelation, stretching all the way back to the the first appearance of the Father and the Son to Joseph Smith in 1820. John Alger, an early Church member, even recalled hearing the Prophet relate that "God touched his eye with his finger and said, 'Joseph, this is my beloved Son hear him.'" Alger remembered Joseph saying that "as soon as the Lord had touched his eyes with his finger he immediately saw the Savior." Alger even recalled seeing Joseph put his finger to his right eye to illustrate how the Father had physically touched him.[81]

In the last sermons of his life, Joseph Smith emphasized the connection between mortal men and women and God in heaven. God's physical body was a way of teaching that God is not a mystical, unknowable force in the universe but a loving father who is deeply concerned with the lives of His children. In one of his final sermons Joseph taught, "God who sits in yonder heavens is a man like yourselves That GOD if you were to see him to day that holds the worlds you would see him like a man in form, like yourselves."[82]

If we really want to know God, we have to know what He is like.

---

81. Diary of Charles Lowell Walker, as told by John Alger, see https://www.fairlatterdaysaints.org/answers/Multiple_accounts_of_the_First_Vision.
82. Discourse, 7 April 1844, as Reported by Wilford Woodruff, *The Joseph Smith Papers*, 134.

He, the Savior, and the Holy Ghost all show what our potential is if we choose to walk the covenant path and enter in His glory.

How does it affect your view of the Father and the Son to know They have physical bodies?

Day 329

Doctrine and Covenants 131:1–3

What Is the New And Everlasting Covenant of Marriage?

> *In the celestial glory there are three heavens or degrees;*
> *And in order to obtain the highest, a man must enter into this order of the priesthood [meaning the new and everlasting covenant of marriage];*
> *And if he does not, he cannot obtain it.*

In May 1843 Joseph Smith visited the home of his close friends Benjamin and Melissa Johnson and told the couple about a marriage that could last beyond this life. Benjamin later recalled, "In the evening he called me and my wife to come and sit down, for he wished to marry us according to the Law of the Lord. I thought it a joke, and said I should not marry my wife again, unless she courted me, for I did it all the first time. He chided my levity, told me he was in earnest, and so it proved, for we stood up and were sealed by the Holy Spirit of Promise."[83]

This simple teaching introduced in the home of one loving couple eventually became one of the most important teachings of the Church. Marriage, love, and eternal relationships do not need to end at death. Joseph even described marriage as an "order of the priesthood" that men and women can enter into together. This order of the priesthood allows our most cherished relationships to continue into the eternities.

How has the knowledge that families can be eternal affected your outlook on life?

---

83. Benjamin Johnson, *My Life's Review*, 96, https://archive.org/stream/BenjaminFJohnsonMyLifesReview/Benjamin+F+Johnson+My+Lifes+Review_djvu.txt

Day 330
Doctrine and Covenants 131:5
What Is the More Sure Word of Prophecy?

(May 17th, 1843.) The more sure word of prophecy means a man's knowing that he is sealed up unto eternal life, by revelation and the spirit of prophecy, through the power of the Holy Priesthood.

Doctrine and Covenants 131:5 was taken from a sermon Joseph Smith gave in Ramus, Illinois, on May 17, 1843. During the sermon, Joseph made reference to 2 Peter 1:19, which reads, "We have also a more sure word of prophecy; whereunto ye do well that ye take heed, as unto a light that shineth in a dark place, until the day dawn, and the day star arise in your hearts." Joseph then remarked that Peter was alluding to a promise of a "man's knowing that he is sealed up unto eternal life." In another passage Peter exhorted the Saints to "make your calling and election sure" (2 Peter 1:10).

Joseph taught that the "more sure word of prophecy" and "having your calling and election made sure" both referred to receiving an assurance from the Lord that you would gain eternal life. Receiving this promise is rare, but it can happen to faithful Church members. On another occasion Joseph remarked that those who had this promise relied on it during times of extreme trials. He taught that "having this promise sealed unto them, it was as an anchor to the soul, sure and steadfast though the thunders might roll; and lightnings flash, and earthquakes bellow, and war gather thick around. Yet this hope and knowledge would support the soul in every hour of trial trouble & tribulation."[84]

Even without formally receiving this promise, every person who remains true to their covenants can expect to have their calling and election made sure after this life. God always keeps His promises, and each one of us has the promise of eternal life if we remain true to our covenants.

How do your covenants sustain you through trials?

---

84. Discourse, 14 May 1843, as Reported by Wilford Woodruff, *The Joseph Smith Papers*, 32; punctuation added.

Day 331
Doctrine and Covenants 131:7–8

What Is the Nature of Matter?

There is no such thing as immaterial matter. All spirit is matter, but it is more fine or pure, and can only be discerned by purer eyes;

We cannot see it; but when our bodies are purified we shall see that it is all matter.

In his sermon given in Ramus, Joseph Smith continued to expound on a theme that runs through the entire Doctrine and Covenants, namely, the connection between the spiritual and the material. In many revelations, the Lord emphasizes that separating the two is an artificial way of seeing the world. Some people may be tempted to see some commandments, such as tithing or the Word of Wisdom, as material. Some may see other actions, such as praying or pondering, as spiritual. The Lord erases the boundary between the two. In an early revelation to Joseph, the Lord declared, "I gave unto him that he should be an agent unto himself; and I gave unto him commandment, but no temporal commandment gave I unto him, for my commandments are spiritual; they are not natural nor temporal, neither carnal nor sensual" (Doctrine and Covenants 29:35).

Another revelation to Joseph spoke of the eternal nature of matter. "For man is spirit. The elements are eternal, and spirit and element, inseparably connected, receive a fulness of joy" (Doctrine and Covenants 93:33). This ties back to the blessing of having a physical body. We typically speak of the spiritual part of us to be eternal, but the Resurrection of Jesus Christ is meant to unite us forever with a perfect physical body that will also last in the eternities. In the end, because of the Savior, every part of us will be eternal, lasting as long as the universe itself lasts.

What are some of the blessings you find in having a physical body?

Day 332
Doctrine and Covenants 132:19

What Are the Promises Made in the New and Everlasting Covenant?

And again, verily I say unto you, if a man marry a wife by my word, which is my law, and by the new and everlasting covenant, and it is sealed unto them by the Holy Spirit of promise, by him who is anointed, unto whom I have appointed this power and the keys of this priesthood; and it shall be said unto them—Ye shall come forth in the first resurrection; and if it be after the first resurrection, in the next resurrection; and shall inherit thrones, kingdoms, principalities, and powers, dominions, all heights and depths.

This revelation, given in July 1843, introduces two of the most well-known and controversial teachings in the history of the Church: eternal marriage and plural marriage. Plural marriage is no longer practiced by the Church, but both teachings are based on the ideas that our relationships with the people we love will continue in the next life. Heaven just isn't heaven without the people who matter to us most.

The new and everlasting covenant explained in this section is the culmination of all of the promises made in the scriptures. It spells out what our ultimate purpose is for our existence. God wants to give us everything that He has. He isn't jealous of His power or His dominions. The purpose of our life is to help us become like Him. For men, it means becoming a divine father. For women, it means becoming a divine mother. For both together, the new and everlasting covenants made between a man, a woman, and God signify the beginning of a new universe. We see these divine couples here on earth only a few years into their ultimate destiny, which is to find a life like the one our Heavenly Parents enjoy.

How do you find meaning in the new and everlasting covenant?

Day 333
Doctrine and Covenants 132:24

What Does It Mean to Gain Eternal Lives?

This is eternal lives—to know the only wise and true God, and Jesus Christ, whom he hath sent. I am he. Receive ye, therefore, my law.

At the beginning of my teaching career, I had a box that students could put questions in. Every few weeks when we had extra time we would pull questions out of the box and answer a few. The questions always surprised me, especially because most of them weren't about historical or doctrinal controversies that I always wondered about. One of the most common questions to show up in the box was, "Will heaven be boring?" My students didn't doubt that there was a heaven, but they wondered how a person could stay sane just sitting on a cloud and singing praises all the day long.

In this revelation, God defines exaltation as eternal lives. The implication is that if we achieve exaltation we become like God Himself. When my students would ask if heaven is boring, I would to ask back, "Well, do you think God is bored?" To obtain eternal lives means to become like God and take on the responsibility of shepherding your own eternal sons and daughters through the plan of salvation. It is most certainly not boring. It is the kind of life where we find the greatest fulfillment and joy. Because of Jesus Christ and His atoning sacrifice, we gain an eternal life of meaning and service. It becomes the kind of life where we have achieved a fulness for ourselves, and we live a life of service helping others to achieve their full potential.

What do you most look forward to about exaltation?

Day 334

Doctrine and Covenants 132:49–50

What Are the Blessings of Abraham?

For I am the Lord thy God, and will be with thee even unto the end of the world, and through all eternity; for verily I seal upon you your exaltation, and prepare a throne for you in the kingdom of my Father, with Abraham your father.

Behold, I have seen your sacrifices, and will forgive all your sins; I have seen your sacrifices in obedience to that which I have told you. Go, therefore, and I make a way for your escape, as I accepted the offering of Abraham of his son Isaac.

Eternal marriage also brought along with it the severe test of plural marriage. The Lord compared the Saints who entered into this practice to Abraham for a number of reasons. Abraham also entered into plural marriage as part of the fulfillment to gain an innumerable posterity. Abraham was given an extreme test. He was asked to give up his only son, Isaac. Ultimately the Lord was only testing Abraham's faith, and the sacrifice of Isaac was not required. But when it came to plural marriage, the Lord did ask difficult sacrifices of the men and women who entered into the practice.

This new covenant was a considerable sacrifice for the early Saints, especially the women involved. Zina Diantha Huntington recalled, "When I heard that God had revealed the law of celestial marriage—that we would have the privilege of associating in family relationship in the worlds to come—I searched the scriptures, and by humble prayer to my Heavenly Father I obtained a testimony for [my]self that God had required that order to be established in his church. I made a greater sacrifice than to give my life, for I never anticipated to again to be looked upon as an honorable woman by those I dearly loved." She then added, "[But] I how could I compromise conscience [and] lay aside the sure testimony of the spirit of God? . . . I heard the words of the Prophet of God saying, at King Follett's funeral, 'All you Saints that will not oppose the doctrine that God reveals through me, I will see that you enter celestial glory.' His teachings were in every respect to benefit the human family."[85]

The Lord does not ask this sacrifice of His Saints today. But He does ask us to do hard things. Living the gospel is not easy, but when we make the sacrifices we are called to make, we can find strength within us we never knew we had.

What sacrifices have you been called to make for the gospel?

Day 335

Doctrine and Covenants 133:2–3

Why Will the Second Coming Be a Surprise to Some People?

> *The Lord who shall suddenly come to his temple; the Lord who shall come down upon the world with a curse to judgment; yea, upon all the nations that forget God, and upon all the ungodly among you.*
>
> *For he shall make bare his holy arm in the eyes of all the nations, and all the ends of the earth shall see the salvation of their God.*

This revelation was actually received the same day that Doctrine and Covenants 1 was received. Sections 1 and 133 were intended to be the bookends of the Doctrine and Covenants. When the book was first published in 1835, section 1 introduced the reader to the Restoration, and section 133 was placed at the end as an appendix to the book. Doctrine and Covenants 133 is a revelation detailing with the signs of the times leading up to the Second Coming of Jesus Christ, and it contains some of the most detailed descriptions of that event found anywhere in scripture.

One word that jumps out at the reader is *sudden*. The section begins by explaining that the Lord will suddenly come to His temple. We are not sure which temple this prophecy is speaking of, but the implication is that His appearance will be a surprise to most of the people. With so many other detailed signs leading up to the Second Coming,

85. Autobiographical Sketches, [1] MS 4780, Church History Library.

how can His appearance be that much of a surprise? To those who have watched the signs carefully, it seems that the immediate moment will be a surprise, not the event itself. However, most of the world will ignore the signs because of unbelief, and His coming will be quite a shock to them. The prophecy states that the Lord will "make bare his holy arm in the eyes of all the nations," suggesting that it will be an event that everyone on earth will be aware of. It will be a great day for some and a terrible day for others. For all men and women it will signal the end of the world of strife and wickedness that we now live in as we move into a world of peace and fulfillment.

What signs of the Second Coming do you see being fulfilled in our time?

Day 336
Doctrine and Covenants 133:8

What Can We Do to Prepare for the Second Coming?

> *Send forth the elders of my church unto the nations which are afar off; unto the islands of the sea; send forth unto foreign lands; call upon all nations, first upon the Gentiles, and then upon the Jews.*

While Doctrine and Covenants 133 suggests that the coming of the Savior will happen suddenly, it also crafts a narrative in which the Saints are working to prepare the world for His return. It does not depict the Saints as just waiting around, watching the world crumble while we wait for a better one to arrive. Instead, the Saints are shown sending forth missionaries to different countries and trying to gather in as many people as possible before the Savior's return. This approach demonstrates two different ways of seeing the Second Coming. First, it is something we are waiting for, and second it is something we are preparing for. Those who are waiting will find less fulfillment than those who work with all their might to prepare the way for the Lord's return.

The Saints were never intended to be on the sidelines in the days leading up to the Second Coming. Instead, the Lord intended His disciples to be in the midst of the fight, doing all they can to bring about righteousness and prepare the way for the Savior. When we read the scriptures, we often focus on the gloom and doom prophecies of upheaval and destructions and overlook the prophecies about the gathering, the building of Zion, and the spread of the gospel. In the times leading up to the Second Coming there will be no shortage of tasks for the Saints to accomplish. We can sit and wait for the end to come, or we can join the fight right now to make the earth a place fit for the King of Kings.

What can you do to help prepare the world for the Second Coming?

Day 337
Doctrine and Covenants 133:53

How Can I Experience the Second Coming Right Now?

> *In all their afflictions he was afflicted. And the angel of his presence saved them; and in his love, and in his pity, he redeemed them, and bore them, and carried them all the days of old.*

Section 133 adds a number of fascinating details to our knowledge of the Savior's Second Coming. For instance, the section reveals that when the Lord appears He will "be red in his apparel, and his garments like him that treadeth in a wine-vat." The Savior will explain His appearance by declaring, "I have trodden the wine-press alone, and have brought judgment upon all people; and none were with me" (Doctrine and Covenants 133:48–50).

But when the Lord meets His disciples, as the revelation says, they will not be thinking of their glorious future with the Savior on the earth but of the past times when He helped them through their trials. The prophecy reads, "They shall mention that loving kindness of their Lord, and all that he has bestowed upon them according to his goodness . . . in all their afflictions he was afflicted. . . . He redeemed them, and bore them, and carried them all the days of old" (Doctrine and Covenants 133:50–53).

This suggests that we don't have to wait for the Second Coming to experience the Savior's salvation or goodness. He can help us and carry us right now. The truth is that while the Second Coming is a real event that will happen in the future, the Savior can be an active presence in our life right now.

How can you make the Savior an active presence in your life?

Day 338

Doctrine and Covenants 134:1

What Is the Purpose of Government?

> *We believe that governments were instituted of God for the benefit of man; and that he holds men accountable for their acts in relation to them, both in making laws and administering them, for the good and safety of society.*

Doctrine and Covenants 133 is not a revelation but an inspired declaration that outlines the relationship of churches and governments. We do not know who wrote the declaration, but most scholars point to Oliver Cowdery because of similarities to other documents he wrote. We also don't know how involved Joseph Smith was in the writing of the declaration, but he wholeheartedly endorsed its contents. Several years after the declaration was written, Joseph included it in its entirety in a letter written to the Chester County *Register and Examiner*. He made no changes to the declaration, except he replaced all "we believe" statements with "I believe."

The statement "we believe that governments were institute of God for the benefit of man" does not teach that we believe that all governments have been instituted of God. Some governments have carried our horrific atrocities and abused the trust and resource of their people. But we do believe that government can be a force for good if it is guided by men and women who follow true principles. Throughout the history of the Church, the Saints have been encouraged to be involved in the governments of their countries.

Despite the many challenges and obstacles in creating good and fair governance, we should be a part of the conversation. If the Lord intends to build Zion, there are a number of ways to accomplish that goal, beginning in our own homes and communities.

How can you get more involved in your local community?

Day 339
Doctrine and Covenants 134:4

What Is the Purpose of Religion?

> *We believe that religion is instituted of God; and that men are amenable to him, and to him only, for the exercise of it, unless their religious opinions prompt them to infringe upon the rights and liberties of others; but we do not believe that human law has a right to interfere in prescribing rules of worship to bind the consciences of men, nor dictate forms for public or private devotion; that the civil magistrate should restrain crime, but never control conscience; should punish guilt, but never suppress the freedom of the soul.*

This inspired declaration also states, "We believe that religion is instituted of God." Again, that does not mean all religions were instituted of God. Unfortunately, religion has been the source of much strife, contention, and suffering. False and apostate religious traditions have caused untold conflicts through the history of mankind. When religion is misused, it can be a source for evil.

Acknowledging that, there is also much good that religion has brought to the world. People in nearly all faith traditions have worked to help their brothers and sister free themselves from poverty, suffering, and ignorance. Latter-day Saints are part of the true Church of Jesus Christ, but we do not hold the monopoly on truth. God loves His children in our faiths, and before we see the bad in other faiths, we need to see the good. Men and women of faith all over the world work every day to make things better for the people around them. Those who are sincere in their religious beliefs will have a place in God's mansions when the end times come.

In the meantime, we can help by reaching out to people of goodwill in all faiths and inviting them to help us see the good, build Zion, and prepare the world for the Second Coming.

What can you do to reach out someone of another religion?

Day 340

Doctrine and Covenants 135:1

How Did Joseph and Hyrum Smith Seal Their Testimonies?

> *To seal the testimony of this book and the Book of Mormon, we announce the martyrdom of Joseph Smith the Prophet, and Hyrum Smith the Patriarch. They were shot in Carthage jail, on the 27th of June, 1844, about five o'clock p.m., by an armed mob—painted black—of from 150 to 200 persons. Hyrum was shot first and fell calmly, exclaiming: I am a dead man! Joseph leaped from the window, and was shot dead in the attempt, exclaiming: O Lord my God! They were both shot after they were dead, in a brutal manner, and both received four balls.*

Doctrine and Covenants 135 serves as a capstone to the lives and ministries of Joseph and Hyrum Smith. It was long attributed to John Taylor, but the introductory heading was revised in the 2013 edition of the Doctrine and Covenants because John never claimed sole authorship, though he probably assisted in writing it. John, along with Willard Richards, was in the jail at the time of the attack and was badly wounded by the mob who stormed the jail. Both he and Willard produced accounts of what happened that fateful day in June 1844, and each reads as a vivid final testimony of the Restoration by Joseph and Hyrum.

According to Doctrine and Covenants 135, Joseph and Hyrum were both reading and studying from the Book of Mormon while they were in Carthage Jail. It even mentions a passage they read in the jail, found in Ether 12. The passage reads in part, "And it came to pass that I prayed unto the Lord that he would give unto the Gentiles grace, that they might have charity. And it came to pass that the Lord said unto me: If they have not charity it mattereth not unto thee, thou hast been faithful; wherefore thy garments shall be made clean" (Ether 12:5). Even in the face of certain death, they continued to share their testimony with the guards in the jail and study from the scriptures revealed to Joseph. Their final acts show the sincerity of their testimony and their faith in Jesus Christ.

If you had to face a trial like Joseph and Hyrum in Carthage Jail, how do you think your testimony would hold up?

Day 341

Doctrine and Covenants 135:3

What Was the Mission of Joseph Smith?

> *Joseph Smith, the Prophet and Seer of the Lord, has done more, save Jesus only, for the salvation of men in this world, than any other man that ever lived in it. In the short space of twenty years, he has brought forth the Book of Mormon, which he translated by the gift and power of God, and has been the means of publishing it on two continents; has sent the fulness of the everlasting gospel, which it contained, to the four quarters of the earth; has brought forth the revelations and commandments which compose this book of Doctrine and Covenants, and many other wise documents and instructions for the benefit of the children of men; gathered many thousands of the Latter-day Saints, founded a great city, and left a fame and name that cannot be slain. He lived great, and he died great in the eyes of God and his people; and like most of the Lord's anointed in ancient times, has sealed his mission and his works with his own blood; and so has his brother Hyrum. In life they were not divided, and in death they were not separated!*

While Jesus Christ is the central figure of our religion, the Restoration of the gospel through the Prophet Joseph Smith is also a critical part of our faith. Doctrine and Covenants 135:3 is one of the finest summaries of Joseph's importance in the Restoration. However, some aspects of his mission go even beyond this text. For instance, Joseph presided over the construction of the first two temples of this dispensation, with hundreds more to follow. Inside those sacred buildings, the ordinances revealed to Joseph Smith continue to allow millions of people, living and dead, to make covenants with God. With nearly two hundred years of hindsight, the mission of Joseph Smith continues to grow in importance. As the gospel continues to spread and grow around the world, Joseph's importance only becomes more clear.

But as important as Joseph Smith is as a historical figure, perhaps his greatest contribution was in helping us to understand the salvational mission of Jesus Christ. The teachings about Christ found in the Book of Mormon, Doctrine and Covenants, and Pearl of Great Price set forth in a clear manner how the entire plan of salvation rises and falls on the perfect life and sacrifice of Jesus. The revelations given to Joseph Smith make clear that Christ was chosen even in the premortal realms, served as a perfect and infinite sacrifice here on earth, and continues as an active presence in the lives of all men and women. Serving as a witness of Jesus Christ is and always will be the most important aspect of Joseph Smith's mission.

How is your life different because of the mission of Joseph Smith?

Day 342
Doctrine and Covenants 135:6

What Was the Cost of the Restoration?

Hyrum Smith was forty-four years old in February, 1844, and Joseph Smith was thirty-eight in December, 1843; and henceforward their names will be classed among the martyrs of religion; and the reader in every nation will be reminded that the Book of Mormon, and this book of Doctrine and Covenants of the church, cost the best blood of the nineteenth century to bring them forth for the salvation of a ruined world; and that if the fire can scathe a green tree for the glory of God, how easy it will burn up the dry trees to purify the vineyard of corruption. They lived for glory; they died for glory; and glory is their eternal reward. From age to age shall their names go down to posterity as gems for the sanctified.

News of the death of Joseph and Hyrum Smith reached Nauvoo quickly, leaving the Saints in a state of shock and disbelief. After all of the close calls over the years, many believed that it was not possible for Joseph and Hyrum to truly be gone. The day after the martyrdom, the bodies of the Prophet and Patriarch arrived in Nauvoo, and funeral arrangements were made. Many had believed that the Lord would not allow the Prophet to be killed. In a revelation given to Brigham Young, the Lord explained the reasons He did not intervene to prevent the deaths of Joseph and Hyrum: "Many have marveled because of his death; but it was needful that he should seal his testimony with his blood, that he might be honored and the wicked might be condemned" (Doctrine and Covenants 136:39).

Dying for what they believed in was the ultimate sign of their sincerity in their beliefs. The authors of Doctrine and Covenants 135 alluded to this teaching in the epistle to the Hebrews, which reads, "For where a testament is, there must also of necessity be the death of the testator. For a testament is of force after men are dead: otherwise it is of no strength at all while the testator liveth" (Hebrews 9:16–17). While the murder of Joseph and Hyrum Smith is a tragedy, their lives are a testament to the Restoration. The testaments brought forth through the labors remain a testament to us today of the power of God to work miracles through ordinary men and women.

How can you demonstrate the sincerity of your testimony?

Day 343

Doctrine and Covenants 136:4

How Do Covenants Help Us Face Trials?

And this shall be our covenant—that we will walk in all the ordinances of the Lord.

The deaths of Joseph and Hyrum Smith meant that the Saints living in Nauvoo and the surrounding areas were on borrowed time. For a time after the martyrdom, the persecution against the Saints abated. But when it became clear that the Church would not disintegrate after the deaths of its beloved leaders, the mobs renewed their efforts to force the Saints from their homes. This revelation was received while the Saints were in exile, living in camps stretched out across Iowa and at a hastily assembled settlement called Winter Quarters in Nebraska. In these trying times Brigham Young received the only revelation of his that is now in the Doctrine and Covenants. With the very survival of the Church at stake, the Lord reminded the Saints where the true source of their power lay—in the strength of their covenants.

Before the Saints left Nauvoo, they labored to complete the temple. Knowing they would only enjoy the temple for a brief season before they departed into the wilderness, Brigham Young and the other Apostles brought as many people as possible through the temple. For a time the temple was in continuous operation. Because of their efforts, more than six thousand Saints received their blessings in the temple before they left Nauvoo. Shortly after the main body of Saints left the city, the temple fell victim to an arsonist who set fire to the sacred structure. But it was not the temple that gave the Saints strength—it was the covenants they made with the Lord. The covenants they made to consecrate what they had, live the law of the gospel, and love and serve God carried them across a continent to found a new city and build hundreds of temple around the world.

Those same covenants and ordinances continue to provide courage and fortitude to the Saints in our time.

How do you find strength in your covenants?

Day 344

Doctrine and Covenants 136:8

How Do I Bear an Equal Proportion?

Let each company bear an equal proportion, according to the dividend of their property, in taking the poor, the widows, the fatherless, and the families of those who have gone into the army, that the cries of the widow and the fatherless come not up into the ears of the Lord against this people.

The journey of the Saints to the West took place primarily in two stages. The first stage was the trip across Iowa in the spring of 1846. By nearly every measure, the trek across Iowa was a near-disaster. Uneven departures, an unusually wet spring, and general disorganization left the Saints scattered across the three hundred miles of prairie between the Mississippi and Missouri Rivers. Some leaders had hoped to go all the way to the Rocky Mountains in 1846, but the trials of Iowa left the Saints straggling into camps across the trail by the time cold weather set in, too exhausted to go much further.

The turning point came when the Lord spoke to Brigham Young at Winter Quarters in Nebraska. Brigham was instructed to organize the Saints into companies, appoint captains, and emphasize the covenants of consecration made in the Nauvoo Temple. Rather than every man or family for themselves, the Saints organized to help the least among them first. They were commanded to look after the widow, the fatherless, and the incomplete families among them and help them make the trek. Placing the the kingdom of God first, the second phase of the trek west went from being the Saints' darkest hour to their finest hour.

What can you do to assist the widows, fatherless, and others in need in your stewardship?

Day 345

Doctrine and Covenants 136:31

How Do Trials Prepare Me for Greater Things?

My people must be tried in all things, that they may be prepared to receive the glory that I have for them, even the glory of Zion; and he that will not bear chastisement is not worthy of my kingdom.

This revelation was received at a time of extreme trial for the Saints. Forced from their homes in Nauvoo, fleeing the United States in the wilderness, and struggling just to survive, some wondered if the Lord had forsaken them. But trials aren't always a sign that you have done something wrong. Sometimes they are a sign that you are being prepared for something greater. God loves all of His children, but He also knows that at times growth happens more quickly in difficult circumstances than in easy ones. The Saints in Winter Quarters would go on to found hundreds of settlements in the Rocky Mountains and lay the foundation for a worldwide movement that exists in hundreds of nations today. They went through a refining process along the way that shaped them into a mighty people.

Think of the times in your life when you have experienced the most growth. Was it when things were easy? While we don't seek out trials, the Lord can use them to shape and refine us. Chastisement sometimes comes because of our own foolish actions and sometimes because the Lord sees us as ready for something greater. Remember that when you are experiencing challenges it might be because you are being shaped and molded into the kind of disciple the Lord can use to perform great works.

What challenges in your life have really helped you to grow?

Day 346

Doctrine and Covenants 137:5–6

How Can I Have Hope for My Loved Ones?

I saw Father Adam and Abraham; and my father and my mother; my brother Alvin, that has long since slept;

And marveled how it was that he had obtained an inheritance in that kingdom, seeing that he had departed this life before the Lord had set his hand to gather Israel the second time, and had not been baptized for the remission of sins.

Though section 137 is a relatively new addition to the Doctrine and Covenants, it was received in 1836 and has been known for nearly two hundred years. During the Pentecostal season surrounding the Kirtland Temple, Joseph Smith and several other priesthood holders were participating in the washings and anointings given in the Kirtland Temple. As Joseph participated in these sacred rites, the heavens were opened and Joseph Smith saw the celestial kingdom. He saw in vision the Father and the Son, surrounded by glory. Next he saw Adam and Abraham, two of the most valiant men to have ever lived. Then he saw his own father and mother. Since Joseph's father was with him in the room where he was seeing the vision, this must have been a vision of the future, after his father and mother had passed on to the next life.

Then came the most surprising part of the vision. Joseph saw his brother Alvin, who died in 1823, seven years before the Church was restored. Joseph had always felt pangs of guilt over his brother's death because Alvin didn't have a chance to join the Church. On his deathbed, Alvin had urged Joseph to do all he could to obtain the gold plates and carry out the work God had given him. Now Joseph was seeing his brother in the celestial kingdom, standing next to the Father, the Son, Adam and Abraham. There was hope after all.

It is sometimes easy to give up hope for people. But in the first temple of this dispensation Joseph learned that hope is never lost for the ones we love. There is a way to reach everyone, even those who have passed on. We never give up because with Jesus Christ there is always hope.

How has the gospel given you hope for your loved ones?

Day 347

Doctrine and Covenants 137:7–8

What Happens to Those Who Never Hear the Gospel?

Thus came the voice of the Lord unto me, saying: All who have died without a knowledge of this gospel, who would have received it if they had been permitted to tarry, shall be heirs of the celestial kingdom of God;

Also all that shall die henceforth without a knowledge of it, who would have received it with all their hearts, shall be heirs of that kingdom.

During Joseph Smith's vision of the celestial kingdom, he saw the Father and the Son, Adam, Abraham, his own mother and father, and his brother Alvin. Knowing the scriptures, Joseph wondered how this was possible when the Lord explained that "all who have died without a knowledge of the this gospel, who would have received it if they had been permitted to tarry, shall be heirs of the celestial kingdom of God." This was clearly in contradiction to other passages found in the scriptures. For instance, Jesus taught that "except a man be born of water and of the spirit, he cannot enter into the kingdom of God" (John 3:5).

Joseph wasn't given the solution to this contradiction at the time. He was only presented with the hope that there was a way for his brother to enter the celestial kingdom. Later in Nauvoo all the pieces came together and Joseph was able to use them to construct our system of temple worship that allows for all men and women, regardless of their background, to have an opportunity to make covenants with God.

It is often the same for us. The Lord doesn't present the whole solution to the problem. He just gives us a few pieces of the puzzle and some encouragement. Then He helps us find our solutions. For Joseph the solution was the most inclusive teaching of the Church: there is a way for all people to be saved. With the Lord there is always a way.

What is a problem you are facing right now? Has the Lord given the pieces to find a solution?

Day 348

Doctrine and Covenants 137:10

What Happens to Children Who Die Before the Age of Accountability?

And I also beheld that all children who die before they arrive at the years of accountability are saved in the celestial kingdom of heaven.

Joseph Smith not only faced the heartache of losing an older brother but also faced the heartache of losing several of his children. He and Emma lost their first child, a son, in 1828 during childbirth. They also lost their next set of children, a pair of twins, in childbirth in 1831. Following this they lost one of their adopted twins, a little boy named Joseph Murdock Smith, who died of measles exacerbated by a mob attack in 1832. The first Smith child to make it to adulthood was Julia Murdock Smith, their other adopted twin. Emma then gave birth to three boys, Joseph Smith III, Frederick Smith, and Alexander Smith, who all survived to adulthood. Next, the Smiths welcomed another baby boy, named Don Carlos after Joseph's brother, who died when he was about eighteen months old. In 1842 they welcomed an unnamed son who was stillborn. Their final child together was David Hyrum Smith, who Emma was carrying when Joseph was killed in Carthage Jail. David Hyrum lived to adulthood but never knew his father.

Losses like these were not unique to the Smith family. Lack of proper medical care, disease, and poor conditions meant that the loss of a child or its mother was quite common. At least as far back as Book of Mormon times, and probably since the beginning of time, the fate of lost children troubled the followers of Christ. The prophet Mormon wrestled with the question, but he later declared that "little children are alive in Christ, even from the foundation of the world" (Moroni 8:12). In the vision recorded in section 137 the Lord reminded Joseph that little children are in His hands, that He has prepared a way for them to be saved before they reach the age of accountability.

Through Jesus Christ all things that are unfair can be made fair. Those who have lost little children will not only know them again but can also live with them again in the celestial kingdom of God.

How does it give you hope to know that little children are saved by Jesus Christ?

Day 349

Doctrine and Covenants 138:11

How Can the Scriptures Help in Challenging Times?

As I pondered over these things which are written, the eyes of my understanding were opened, and the Spirit of the Lord rested upon me, and I saw the hosts of the dead, both small and great.

The year 1918 was momentous for the Church and for humanity in general. It saw the end of the most destructive war in human history up until that time. Simply called the Great War by most people at the time, World War I had cost the lives of more people, both soldier and civilian, than any other war in human history. It would draw to its bloody end just over a month after this revelation was received. The end of the war marked the beginning of an even greater tragedy as the returning soldiers from the conflict helped spread a dangerous form of influenza that resulted in a global pandemic that ultimately killed more people than the war. Doctrine and Covenants 138, a revelation about the fate of the dead, was received in the middle of this momentous series of events.

It was also the last revelation given to the prophet Joseph F. Smith. President Smith presided over the Church through a number of challenging events, but in the last year of his life he was overwhelmed by a collection of devastating losses that tested his faith. In January of 1918, President Smith suddenly lost his son Hyrum to a burst appendix. Just a few months later, Hyrum's wife, Ida, also passed away suddenly, leaving five children orphaned. This devastating series of events left President Smith in a deep state of depression, where he retreated into himself and spent days poring over the scriptures in an attempt to find solace for his losses. During one of these scripture study sessions President Smith was studying passages in the New Testament about the visit of Jesus Christ to the spirit world. The scriptures opened the way for him to receive one of the most profound revelations in the Doctrine and Covenants.

How have the scriptures helped you received personal revelation?

Day 350

Doctrine and Covenants 138:30

How Is the Gospel Preached in the Spirit World?

But behold, from among the righteous, he organized his forces and appointed messengers, clothed with power and authority, and

> *commissioned them to go forth and carry the light of the gospel to them that were in darkness, even to all the spirits of men; and thus was the gospel preached to the dead.*

Joseph F. Smith's vision was of a different place and a different time. He saw the spirit world on the day Jesus Christ died as part of His atoning sacrifice. He also saw that in the spirit world a host of the righteous had gathered, awaiting the advent of the Savior. Among this number President Smith saw Adam, along with Eve, and "many of her faithful daughters who had lived through the ages and worshiped the true and living God" (Doctrine and Covenants 138:39). He saw numerous prophets from the Old Testament, including, Abel, Seth, Noah, Shem, Abraham, Isaac, Jacob, Moses, Isaiah, Ezekiel, Daniel, Elias, and Malachi. He also testified that he saw "the prophets who dwelt among the Nephites and testified of the coming of the Son of God" (Doctrine and Covenants 138:40–49).

The Savior's reunion with these faithful witnesses must have been a joyous site to behold, but that was not the point of the Savior's visit to the spirit world. President Smith saw that from among this dream team of disciples, the Savior "organized his forces and appointed messengers, clothed with power and authority," sending them to preach the gospel "to them that were in darkness, even to all the spirits of men" (Doctrine and Covenants 138:30). This is a part of the atoning work of Jesus Christ that is as important as His death and Resurrection. The missionary work initiated in the spirit world by the Son of God opened the door to every child of God, regardless of their background.

This work continues on both sides of the veil. Missionaries teach the gospel in the spirit world, while Latter-day Saints here on earth play their part by performing proxy ordinances in temples around the world. Those who participate in this great work open the door for everyone to have the chance to gain eternal life.

How has the Savior's work in the spirit world blessed you and your family?

Day 351

Doctrine and Covenants 138:57

What Happens to the Faithful After Death?

I beheld that the faithful elders of this dispensation, when they depart from mortal life, continue their labors in the preaching of the gospel of repentance and redemption, through the sacrifice of the Only Begotten Son of God, among those who are in darkness and under the bondage of sin in the great world of the spirits of the dead.

The vision of the redemption of the dead, as Doctrine and Covenants 138 is known, was received when Joseph F. Smith was on death's door. He passed into the next life just over a month after the revelation was given. When President Smith appeared in the October 1918 general conference, he only spoke briefly, striking a cryptic tone about what the Lord had shown him. Approaching the pulpit, he said, "I will not, I dare not, attempt to enter upon many things that are resting upon my mind this morning, and I shall postpone until some future time, the Lord being willing, my attempt to tell you some of the things that are in my mind, and that dwell in my heart. I have not lived alone these five months."[86] After the conference, President Smith sat down with his son Joseph Fielding Smith, another future president of the Church. President Smith carefully dictated the revelation while his son recorded it with a typewriter.

The revelation was also received in the shadow of death. The passing of President Smith's son Hyrum and his daughter-in-law Ida loomed large in his mind. The text of the revelation shows at least three temporal shifts that took place. First, he saw the spirit world on the day of the Savior's crucifixion. Second, the vision shifted and he saw the Prophet Joseph Smith; his own father, Hyrum Smith; Brigham Young; and other modern prophets taking part of the work in the spirit world (Doctrine and Covenants 138:53). Finally, one final shift in time took place and he saw the spirit world in his own day. "I beheld that the faithful elders of this dispensation, when they depart from mortal life,

86. Conference Report, October 1918.

continue their labors in the preaching of the gospel of repentance and redemption, through the sacrifice of the Only Begotten Son of God, among those who are in darkness and under the bondage of sin in the great world of the spirits of the dead" (Doctrine and Covenants 138:57).

President Smith's vision assures us that death isn't the end of our lives. It isn't even the end of our work. When they die, faithful men and women continue their labors in the world of the spirits. Some of our most important work will take place in the spirit world. For a prophet who was only a few days from departing this life, it must have been fulfilling to know that the work which provided meaning and purpose to his life on earth would only continue.

What do you look forward to about the next life?

Day 352
Official Declaration 2

How Can I Be Patient When Waiting for Blessings?

> *He has heard our prayers, and by revelation has confirmed that the long-promised day has come when every faithful, worthy man in the Church may receive the holy priesthood, with power to exercise its divine authority, and enjoy with his loved ones every blessing that flows therefrom, including the blessings of the temple.*

Official Declaration 2 marks the revelation given to Spencer W. Kimball in 1978 extending the blessings of the priesthood to all worthy people. Since the revelation was given, the blessings of the gospel have been extended to millions of people around the globe. But even before the revelation was given, there were members of African ancestry who joined the Church and endured in the faith in spite of not being able to fully partake of all of its blessings.

Helvécio and Rudá Martins were Black members of the Church in Brazil when the 1978 revelation was received. As faithful Church members for many years, they were stunned when they heard news of the revelation. "I could not contain my emotions," Helvécio later recalled. "Ruda and I went into our bedroom, knelt down, and prayed. We wept as we thanked our Father in Heaven for an event we had only dreamed about." Just a few weeks later Helvécio and his son Marcus both received the Aaronic Priesthood. Shortly after, he received the Melchizedek priesthood and ordained his son. He later wrote, "I felt I would explode with joy happiness and contentment. What an incredible experience."[87] In 1990 Helvécio became the first person of African ancestry called as a General Authority.

Faithful Saints like the Martin family waited years to receive their full blessings. We may not fully understand the reasons behind all of the challenges we face in life. But we know that if we trust in the Lord, He will hear our prayers and answer them in time.

How can you find joy in patience?

Day 353
Article of Faith 1

What Is the Godhead?

> *We believe in God, the Eternal Father, and in His Son, Jesus Christ, and in the Holy Ghost.*

The Articles of Faith were written by Joseph Smith in 1842 as part of a letter written to John Wentworth, the editor of the *Chicago Democrat.* The letter included a history of Joseph Smith beginning with his First Vision and then recounting the growth and progress of the Church. At the end of the letter, Joseph included the thirteen articles of faith. Over the years, the Articles of Faith have come to be valued as one of the finest short summaries of the beliefs of the Latter-day Saints ever written. The Articles of Faith do not discuss every part of the Church, but they are a great introduction to the basic beliefs of our faith.

87. Helvecio Martins and Mark Grover, *Elder Helvecio Martins,* 1994, 69–71, 117, 121–122.

Joseph starts with the most fundamental belief, that there is a God who is our Father, that His Son, Jesus Christ, is our Savior, and there is a Holy Spirit who provides us with guidance. Latter-day Saints differ from other Christians in that we don't accept the doctrine of the Trinity, which posits that the Father, the Son, and the Holy Ghost are all the same being. Latter-day revelation, beginning with the First Vision, reveals that God and Jesus are separate beings. Further revelations opened the way to an understanding of the literal fatherhood of God and brotherhood of Christ. All of the members of Godhead devote their time and their gifts toward helping ordinary men and women achieve their true potential. But perhaps the most important revelation of all is coming to know that They know each of us personally and can be deeply involved in our lives if we allow Them to be.

How can you draw closer to the Father, the Son, and the Holy Ghost?

Day 354
Article of Faith 2

How Do Latter-day Saints View the Fall of Adam And Eve?

We believe that men will be punished for their own sins, and not for Adam's transgression.

Most people who believe in the Bible interpret the Fall of Adam and Eve as a tale of woe and despair. Because of the Book of Mormon, Latter-day Saints believe in a fortunate Fall. The Fall was not contrary to God's will, and mankind is not forever stained because of the transgressions of their ancestors. The Fall was not about sin; it was about choice. The Lord placed Adam and Eve in the Garden of Eden and then allowed them to make a choice. They chose to partake of the fruit, leading to death and sin but also to a chance to progress, grow, and become like God. The revelations given to Joseph Smith also make it clear that Adam and Eve were not left without comfort or guidance but were instead taught the plan of salvation.

Eve summarized her joy over the plan when she declared, "Were it not for our transgression we never should have had seed, and never should have known good and evil, and the joy of our redemption, and the eternal life which God giveth unto all the obedient" (Moses 5:11).

Adam and Eve learned that any sin or transgression can become an opportunity for growth if we choose to turn to God and allow the Savior to help us. None of us are condemned by our past transgressions or the transgressions of our ancestors. Jesus Christ can help us recover from all of the negative things in this world. With this knowledge we can see the Fall as a glorious part of the plan of happiness, knowing that "Adam fell that men might be, and men are that they might have joy" (2 Nephi 2:25).

How does your knowledge of the Fall of Adam and Eve help you find joy and purpose in your life?

Day 355
Article of Faith 3

How Does Jesus Christ Save All Mankind?

We believe that through the Atonement of Christ, all mankind may be saved, by obedience to the laws and ordinances of the Gospel.

When Joseph Smith was asked what Latter-day Saints believe, he wrote, "The fundamental principles of our religion is the testimony of the apostles and prophets concerning Jesus Christ, 'that he died, was buried, and rose again the third day, and ascended up into heaven;' and all other things are only appendages to these, which pertain to our religion."[88]

This statement illustrates how central the Atonement of Jesus Christ is to our faith. In Joseph Smith's mind, if our teachings are a tree, the trunk of the tree is what Jesus did for us, and everything else is a branch. Everything in the Church from sacrament meetings, to temples, to socials with potluck dinners gains its significance from the

88. Questions and Answers, 8 May 1838, *The Joseph Smith Papers*, 44.

fact that Jesus died for our sins and was resurrected. This not only gives meaning to our lives, but it also gives meaning and purpose to the lives of all of our brothers and sisters everywhere in the world, regardless of beliefs or background.

Gospel is the Greek word for "glad tidings" or "good news." Informing every person of the good news is the central mission of the Church. We need to keep this in mind when we speak, teach, and share our faith. Jesus is central to everything we teach and believe. Without Him, everything else loses its meaning. With Him, we have the promise of joy in this life and a life of fulfillment in the eternities.

How does the Atonement of Jesus Christ provide meaning to your life?

Day 356
Article of Faith 4

What Are the First Principles and Ordinances of the Gospel?

> *We believe that the first principles and ordinances of the Gospel are: first, Faith in the Lord Jesus Christ; second, Repentance; third, Baptism by immersion for the remission of sins; fourth, Laying on of hands for the gift of the Holy Ghost.*

The gospel of Jesus Christ may, at times, seem complex with its numerous doctrines, many books of scripture, and dense history. But at its core, it is remarkably simple. By focusing primarily on these four foundational principles and ordinances, we can live the gospel of Christ in its purest form. Wholeheartedly embracing these principles leads us to live according to the higher law, making the gospel straightforward.

Focusing on these principles not only brings us clarity but also qualifies us for salvation. Second Nephi 9:23 states, "And [Christ] commandeth all man that they must repent, and be baptized in his name, having perfect faith in the Holy One of Israel, or they cannot be saved in the kingdom of God."

Jesus Christ and His prophets repeatedly teach these principles and ordinances throughout scripture. In fact, if Christ were to appear to us today, He would likely teach about the necessity of faith, repentance, baptism, and the gift of the Holy Ghost. In the Book of Mormon when Christ appeared to the Nephites, He first testified of His divine mission and ministered to the multitude one by one. He then called Apostles and gave them authority to perform baptisms, teaching "that whoso repenteth of his sins through your words, and desire to be baptized in my name, on this wise shall ye baptize them" (3 Nephi 11:23). In the same sense that these four principles and ordinances are significant because they are listed as "the first" of the gospel, it is impactful that repentance and baptism are two of the first things that Jesus teaches to the people of Nephi.

How can focusing on these principles help make living the gospel more simple?

Day 357
Article of Faith 5

How Does a Person Enter into the Priesthood?

> *We believe that a man must be called of God, by prophecy, and by the laying on of hands by those who are in authority, to preach the Gospel and administer in the ordinances thereof.*

Priesthood is a very unique thing for Latter-day Saints. In most religions, priesthood comes as a results of years of study, advanced degrees, and sometimes lengthy apprenticeships. By contrast, Latter-day Saints sometimes give priesthood authority to boys as young as eleven years old! Which of these approaches is more in line with the scriptures? Moses longed for a priestly people, declaring, "Would God that all the Lord's people were prophets, and that the Lord would put his spirit upon them!" (Numbers 11:29). Jesus recruited simple fishermen to serve as the leaders of His church. The writer of Hebrews, speaking of the priesthood, taught that "man taketh this honour unto himself, but he that is called of God, as was Aaron" (Hebrews 5:4). Education can be a great help to those who serve in the Church, but education is not the deciding factor in who receives priesthood authority. Power in the priesthood comes through revelation and worthiness.

In the Lord's church nearly every man and woman is given priesthood authority to carry out the purposes of the Church. A deacon's quorum president is given the keys necessary to carry out the work of his quorum. A sister missionary is given priesthood authority to teach the gospel. This might mean that our meetings are a little less professional or that the sermons aren't as polished as they are in other churches. But there is deep sincerity in the lessons taught and the testimonies shared by members of the Church. In the end, what the Savior wanted wasn't a gathering of disciples where one person taught, spoke, and managed everything. He wanted a kingdom of priests and priestesses, all flawed but striving to follow the Master.

How has serving in the Church been a blessing in your life?

Day 358
Article of Faith 6

What Is the Purpose of Prophets and Apostles?

> *We believe in the same organization that existed in the Primitive Church, namely, apostles, prophets, pastors, teachers, evangelists, and so forth.*

The Savior said that His Church is "the only *true* and *living* church upon the face of the whole earth, with which I, the Lord, am well pleased" (Doctrine and Covenants 1:30; emphasis added). We often emphasize one of those words in our testimonies, declaring that the Church is *true*, but we often neglect to mention that the Church is also *living*.

A living church is led by living revelations. These revelations come to men and women who receive inspiration from God to lead and guide the Church. While the Church embraces the organization that existed in New Testament times, further revelation has led us to expand the organization. New offices in the Church have been created by inspiration to serve the needs of youth, women, and children. The Church is a living faith that will continue to expand and grow in the future as well. The blueprint of the ancient Church established the foundations we build on, but we look forward to further revelations that will allow the Church to carry out its divine mission to prepare the world for the Second Coming of Christ. The revelations given to prophets and apostles are a key component of the living Church.

Why is it important to see the Church as both true and living?

Day 359
Article of Faith 7

What Are the Gifts of the Spirit?

We believe in the gift of tongues, prophecy, revelation, visions, healing, interpretation of tongues, and so forth.

One of the most chilling prophecies found in the Book of Mormon is that in the last days "it shall be said that miracles are done away" (Mormon 8:26). But miracles still happen on a daily basis. The gifts of the spirit are still active in the Church. Every day men and women of faith perform miracles in blessing the lives of the people around them. Often these miracles are quiet and take place away from the attention of the world. But in my own life I have witnessed on a regular basis the power of faith and miracles in changing the world around us. I have seen people healed by the power of faith. I have given blessings where prophecies and counsel directly from God have come through my voice.

The key to understanding the gifts of the spirit is to recognize that those who perform these miraculous acts are not the source of the miracles. They are instruments that God works through to perform miracles. The power of God is just as present in our time as it was in ancient times. But we need to recognize that miracles like the parting of the Red Sea by Moses are the kind of events that happen rarely. The real miracles happen every day, but they are usually more subtle and quiet. It takes faith to perform miracles, but it also takes faith to see them. Once you have the right vision, you can see miracles all around you nearly every day.

What miracles have you seen in your life?

Day 360
Article of Faith 8

What Do We Believe Is the Word of God?

We believe the Bible to be the word of God as far as it is translated correctly; we also believe the Book of Mormon to be the word of God.

One of the key differences between Latter-day Saints and their friends of other faiths is that we believe in an open canon of scripture. We also take a different approach toward scripture, accepting that there can be errors in the text of these sacred books. Scriptural authors are human and can make mistakes, but the principles taught in the Bible and the Book of Mormon lead people to God. We also accept other canonical books such as the Doctrine and Covenants and the Pearl of Great Price.

One of the most valuable contributions of these books is that they show that the words of God can come to people in different places and different times. The Book of Mormon states one of its purposes as "to the convincing of the Jew and Gentile that Jesus is the Christ, the Eternal God, manifesting himself unto all nations" (Book of Mormon title page). I was once in an intense discussion with a person from a different faith who said that he didn't like the Book of Mormon because it teaches that America is special. I was inspired to reply that the message of the Book of Mormon isn't just that America is a chosen land but that any land can be chosen by God. The children of God are found in all nations. These two books of scripture tell the story of God's dealing with the house of Israel in Palestine and America, but they also promise a larger story that take place among all people and continues to this day.

The words of God never end, and having multiple scriptural testimonies of the divinity of Jesus Christ is one of the greatest blessings given to the Latter-day Saints!

How has the Book of Mormon and other scripture affected your life?

Day 361
Article of Faith 9

Why Is Revelation Important to the Gospel?

We believe all that God has revealed, all that He does now reveal, and we believe that He will yet reveal many great and important things pertaining to the Kingdom of God.

Part of our belief in an open canon of scripture is reflected in the ninth article of faith's declaration that "we believe that [God] will yet reveal many great and important things pertaining to the Kingdom of God." As a living Church, we look forward to future revelations to come. We also believe that the leaders of the Church are led by revelation as well. Revelation comes at all levels of the Church. A newly baptized member of the Church can kneel in prayer and seek revelation to direct them in their own life. The president of the Church can receive revelation for the entire world, even as Moses received direction and guidance from God in his time (see Doctrine and Covenants 28:2).

There are checks and balances to this system of revelation. Revelation comes within a person's stewardship and not at random. Revelations must be measured for validity against the canon of scripture. But revelation flows continually from God to His sons and daughter. "As well might man stretch forth his puny arm to stop the Missouri river in its decreed course, or to turn it up stream," the Lord told Joseph Smith, "as to hinder the Almighty from pouring down knowledge from heaven upon the heads of the Latter-day Saints" (Doctrine and Covenants 121:33).

While we need approach revelation wisely and at times with caution, we can also embrace the fact that Heavenly Father wants to communicate light and knowledge to His children. On one occasion Joseph Smith taught, "I believe all that God ever revealed, and I never hear of a man being damned for believing too much; but they are damned for unbelief."[89]

When have you received a revelation and how did it bless your life?

---

89. *Teachings of the Presidents of the Church: Joseph Smith* (2007), chapter 22.

Day 362
Article of Faith 10

What Is the Gathering of Israel?

We believe in the literal gathering of Israel and in the restoration of the Ten Tribes; that Zion (the New Jerusalem) will be built upon the American continent; that Christ will reign personally upon the earth; and, that the earth will be renewed and receive its paradisiacal glory.

Latter-day Saints believe that history has a purpose. It is not just one endless cycle that repeats over and over again. History is coming to a conclusion, and it is rapidly approaching. In the tenth article of faith, Joseph Smith uses the word *literally* to describe our belief in a number of events leading up to the Second Coming of Jesus Christ. The house of Israel will be gathered again, physically and spiritually (see 2 Nephi 9:1–2). God will build two great holy cities, one in the Western hemisphere (Zion) and one in the Eastern hemisphere (Jerusalem). We believe that Jesus will return and reign as the true king of the earth for a thousand years. His very presence will cause the earth to be healed and once again become a paradisiacal place of safety for all of God's creations. We believe all of this will happen in a very literal sense.

But while we believe in the literal events linked to the Second Coming of Christ, we don't know precisely how these events will come to pass. Signs can be fulfilled in surprising ways, and there are many signs surrounding the Second Coming that have yet to be fulfilled. The gathering of Israel and the building of Zion will be miracles indeed. But our history has shown that they are the kind of miracles that will happen because of a thousand little miracles that occur along the way. Creating a new world is hard work, but Latter-day Saints have never been shy about hard work.

This is a fundamentally optimistic way of seeing the world. We believe that a better world is coming. We believe that the Savior will end the suffering and injustice that we now see in the world. But we also believe that we can't just wait for the Savior to come. We have to join in the work of building a paradisiacal world right now.

What can you do right now to help create a paradisiacal world?

Day 363
Article of Faith 11

Why Is Religious Freedom Important?

We claim the privilege of worshiping Almighty God according to the dictates of our own conscience, and allow all men the same privilege, let them worship how, where, or what they may.

The Church was founded in a country with religious freedom built into its constitution. Even with these protections, the Saints suffered horrific persecutions at the hands of other American citizens and eventually were forced to flee the country to seek refuge. Since Latter-day Saints have suffered so much at the hands of those who would take away their rights of worship, they have in turn sought to find ways to protect all people from persecution based on religious beliefs. While seeking to secure rights to protect our freedom to worship, we must also stamp out any feeling of religious bigotry we may feel against other faiths.

During a council meeting held in Nauvoo, Joseph Smith explained his feelings on religious freedom: "God cannot save or damn a man only on the principle that every man acts, chooses and worships for himself; hence the importance of thrusting from us every spirit of bigotry and intolerance towards a mans religious sentiments, that spirit which has drenched the earth with blood— When a man feels the least temptation to such intolerance he ought to spurn it from him. . . . Nothing can reclaim the human mind from its ignorance, bigotry, superstition &c but those grand and sublime principles of equal rights and universal freedom to all men."[90]

If the Saints wish to retain their rights of worship, they must protect the rights of others.

Why is it important to protect the rights of all people, even if you might disagree with them?

---

90. Council of Fifty, Minutes, March 1844–January 1846; Volume 1, 10 March 1844–1 March 1845, *The Joseph Smith Papers*, 119.

Day 364
Article of Faith 12

Why Is It Important to Be a Good Citizen?

We believe in being subject to kings, presidents, rulers, and magistrates, in obeying, honoring, and sustaining the law.

While most Latter-day Saints see themselves first and foremost as children of God and citizens of the kingdom of God, we also believe in working to make the countries and communities we live in a better place. Church members have been urged by prophets and apostles to be active citizens, to vote, and to work to support governments that uphold righteous principles.

That is not to say that we always agree with the law, but we seek to uphold the law. N. Eldon Tanner, a counselor in the First Presidency once quoted Abraham Lincoln, who taught, "'Bad laws, if they exist, should be repealed as soon as possible; still, while they continue in force, they should be religiously observed." President Tanner then added, "There is no reason or justification for men to disregard or break the law or try to take it into their own hands. It is the duty of citizens of any country to remember that they have individual responsibilities, and that they must operate within the law of the country in which they have chosen to live."[91]

Another part of being a good citizen is to learn to disagree without being disagreeable. The Saints come from all backgrounds and all kinds of political persuasions. One of the wonderful things about going to Church every Sunday is spending time with people who might have different views than you do. The Church can be a great blessing to any society as long as it is safe place for everyone.

How can you be a better citizen?

---

91. N. Eldon Tanner, Conference Report, October 1975, 126.

Day 365
Article of Faith 13

How Can I Seek After Good Things?

We believe in being honest, true, chaste, benevolent, virtuous, and in doing good to all men; indeed, we may say that we follow the admonition of Paul—We believe all things, we hope all things, we have endured many things, and hope to be able to endure all things. If there is anything virtuous, lovely, or of good report or praiseworthy, we seek after these things.

One of the blessings of being a member of the Church is that we seek not only religious truth but all truth and all good things. Brigham Young once taught that "all truth belongs to Mormonism," adding that "every accomplishment, every polished grace, every useful attainment in mathematics, music, and in all sciences and art belong to the saints."[92]

An important part of our faith is to seek out the good, wherever it can be found. There is a way to make all good things a part of the gospel of Jesus Christ. The Savior Himself is the source of all good things in this world. All good things eventually trace themselves back to Him and His teachings.

We find the good not only in the Church but in every setting in which we find ourselves. And we don't just seek out the good; we can create the good. The mission of the Saints is to build, lift, and help everyone that we can.

Our faith in Jesus Christ unlocks our power to see the good everywhere we can.

How can you seek out the good in the world around you?

---

92. Brigham Young, *Journal of Discourses*, 224.

About the Author

Casey Paul Griffiths is an associate professor of Church history and doctrine at Brigham Young University in Provo, Utah. He holds a bachelor's degree in history, a master's degree in religious education, and a PhD in educational leadership and foundations, all from BYU. He has served as president of the John Whitmer Historical Association and the BYU Education Society.

Prior to his employment at BYU, he served as a teacher and curriculum writer in the Seminaries and Institutes of Religion Department of The Church of Jesus Christ of Latter-day Saints. He also serves as a managing editor of Doctrine and Covenants Central, a website designed to build faith in Jesus Christ by making the Doctrine and Covenants accessible, comprehensible, and defensible to people everywhere. He lives in Saratoga Springs, Utah, with his wife, Elizabeth, and their four wonderful children.